The Policy Process in the
Modern Capitalist State

D0543619

The Policy Process in the Modern Capitalist State

Second Edition

Christopher Ham
*Professor of Health Policy and Management,
University of Birmingham*

Michael Hill
*Professor of Social Policy,
University of Newcastle upon Tyne*

 HARVESTER
WHEATSHEAF

New York   London   Toronto   Sydney   Tokyo   Singapore

First published 1984 by
Prentice Hall / Harvester Wheatsheaf
This edition published 1993 by
Harvester Wheatsheaf
Campus 400, Maylands Avenue
Hemel Hempstead
Hertfordshire. HP2 7EZ
A division of
Simon & Schuster International Group

Typeset in 10/12pt Times
by Inforum, Rowlands Castle, Hants

Printed and bound in Great Britain by
Hartnolls Ltd, Bodmin Cornwall

British Library Cataloguing in Publication Data

A catalogue record for this book is available from
the British Library

ISBN 0-7450-1106-3

6 7 8 9 10 00 99 98 97 96

To Alexander, Julia and David

CONTENTS

LIST OF FIGURES

PREFACE

The immediate origins of this book lie in work we undertook in establishing and running a master's course in public policy studies at the School for Advanced Urban Studies (SAUS), University of Bristol. The course, which started admitting students in 1979, was designed for people working in government agencies, voluntary organisations concerned with the operation of government agencies and teachers of policy studies in further and higher education. The intention behind the course, consistent with the School's mission to be a centre of excellence in the field of public policy-making, was to bring to bear a range of ideas, concepts and theories from a number of social science disciplines in a way which would both further understanding of the problems of government and help policy-makers tackle those problems more effectively. Although there is not an exact fit between the contents of this book and the course curriculum, the chapters which follow give some indication of how that intention was translated into practice. As such, the book provides an account of a significant element in the approach to public policy studies teaching at master's degree level adopted at the School.

Our students were taught that it is rarely possible to agree on one version of events: the most that can be achieved is a plausible interpretation. The reason for this, of course, is that we each see the world in a particular way, and bring our personal histories and biases to bear in interpreting events. What then are the histories and biases of the authors? Chris Ham trained as a political scientist and his early studies focused on the role of pressure groups, the relevance of pluralist theory as a way of understanding political behaviour and the literature on community power. These interests were given a sharper focus in an empirical study of policy-making in the British National Health Service (Ham, 1981), and in a more general attempt to analyse health policy and health services in Britain from a political science perspective (Ham, 1982, 1992). In parallel, Ham developed an interest in policy analysis as a field of study, and as the first graduate tutor at the School for Advanced Urban Studies, took overall responsibility for organising the policy analysis core course which formed the major part of the School's master's programme. Subsequently, he undertook further research into the process of health policy making and implementation, both in the United Kingdom and in a comparative context. Some of this research focused on interaction between different levels of analysis in explaining policy outcomes (Ham, 1986), other studies concentrated on particular aspects of the policy process, such as policy-making (Ham, 1988).

Most recently, Ham has worked as a health policy analyst in an independent think-tank, the King's Fund Institute, and has reflected on the experience of undertaking analysis for polity (Ham, 1991). In his current post at Birmingham University, he combines an interest in teaching and research on health policy. This includes a continuing interest in using the results of research to contribute to policy-making.

Michael Hill studied sociology while working as a civil servant in the National Assistance Board. In his subsequent career as a lecturer and researcher he has endeavoured both to advance the academic study of public policy and to make a practical contribution to policy analysis, mainly in the field of social policy. The master's course at SAUS provided a splendid opportunity to try to do this. In 1986 Michael Hill moved to the University of Newcastle, where he has used this book as the main text for a third-year undergraduate course on policy making and implementation. This has provided an opportunity to test whether the ideas in the book are comprehensible to undergraduate students, most of whom lack any relevant practical experience. It has accordingly influenced this second edition.

Very early in his academic life Michael Hill explored, in *The Sociology of Public Administration*, some of the main contributions he felt organisational and political sociology could make to the understanding of the policy process. By the time the master's course started at SAUS that book was out of print. Hence we decided that we should collaborate in making the material we were drawing on in our teaching available to a wider audience. *The Sociology of Public Administration* had been rendered out of date by advances in relevant theory. It is further advances in theory which have made it necessary to produce this second edition: advances which explore the relevance of economic models for the understanding of the policy process, extend the analysis of power inequalities to give more attention to gender and race and elaborate the complexities of inter- and intra-organisational relationships.

The book has been written with the needs of postgraduate students, advanced undergraduate students and their teachers in mind. Given the eclectic nature of policy analysis as a field of study (see Chapter 1), we would expect these students to be following courses in a variety of disciplines and areas, including political science, sociology, public administration, social administration, policy studies and organisation theory.

In writing the book we have incurred debts to both colleagues and students. Colleagues have provided much support and encouragement, and we would particularly like to acknowledge the help given by our many former colleagues at SAUS. In preparing this revised edition comments from many people who use the book for courses in Britain, the Netherlands, Scandinavia and Australasia have been helpful to us, particularly comments from the group who attended the seminar on New Agendas in the Study of the Policy Process in 1991. That seminar was the starting point for the production of a collection of essays which deal with developments in various countries which is to be published by Harvester Wheatsheaf in a collection which will complement this volume.

Thanks are also due to Edward Elgar who commissioned the original book and to Clare Grist who has been responsible for the publication of this revised version. We would also like to acknowledge the support given by our respective families, in particular by Ioanna Burnell and Betty Hill.

Chris Ham, Michael Hill
London and Newcastle
March 1992

CHAPTER 1

POLICY AND POLICY ANALYSIS

Introduction

Interest in policy analysis has grown steadily in recent years. Beginning in the United States in the 1960s, the public policy movement arose from two sources of concern. First, the scale and apparent intractability of the problems facing governments in Western industrialised societies led policy-makers to seek help in the solution of those problems. Second, academic researchers, particularly in social science disciplines, increasingly turned their attention to policy-related issues, and sought to apply their knowledge to the illumination of those issues. It is important not to exaggerate either of these trends. There was no sudden rush by policy-makers to draw on academic research, nor was there an immediate reorientation among researchers towards policy analysis activities. What did happen was that over a period of years new university teaching programmes were developed in public policy; a number of academic journals devoted to policy analysis, policy studies and policy sciences were launched; and teachers and researchers in such established disciplines as political science, economics and sociology began producing publications on policy-related themes. At the same time, government agencies started employing policy analysts, and took on board some of the techniques and skills that were to become the policy analyst's stock in trade; for example, cost-benefit analysis, programme budgeting and impact analysis.

Writing of these developments in 1972, Heclo referred to the

'renewed fashionability' (p. 83) of policy analysis, a useful reminder that although the field was expanding it was not entirely
new. Echoing these comments Rhodes has observed that much of
the work that claimed to be new was 'all very familiar' (1979,
p. 26). This familiarity sprang in part from the long-standing interest in the operation of government and in policy issues among
academics and researchers. Studies which had originally developed
out of the work of political scientists, economists and others were
now embraced by the emerging policy analysis perspective.
Equally, the attempt to apply social science knowledge to problems of government and to influence the activities and decisions
of government drew on a tradition involving individuals such as
Keynes, the Webbs and even Marx. While much was therefore
familiar, the scale of concern with policy issues was new. A comparison between the limited response to Lasswell's call to academics to pursue a policy orientation in a book published in 1951
(Lasswell, 1951) with the much greater rate of activity which developed in the 1960s and 1970s illustrates this. A further difference
was that the public policy movement claimed to offer a new approach to the problems of government, not least when compared
with public administration whose perceived failings provided the
stimulus for the development of policy analysis courses in American universities in the late 1960s. Many of the master's programmes in public policy took as their model the master's in
business administration programmes run by the business schools.
The emphasis was on quantitative methods combined with organisational analysis and the development of management skills
through case-study approaches. Ethics and values also found a
place in some programmes. Yet despite the claim that these programmes overcame the narrowness and lack of rigour of public
administration courses, some observers remained unconvinced
that the two were really that different (Rhodes, 1979).

If the United States was in the forefront of these developments,
the United Kingdom followed not far behind. University teaching
and research programmes evolved from the mid-1970s; in parallel
there were established a number of journals and publications with a
policy focus; and for a time discussions were held on the formation
of a British Brookings, modelled on the Brookings Institution in
Washington. The intention was to establish an independent centre
for policy research to carry out high-quality work on the problems of

government. Although the plan never materialised, two existing research units – the Centre for Studies in Social Policy and Political and Economic Planning – combined to form the Policy Studies Institute, and the Social Science Research Council placed a new emphasis on policy-relevant research. One of the significant differences between the public policy movement as it developed in the United Kingdom and in the United States was that in the United States government attitudes towards the social sciences were much more favourable than in the United Kingdom. As a result, government funding of social science research and the appointment of academics to government posts occurred on a much greater scale in the United States (Sharpe, 1975). A further difference was that in the United Kingdom policy analysts as such were rarely employed by government agencies. Rather, civil servants, administrators and specialists in government acquired, to a greater or lesser extent, policy analysis skills (Gunn, 1980).

In the 1980s interest in policy analysis continued to develop, despite a tendency for a shift in the terms of the debate. The attack upon the public sector led to a search for market devices to solve social allocation problems, and an emphasis upon the need for solutions to public sector inefficiencies rooted in the application of private sector management techniques. Thus, public administration came increasingly to be described as public management (Pollitt, 1990; Hood, 1991). Curiously, whilst such an emphasis tended to involve an assertion of the need to apply traditional formal managerial control devices rooted in a belief that policy implementation is a straightforward process, the academic scepticism about the limits to the use of policy analysis in practice tended in another sense to be taken on board by the politicians. Thus, in Britain, no Royal Commission (to engage in the careful study of a policy problem) was appointed throughout Mrs Thatcher's period as Prime Minister. Rather, brief policy analysis exercises were conducted with an explicit political brief and the use of a limited number of ideologically trusted advisers.

From what has been said so far, it is clear that policy analysis is a term which describes a range of activities. Indeed, these activities are so varied that one writer has argued that 'there can be no one definition of policy analysis' (Wildavsky, 1979, p. 15). In Wildavsky's view, it is more important to practise policy analysis than to spend time defining it. As he comments, 'analysis should be shown not just defined. Nothing is more stultifying than a futile search for Aristotelian essences' (p. 410). While we have considerable sympathy for this point of view, it behoves us as authors of another contribution to the burgeoning literature on policy analysis to attempt some clarification of basic concepts and terms. This is necessary not least because it will indicate the scope of policy analysis and those aspects of the field which are encompassed in this book.

The scope of policy analysis

One of the problems facing students of policy analysis is the bewildering variety of terms used in the literature. Policy sciences, policy studies and policy analysis are three of the terms which are more commonly used to describe the field as a whole. Sometimes these terms are used in specific, well-defined senses, sometimes they are used interchangeably. When the terms are defined, there is often little consistency in the definitions employed by different writers. It is small wonder that Wildavsky and others seek to avoid becoming embroiled in definitional debates.

Our preference is for policy analysis as a general description of the subject matter with which we are concerned. One reason for this is that, after a period in which policy sciences seemed to be gaining ascendancy (Dror, 1971; Lasswell, 1951), policy analysis emerged as the favoured term among the authors of a number of significant contributions to the literature (Wildavsky, 1979; Jenkins, 1978; Hogwood and Gunn, 1984). Unless there are convincing reasons to the contrary, it seems to us wise to accept the existing terminology. A second reason for using policy analysis is that it enables the field to be divided into analysis *of* policy and analysis *for* policy (Gordon, Lewis and Young, 1977). This distinction is important in drawing attention to policy analysis as an academic activity concerned primarily with advancing understanding, and policy analysis as an applied activity concerned mainly with contributing to the solution of social problems. We will elaborate this distinction shortly. Before doing so, however, let us consider in more detail the subject matter of policy analysis.

'Policy analysis', writes Thomas Dye, 'is finding out what governments do, why they do it, and what difference it makes' (1976, p. 1). In Dye's view, all definitions of policy analysis really boil down to the same thing – 'the description and explanation of the causes and consequences of government action' (*ibid.*). On first reading, this definition appears to describe the subject matter of political science as much as policy analysis. After all, political scientists are interested in the causes and consequences of government action and have expended much effort seeking to describe and explain such action. Yet, as Dye points out, traditionally political scientists concentrated on examining the institutions and structures of government. Only in its later development has political science shifted from an institutional to a behavioural focus. And only recently has public policy become a significant concern of political scientists. What distinguishes policy analysis from much political science in Dye's interpretation is the preoccupation of policy analysts with *what* government does. It can be added that policy analysis is also distinguished by its use of concepts from a number of different disciplines, a point we develop later in the chapter.

While Dye's definition emphasises the role of analysis in increasing knowledge of government action, he notes that analysis may also help policy-makers 'to improve the quality of public policy' (p. 108). Dye is here echoing the views of a number of other writers who have argued that policy analysis is a prescriptive as well as a descriptive activity. One of the founders of policy analysis, Harold Lasswell, notes the growth of 'a policy orientation' (Lasswell, 1951) in the social sciences and other disciplines. This comprises two elements: the development of knowledge about the policy process itself, and the improvement of information available to policy-makers. Lasswell also describes the policy orientation as the policy science approach, a term borrowed by Yehezkel Dror to refer to 'the contribution of systematic knowledge, structured rationality and organised creativity to better policy making' (1971, p. ix). Like Lasswell, Dror holds out high hopes for the contribution which the policy scientist can make to the improvement of policy-making and the alleviation of social problems. Thus, while Lasswell argues that the policy scientist should concentrate on 'the fundamental problems of man in society' (p. 8) and aim to assist in the achievement of 'the realisation of human dignity in theory and fact' (p. 15), Dror asserts that 'policy sciences is essential for improvement of the human condition, and, indeed, for avoidance of catastrophe' (*sic*) (1971, p. ix).

The prescriptive orientation of policy analysis is also stressed by Aaron Wildavsky, although it is noticeable that Wildavsky is more modest in the claims that he makes for analysis. As we have noted, Wildavsky rejects the idea that it is possible to agree on a single definition of policy analysis. Instead, he outlines the main features of policy analysis, paying particular attention to policy analysis as a problem-centred activity. That is, analysis takes as its subject matter problems facing policy-makers and aims to ameliorate those problems through a process of creativity, imagination and craftsmanship. In Wildavsky's view, problems are not so much solved as superseded. Given the intractability of many social problems, the role of analysis is to locate problems where solutions might be tried. If the analyst is able to redefine problems in a way which makes some improvement possible then this is as much as can be expected. As part of this process Wildavsky argues that the analyst should engage in action. Thinking about problems and seeking solutions – in Wildavsky's terms 'intellectual cogitation' – must be joined with 'social interaction' if analysis is to have an impact (Wildavsky, 1979, p. 17). Policy analysis is therefore concerned with both planning and politics, and 'The highest form of analysis is using intellect to aid interaction between people' (*ibid.*).

Seen in these terms, policy analysis is as much to do with advocacy, or 'salesmanship' (Wildavsky, 1979, p. 10), as with understanding. How far academic policy analysts should engage in advocacy is an issue of some dispute. Lasswell takes an unequivocal stance on this issue, maintaining that social scientists pursuing the policy orientation should neither engage full time in practical politics nor spend time advising policy-makers on immediate questions. His argument is that social scientists should concentrate on major problems and should communicate their ideas and findings to policy-makers through seminars at existing institutions and through the establishment of new institutions (Lasswell, 1951). In a similar vein, Dye contends that 'policy advocacy and policy analysis are separate endeavours' (1976, p. 3). He goes on to argue that social scientists should not actively engage in politics but rather should concentrate on 'the systematic application of social science theory, methodology and findings to contemporary societal problems' (*ibid.*). This argument finds echoes in the writings of two English commentators, Sharpe (1975) and Donnison (1972). Sharpe concludes a review of the relationship between social science and policy-making by suggesting that social science may make an increased contribution to policy-making if academics concentrate on doing good research rather than decamp to Whitehall, while Donnison qualifies his call for an increase in policy-oriented research by warning that researchers 'should remain firmly rooted in the academic world' (1972, p. 532).

Wildavsky has some sympathy with these views, but goes a stage further to argue that analysis must include consideration of how the ideas emerging from analysis can be applied. Good craftsmanship – in Dye's terms the application of theory to social problems – requires that the anticipated difficulties of implementing the results of analysis are taken into account. Going beyond this by 'acting to implement the analysis' (1979, p. 10) and 'actively helping policy ideas make their way in this world' (*ibid.*) is for Wildavsky an optional extra – but an option for which he expresses a strong preference.

The academic analyst who engages in salesmanship is clearly operating in a similar way to many policy analysts who work in government. As a government activity, policy analysis typically involves giving information and providing advice in order to assist policy-makers in the process of choosing between alternatives. The working style of policy analysts in government varies considerably. Meltsner (1976), in his study of analysts in the American federal bureaucracy, identifies three types: the technician, interested in doing good quality – policy-oriented – research and essentially an academic in bureaucratic residence; the politician, concerned to achieve advancement and personal influence and interested in analysis only in so far as it furthers these ends; and the entrepreneur, interested in using analysis to influence policy – and improve policy impact. One point to note is that academic analysts have increasingly crossed the threshold into government, thereby ignoring Lasswell's warning that they should not become directly involved in advising politicians. This is true not only in the United States but also in the United Kingdom, where, as we have noted, policy analysts as such have rarely been employed by government agencies. Academics in the United Kingdom have acted as specialist political advisers to ministers and parliamentary select committees, and they have played a part in the work of the Central Policy Review Staff, established in 1970 as a think-tank within central government. As a result, the dividing line between policy analysts

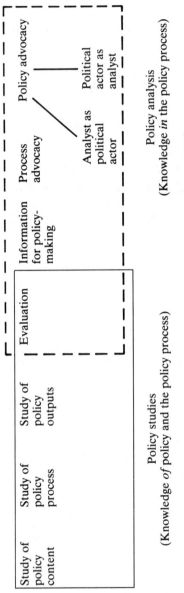

Figure 1.1 Types of study of public policy-making (Source: Hogwood and Gunn, 1981)

inside and outside government has become increasingly blurred. At the same time, academic policy analysts have in some cases used their expertise to assist pressure groups in the pursuit of particular policy preferences. It is this range of activity carried out in different settings which makes policy analysis such a difficult subject to tie down and define.

Nevertheless, the discussion may be advanced by returning to the distinction between analysis of policy and analysis for policy mentioned earlier in the chapter. If, as we have suggested, some policy analysts are interested in furthering understanding of policy, some are interested in improving the quality of policy, and some are interested in both activities, is it possible to make more precise distinctions between different kinds of policy analysis work? We believe it is. In particular, the typology proposed by Hogwood and Gunn (1981, see also their book, 1984) which draws on an earlier analysis by Gordon, Lewis and Young (1977) points to seven varieties of policy analysis, illustrated in Figure 1.1. First, there are *studies of policy content* in which analysts seek to describe and explain the genesis and development of particular policies. In the United Kingdom, much social policy and administration work is of this kind. The analyst interested in policy content usually investigates one or more cases in order to trace how a policy emerged, how it was implemented and what the results were. Second, there are *studies of policy process* in which attention is focused on the stages through which issues pass and attempts are made to assess the influence of different factors on the development of the issue. Studies of the policy process invariably show some concern with policy content, but in the main they are interested in uncovering the various influences on policy formulation. A classic example is Graham Allison's (1971) book on the Cuban missile crisis which uses the missile crisis to test out the strengths and weaknesses of a number of models of the policy process. Studies of the policy process are often concerned with single issues of this kind or with specific policy areas, but they may also focus on the policy process within an organisation or on the influences on policy within a particular community or society. Third, there are *studies of policy outputs* which seek to explain why levels of expenditure or service provision vary between areas. In Dye's terminology, these are studies of policy determination (1976, p. 5), studies which take policies as dependent variables and attempt to understand these policies in terms of social, economic, technological and other factors. Output studies have received much attention in the United States, not least in Dye's own work, but they have been undertaken increasingly in the United Kingdom and other Western European countries. A particularly complex area of application of this approach is to be found in the vast literature which attempts to explain national differences in the development of social welfare policies (for a succinct review of this see Baldwin, 1990). The fourth category, *evaluation studies*, marks the borderline between analysis of policy and analysis for policy. Evaluation studies are also sometimes referred to as impact studies as they are concerned to analyse the impact policies have on the population. Evaluation studies may be either descriptive or prescriptive. Fifth, there is *information for policy-making* in which data are marshalled in order to assist policy-makers reach decisions. Information for policy may derive from reviews carried out within government as part of a regular monitoring process; or it may be provided by academic policy analysts concerned to apply their knowledge to practical problems. Sixth, there is *process advocacy*, a variant of analysis for policy in which analysts seek to improve the nature of policy-making systems. Process advocacy is manifested in attempts to improve the machinery of government through the reallocation of functions and tasks, and in efforts to enhance the basis for policy choice through the development of planning systems and new approaches to option appraisal. Finally, there is *policy advocacy*, the activity which involves the analyst in pressing specific options and ideas in the policy process, either individually or in association with others, perhaps through a pressure group.

The policy orientation

Having clarified the meaning of policy analysis and the various forms it takes, we are now in a position to specify the areas which are of particular concern to us in this book. Our main interest is in the analysis of policy. This implies that we are concerned specifically with studies of the policy process, but cannot, of course, disregard insights from studies in others of Hogwood and Gunn's categories, particularly studies of policy outputs which provide insights into process. We are therefore concerned with a specific important part of the whole field of policy analysis. In studying the policy process we find it useful to draw on ideas and insights from a number of academic disciplines, particularly political science and sociology. We do not agree with Dror that policy analysis (in his terminology policy sciences) is 'a new supra discipline' (1971, p. ix). Rather, we endorse Wildavsky's view that 'Policy analysis is an applied sub-field whose content cannot be determined by disciplinary boundaries but by whatever appears appropriate to the circumstances of the time and the nature of problem' (1979, p. 15). Even those with only a passing knowledge of the policy analysis literature will readily recognise the problems of locating policy analysis in existing disciplinary categories. It is for this reason that Lasswell refers to a policy *orientation* – an orientation 'that cuts across the existing specialisations' (1951, p. 3). This is a formulation we propose to follow.

As we see it, the purpose of policy analysis is to draw on ideas from a range of disciplines in order to interpret the causes and consequences of government action, in particular by focusing on the processes of policy formulation. But what is policy? Again this is a question that has attracted much interest but little agreement. Heclo notes that 'Policy is not . . . a self evident term' (1972, p. 84) and he suggests that 'A policy may usefully be considered as a course of action or inaction rather than specific decisions or actions' (p. 85). As a variant on this, David Easton notes that 'a policy . . . consists of a web of decisions and actions that allocate . . . values' (1953, p. 130). A further definition is offered by Jenkins who sees policy as 'a set of interrelated decisions . . . concerning the selection of goals and the means of achieving them within a specified situation . . .' (1978, p. 15). Other writers have suggested even vaguer definitions: Friend and his colleagues say 'policy is essentially a *stance* which, once articulated, contributes to the context within which a succession of future decisions will be made' (1974, p. 40); and Cunningham, a former top British civil servant, argues 'Policy is rather like the elephant – you recognise it when you see it but cannot easily define it' (1963, p. 229). The definitional problems posed by the concept of policy suggest that it is difficult to treat it as a very specific and concrete phenomenon. Policy may sometimes be identifiable in terms of a decision, but very often it involves either groups of decisions or what may be seen as little more than an orientation. The attempts at definition also imply that it is hard to identify particular occasions when policy is made. Policy will often continue to evolve within what is conventionally described as the implementation phase rather than the policy-making phase of the policy process.

Let us look a little more at the implications of the fact that policy involves a course of action or a web of decisions rather than one decision. There are several aspects to this. First, a decision network, often of considerable complexity, may be involved in producing action, and a web of decisions taking place over a long period of time and extending far beyond the initial policy-making process may form part of the network. A second aspect is that even at the policy-making level, policy is not usually expressed in a single decision. It tends to be defined in terms of a series of decisions which, taken together, comprise a more or less common understanding of what policy is. Third, policies invariably change over time. Yesterday's statements of intent may not be the same as today's, either because of incremental adjustments to earlier decisions, or because of major changes of direction. Also, experience of implementing a decision may feed back into the decision-making process, thereby creating or leading to changes in the allocation of values. This is not to say that policies are always changing, but simply that the policy process is dynamic rather than static and that we need to be aware of shifting definitions of issues. Fourth, a development of this point is that much policy decision-making is concerned, as Hogwood and Gunn (1984) have stressed, with attempting the difficult task of 'policy termination' or determining 'policy succession' (see also Hogwood and Peters, 1983).

Fifth, the corollary of the last two points is the need to recognise that the study of policy has as one of its main concerns the examination of nondecisions. This is what Heclo is pointing to in his reference to inaction. The concept of nondecision-making has become increasingly important in recent years, and it has been argued that much political activity is concerned with maintaining the *status quo* and resisting challenges to the existing allocation of values. Analysis of this activity is a necessary part of the examination of the dynamics of the policy process, and we investigate nondecision-making in Chapter 4. Finally, the definitions cited above raise the question of whether policy can be seen as action without decisions. Can it be said that a pattern of actions over a period of time constitutes a policy, even if these actions have not

Figure 1.2 A simplified model of a political system (Source: Easton, 1965a)

been formally sanctioned by a decision? Writers on policy have increasingly turned their attention to the action of lower-level actors, sometimes called street-level bureaucrats (Lipsky, 1980), in order to gain a better understanding of policy-making and implementation. In some circumstances it is suggested that it is at this level in the system that policy is actually made. It would seem to be important to balance a decisional top-down perspective on policy with an action-oriented bottom-up perspective. Actions as well as decisions may therefore be said to be the proper focus of policy analysis, and we explore the influence of street-level bureaucrats on policy later in the book.

We have so far discussed policy as the output of a political process. Wildavsky reminds us that 'Policy is a process as well as a product. It is used to refer to a process of decision-making and also to the product of that process' (1979, p. 387). In seeking to comprehend the complexities of the process of decision-making, writers have put forward a number of models among which the systems approach outlined by David Easton (1953, 1965a and b) has received considerable prominence. Easton argues that political activity can be analysed in terms of a system containing a number of processes which must remain in balance if the activity is to survive. The paradigm that he employs is the biological system whose life processes interact with each other and with the environment to produce a changing but none the less stable bodily state. Political systems are like biological systems, argues Easton, and exist in an environment which contains a variety of other systems, including social systems and ecological systems.

One of the key processes of political systems is inputs, which take the form of demands and supports. Demands involve actions by individuals and groups seeking authoritative allocations of values from the authorities. Supports comprise actions such as voting, obedience to the law, and the payment of taxes. These feed into the black box of decision-making, also known as the conversion process, to produce outputs, the decisions and policies of the authorities. Outputs may be distinguished from outcomes, which are the effects policies have on citizens. Easton's analysis does not end here, for within the systems framework there is allowance for feedback, through which the outputs of the political system influence future inputs into the system. The whole process is represented in Figure 1.2.

The main merit of systems theory is that it provides a way of conceptualising what are often complex political phenomena. In emphasising processes as opposed to institutions or structures, Easton's approach represents an advance over more traditional analyses within political science and public administration. The approach is also useful in disaggregating the policy process into a number of different stages, each of which becomes amenable to more detailed analysis. For all of these reasons the systems model is of value, and this no doubt helps to account for its prominence in the literature. Yet the model is not without its drawbacks, and our understanding of policy and the policy process may be developed further by examining various points of criticism.

First, it would be wrong to accept Easton's conceptualisation of the political system as an accurate description of the way systems work in practice. While Easton's identification of processes is valuable, the neat, logical ordering of those processes in terms of demand initiation, through the conversion process to outputs, rarely occurs so simply in the practical world of policy-making. For example, policy-makers themselves may be the source of demands, and although Easton recognises the significance of what he terms 'withinputs', consideration needs to be given to the manner in which individual and group behaviour may be shaped by political leaders. A growing body of work suggests that, far from arising autonomously in the community, political demands may be manufactured by leaders, who thereby create conditions for their own action (Edelman, 1971). Through the manipulation of language and the creation of crises the authorities may impose their own definitions of problems and help to frame the political agenda. Recognition of these processes is an important corrective to the naive assumptions found in some applications of systems theory. Edelman's work also draws attention to the way in which policies serve symbolic purposes. That is, policies may often be more effective in giving the impression that government is taking action, and therefore in maintaining political support, than in tackling social problems. As Dye has pointed out, it is a weakness of policy analysis that it concentrates 'primarily upon activities of governments, rather than the rhetoric of governments' (1976, p. 21). What this suggests is that students of the policy process should be wary of taking policy-makers too seriously. Policies may be intended to improve social conditions, but this should be part of the object of enquiry rather than an assumption of research.

A second criticism of the systems framework is that it highlights the central importance of the conversion process, the black box of decision-making, but gives it relatively little attention when compared with the detailed consideration of demands and supports. This indicates the need to draw not only on systems analysis but also on work which has explored the dynamics of decision-making. A considerable amount of this book is about penetrating the black box. Included within the political system, as used in general terms here, there is likely to be a great deal of political activity. This may involve inter-organisational politics – between levels of government (central and local) and between different departments at the same level. It may also involve intra-organisational politics, in which the roles of, for example, public servants will be important. These political relationships will be channelled by structures and rules, which will themselves be the subject of continuous political action.

A third criticism which follows from that last point is that the system, and in particular the way processes occur within the 'black box' may itself be the object of political action. There will be various place in this book where we will want to note the importance of what has been called 'meta-policy'-making (Dror, 1986; see also Hupe, 1990). This is concerned with setting and changing the systems and structures within which the processes which are concerned with substantive policy outputs occur. Of course political science gives considerable attention to the big examples of meta-policy-making: the determination of constitutions and the battles for political power characteristic of nation-building or the disintegration of empires. What may be overlooked, however, is the way in which the relationships between units of government are subject to continual adjustment as powers and duties or financing arrangements are altered. Systematic presentations of the policy process tend to give a game-like appearance to conflicts, the problem is that politics may both be about securing a specific outcome but also about the changing the 'rules of the game'. Moreover, the latter may be prompted both by an interest in influencing a current outcome and by a concern to influence future outcomes. The systems model tends to treat the system itself as something static and uncontested, or at least only subject to rare fundamental change within the more stable nation-states.

The very emphasis in system theory on the idea of the black box is instructive. The imagery reminds us that these processes are often difficult to penetrate, and thus to research. It is important, therefore, to try to develop models of the way decisions are made, and to compare and contrast those models to see the different ways in which they help us to understand processes. Allison (1971) offers a useful approach here. Allison suggests that three models are of relevance. There is, first, the rational actor model, which sees actions as being formed by purposeful agents with certain goals and objectives. These agents have to choose between alternative courses of action in order to achieve their goals. Alternatives are assumed to have a set of consequences attached, and rational choice consists of selecting that alternative whose consequences rank highest. Second, there is the organisational process model which sees action not as rational choice, but as the output of organisational behaviour. This behaviour is largely the enactment of established routines in which sequential attention is given to goals and standard operating procedures are adopted. In contrast, the bureaucratic politics model sees action neither as choice nor output but rather as the result of bargaining between groups and individuals in the political system. There are other ways of formulating Allison's alternatives. What we would stress here is the value of the method, which may use various kinds of decision and organisation theory. We will discuss and develop it in later chapters.

One of the merits of the systems model is that it draws attention to the relationship between political systems and other systems. In Figure 1.2, these other systems are referred to simply as the environment of the political system. The environment of the political system and its influence on policy is a major concern in studies of policy outputs. The work of Thomas Dye (1976) and others seeks to explain the policies which emerge from political systems in terms of a range of characteristics in the environment, including levels of urbanisation, per capita income, educational attainment and so on. While they do not ignore political variables, output studies attempt to place these variables in context and assess their importance relative to the social and economic characteristics of the particular population under investigation. Output studies serve as a useful reminder that politics cannot be considered in isolation from the economy and society. As Minogue comments

'what governments do' embraces the whole of social, economic and political life, either in practice or potentially. Public policy is self-evidently not a narrow field of enquiry, though policy analysts may well focus only on narrow areas of the broad field. Public policies do things to economies and societies, so that ultimately any satisfactory explanatory theory of public policy must also explain the interrelations between the state, politics, economy and society. (Minogue, n.d., p. 5)

We would endorse this view, adding only that economies and societies 'do things' to policies as well as vice versa. It follows that policy analysis should give due consideration to the social, political and economic contexts within which problems are tackled. It also follows that the student of the policy process should stand back from the world of everyday politics in order to ask some of the bigger questions about the role of the state in contemporary society and the distribution of power between different social groups. Unless this is done then policy analysis must remain at best a partial enterprise.

While there is increasing recognition of the importance of these bigger questions in the policy analysis literature, it remains the case that many writers ignore this level of analysis. In short, what we are suggesting is the need to combine systems analysis with systemic analysis in order to provide an adequate understanding of government action. This points to the importance of giving attention to issues about how decisions are taken within the organisations comprising the policy-making and implementation system, issues about the institutional arrangements comprising the system and issues about the role of the state and its relationship to society. In addition there are clearly issues about the ways in which these three concerns fit together which are particularly significant and problematic.

Conclusion

Much of the discussion in this chapter has been based on the distinction between analysis of policy and analysis for policy. We have argued that policy analysis is concerned both with furthering understanding of policy and the policy process, and with prescribing how policy might be improved. In conclusion, we want to draw attention to the difficulty of maintaining this distinction. Our experience of teaching and writing about policy analysis over a number of years suggests that students and readers almost invariably seek to draw lessons from analysis, however much the analysis is presented as simply explanation. For this reason, the academic analyst – like his or her bureaucratic counterpart – may not be able to avoid becoming a policy advocate. We are also conscious that analysis cannot be value-free. As Rein (1976 and 1983) has observed, the idea that analysis is scientific, dispassionate and value-neutral is a myth because research is inevitably influenced by the beliefs and assumptions of the researcher. The framework within which policy research is carried out also has a bearing on the issues that are investigated and the questions that are asked. The fact that policy research is often funded by government agencies means that the research agenda is set by politicians and bureaucrats rather than academics. For all of these reasons Rein disputes the view that analysis can be devoid of values, and he advocates a value-critical stance in which the researcher adopts a sceptical approach and continually questions the assumptions of policy-makers. The value-critical stance implies that for policy analysts the 'most demanding task is identification of their own values' (1976, p. 169). If this is the case, then what values does the policy analyst pursue, and what is the implicit ideology of policy analysis?

Rein is but one of a number of comparatively recent American policy analysts who have contributed to shifting this activity in their country from a comparatively naive concern with problem-solving technologies towards a recognition of the extent to which they are engaged in an activity constrained by politics and deeply penetrated by value concerns (see Heineman *et al.*, 1990). Aaron Wildavsky's work also provides a reference point for addressing these questions. Reflecting on the failure of social programmes in the United States in the 1960s, in his *Speaking Truth to Power,* Wildavsky comments, 'Much of the scholarship of the seventies, my own included, has been an effort to understand what went wrong and to learn how things might be made to work better' (1979, p. 4). Wildavsky goes on to argue that policy analysis is about learning from experience, particularly from the experience of failure, and correcting errors when they arise. Too much should not be expected of analysis, and in contrast to the large claims for policy analysis made by Lasswell and Dror, Wildavsky rejects the idea that analysis should be concerned with the 'presentation of utopian scenarios' (p. 396). Instead he argues that analysis 'must remain anchored in the current pattern of social relationships' (*ibid.*). Analysis is therefore less concerned with how to realise people's objectives and preferences than with how to modify and scale down preferences so that they can be realised. Accordingly Wildavsky maintains that 'policy analysis is about improvement, about improving citizen preferences for the policies they – the people – ought to prefer' (p. 19). Within this framework, it is the feasibility of policies which provides the test of their goodness. If policies and problems can be accommodated to preferences and objectives, then the analyst will have succeeded.

The values which Wildavsky articulates are clearly of a conservative nature – a point he himself acknowledges. If policy analysis is located in the existing structure of social relationships, and if the scope of analysis is limited to problems already on the agenda for discussion, then significant issues may be ignored and the needs of particular groups may be overlooked. Although Wildavsky argues that social interaction and intellectual cogitation should be linked, his own preference is for interaction to play a greater role in policy-making than planning. Yet because governments have not been notably successful in tackling social problems, Wildavsky argues for a limited role for governments and for interaction to be enhanced through markets as well as politics. As one reviewer has commented, the 'general preference for market solutions over public planning' (Premfors, 1981, p. 222) is a key part of the ideology of policy analysis espoused by Wildavsky. As Minogue points out, turning the title of Wildavsky's book on its head, 'Power decides what Truth is' (Minogue, 1983, p.79).

Our own stance is somewhat different. While acknowledging the virtues of the pragmatic approach favoured by Wildavsky, we believe that policy analysts should not restrict themselves to examining how policies may be improved within existing social and political relationships. Rather, these relationships themselves should be part of the field of enquiry. Policy analysis need not be conservative if it focuses on nondecisions as well as decisions, and if some of the utopian scenarios which Wildavsky deliberately leaves out of his analysis are examined. Our preference is for politics over markets as a means of arriving at decisions, and we do not accept that governments have been entirely unsuccessful in their attempts to ameliorate social problems. As Wildavsky himself comments, 'Comparing the social state of the nation before and after these social policies [of the 1960s] . . . I wonder if we would be willing to trade current problems for those we used to have. I would not. I don't consider the sixties a disastrous decade' (1979, p. 5). In any case, even if government has failed in a number of policy areas, then the path to more effective action may lie less in the direction of government disengagement and withdrawal and more in the direction of acting upon the economic and social constraints which limit government effectiveness. It is for precisely this reason that we have argued the case for an approach to policy analysis which recognises these wider considerations. The effectiveness of policies and policy-making processes cannot be assessed independently of analysis of the distribution of economic and political power within political systems.

In support of our argument, and as a concluding comment, we cite the work of Charles Lindblom. For a long time Lindblom's major contribution to the policy analysis literature was widely regarded to be his work on incrementalism (Lindblom, 1959). Lindblom's critique of comprehensive rationality as a method of decision-making, and his exposition of muddling through as a preferable alternative, is a classic commentary on the process of decision-making. Later, Lindblom (1977) turned his attention to analysing the role of the state in contemporary society and he located the incrementalist thesis within a wider context. Specifically, Lindblom points to the power of business corporations in Western industrialised societies and their ability to block far-reaching changes. In this way Lindblom is able to suggest how incremental politics are related to particular kinds of social, economic and political arrangements. This is the kind of policy analysis work we favour since detailed analysis of specific issues is combined with an analysis of the role of the state. It is surely work of this kind that Lasswell had in mind when he argued that the policy orientation should examine fundamental and major questions in society rather than topical issues of the moment.

CHAPTER 2

THE ROLE OF THE STATE

The state in contemporary society has a profound impact on people's lives. From the moment of birth to the instant of death, the destinies of individuals are regulated and controlled by government agencies to an extent previously unknown. Yet state intervention is not a completely new phenomenon. Even in the nineteenth century complaints were voiced in Britain about the growth of regulation by the state, and what is distinctive about the modern state is the character and scope of its intervention. As Saunders notes, the state's 'character has been increasingly positive and directive while its scope has broadened to encompass areas of economic activity which have traditionally been considered private and thus inviolable' (1980, p. 140).

The growth of state intervention in advanced industrialised societies has been accompanied until recently by a curious neglect on the part of social scientists of the role of the state and its relationship to groups and individuals. To a considerable extent, mainstream approaches within established disciplines such as political science have concentrated on examining phenomena such as voting behaviour, electoral systems and pressure groups while ignoring the wider context within which these phenomena are located. It is significant that, in reacting to this neglect, the American editors of a recent volume of essays entitled their contribution 'Bringing the State Back In' (Evans, Rueschemeyer and Skocpol, 1985). In our view it is necessary to give the state a central position in policy analysis. The case for doing so has been expressed clearly by Wolfe who has asserted, 'If state power is ever to be understood, the term itself must be brought back into existence; to resurrect the state is to make a political declaration about the centrality of organised political power in modern societies' (1977, p. ix). We therefore focus specifically on the role of the state and theories of the power structure in this chapter, beginning with a definition of the state and a description of its functions.

What is the state?

The state can be defined both in terms of the institutions which make it up and the functions these institutions perform. State institutions comprise legislative bodies, including parliamentary assemblies and subordinate law-making institutions; executive bodies, including governmental bureaux and departments of state; and judicial bodies – principally courts of law – with responsibility for enforcing and, through their decisions, developing the law. There are variations between political systems in the extent to which legislative, executive and judicial institutions are separate from one another or overlap. In the United Kingdom there is considerable overlap between the Cabinet, Parliament and the House of Lords as the highest branch of the judiciary, while in the United States, the presidency, Congress and the Supreme Court are distinctive institutions, kept apart by the separation-of-powers principle. To support and maintain legislative, executive and judicial institutions, all political systems employ police and armed forces to guarantee internal and external security.

State institutions are located at various levels – national, regional and local. Peripheral institutions vary considerably in the degree of freedom they enjoy from central agencies. The autonomy of peripheral bodies is important, not least because this will influence whether central policies are implemented at the local level. The growth of state intervention has tended to increase the powers of central institutions, although there are important variations between political systems on this point. The existence of state agencies at different levels means that consideration must be given to the role of the local state as well as to the role of the national state. We comment on theories of the local state later in the chapter, noting in particular Cawson and Saunders' (1981) argument that different agencies of the state may be subject to different political influences.

Whilst this is a book which aims to generalise across the varied political systems of modern capitalist states, its authors come from one of the most unified of those states. This inevitably colours the way the topic of the state is treated here. It is important that readers of this book recognise that characteristics of the state, determined at an earlier stage in the history of each nation state, provide a framework of constitutional rules and procedures, albeit continuously renegotiable, within which political competition occurs. Dearlove and Saunders sum up this point as follows: 'The constitution sets the context within which politics operate; it is itself an object of political debate and conflict; and it provides a theory of how political processes should and do work' (Dearlove and Saunders, 1991, p. 538).

This is particularly important where federal systems make the respective layers of government significant actors in relation to each other. And even without federalism supra-national organisations may be important for the internal politics of a nation-state. Similarly, voting systems and constitutional relationships within bicameral legislative arrangements will structure the way in which the power game is played in a specific society. Thus, when we recognise, below, issues of choice between theories of the state our readers should realise that these structural considerations may affect the plausibility of specific theories (this is particularly true of the arguments about corporatism).

The bodies which make up the state perform several functions. The main role of the police and armed forces is the maintenance of law, order and peace. These functions are clearly fundamental to the persistence of stable relationships within a society, and they were among the earliest responsibilities taken on by the state. Indeed, it can be argued, following Weber (see Gerth and Mills, 1948), that having a monopoly of the legitimate use of force is what distinguishes state from non-state institutions. Equally important as the maintenance of internal and external security has been the state's role in protecting property rights, and its intervention, through the creation of judicial machinery, in establishing a system for dispensing justice between citizens. Until the twentieth century the state impinged on individuals mainly through its control, regulative and judicial activities. Only in relatively recent times has the state become heavily involved in the provision of services and in the operation of the economy. One of the consequences of state intervention in service provision and economic management has been the need to increase and extend the powers of taxation in order to finance state activities.

Although there are moves in a number of political systems to reverse these developments by cutting taxation and privatising functions previously performed by the state, it remains the case that individuals are affected in almost all aspects of their lives by what the state does. In contemporary terms, three areas of state intervention are of particular importance. First, there is the range of public services often referred to as 'the welfare state'. This area of intervention is manifested in the provision of services such as education, public health, pensions, income maintenance and housing. Second, following the widespread adoption of Keynesian economic management policies, the modern state has become more closely involved in regulating the operation of the economy. State intervention in this area ranges from facilitating industrial development through subsidies and tax concessions, to direct involvement in the productive process through public ownership of certain industries. Third, the complexity of economic and urban life makes it necessary for the state to engage in a range of regulatory activities to limit the collective impact of individual behaviour. These activities go far beyond the basic forms of social control required in simpler societies to embrace the prevention of the consequences of unrestrained economic activities: in particular, environmental protection, consumer protection and the limitation of the exploitative potential of monopolies and cartels. Significantly, inasmuch as there has been some state withdrawal from the direct provision of services and benefits this has increased the importance of these regulatory activities.

These points draw attention to the fact that the political activities of the state are inextricably bound up with economic developments within society. From an historical perspective, much of the growth of state intervention can be explained in terms of changes in the economy. For example, in Britain in the nineteenth century the Factory Acts which regulated working conditions were a response to perceived deficiencies in the way in which factory owners organised production processes. When attention was drawn to the existence of harmful and damaging working environments, the state intervened to curb the unbridled enthusiasm of entrepreneurs and introduced some measure of protection for industrial workers. Again, in the twentieth century the apparent failure of private enterprise and market mechanisms to maintain high levels of employment has resulted in state intervention in the economy through such measures as demand management, public works programmes and state ownership of industry in an attempt to create jobs. It should not be concluded from these comments that there is a direct and deterministic relationship between changes in the economy and state intervention. Clearly, no such relationship exists in practice, and economic changes have to be perceived and acted upon before there is any possibility of state intervention. Nevertheless, what the state does will be influenced in important respects by economic factors.

One of the issues this raises is the relative influence of state and societal factors in explaining the development of public policy. Nordlinger (1981) argues that the four main bodies of theory which have tackled this issue have all given 'society-centred' answers. Thus, pluralism emphasises the constraints imposed on the state by a wide range of groups and maintains that public policy is largely a reflection of the preferences of these groups; neo-pluralism or elitism stresses the power exercised by a small number of well-organised societal interests and notes the ability of these interests to achieve their goals; Marxism points to the influence of economic interests on political action and sees the state as an important means of maintaining the dominance of particular social classes; and corporatist theories also point to economic changes in industrial society as having a major impact on the role of the state and its interaction with outside groups. Nordlinger contends that none of these theories gives 'state-centred' explanations of public policy sufficient prominence. To explore these ideas in more detail, and to test the validity of Nordlinger's arguments, we will examine the different theories in order to understand better how the state operates in contemporary society.

Pluralist theory

The political systems of Western industrialised societies are often described as democratic. As Parry has noted,

> 'Democracy' and 'democratic' have become in the twentieth century words which imply approval of the society or institutions so

described. This has necessarily meant that the words have become debased in that they have almost ceased without further definition to be of any use in distinguishing one particular form of government from another. (1969, p. 141)

Parry goes on to comment that the classical liberal theory of democracy, represented by writers such as Mill and Rousseau, emphasises the importance of widespread political participation on the part of individuals. Inspired by Greek models of democracy, both Mill and Rousseau stress the need for direct and active involvement by citizens if democratic government is to be achieved. More recent theorists in the liberal tradition have played down the importance of participation, and have pointed instead to the role of regular competitive elections in democratic governments. Schumpeter (1947) exemplifies this body of work, defining democracy as 'that institutional arrangement for arriving at political decisions in which individuals acquire the power to decide by means of a competitive struggle for the people's vote' (p. 269).

Later contributions to the reinterpretation of democracy point to the representation of opinion through pressure groups as well as open elections as a key feature of democracies. Thus, it is argued that the pressure groups which have grown up alongside the formal institutions of government have come to play an important part in representing the views of specific interests. In the British context, Beer (1965) has noted the development of a collectivist theory of representation legitimising a much greater role for groups than earlier conceptions of representative government. Beer argues that as governments sought to manage the economy they were led to bargain with organised groups of producers, in particular worker and employer associations. Governments of both political parties sought the consent and cooperation of these associations, and needed their advice, acquiescence and approval. Similarly, the evolution of the welfare state stimulated action by organised groups of consumers, such as tenants, parents and patients. The desire by governments to retain office led them to consult and bargain with these consumer groups in an attempt to win support and votes. Beer's thesis has been developed in the work of Richardson and Jordan (1979, see also Jordan and Richardson, 1987), who have argued that Britain is a 'post-parliamentary democracy' in which policies are developed in negotiation between government agencies and pressure groups organised into policy communities.

According to Richardson and Jordan, pressure groups influence public policy from the point at which issues emerge on to the agenda to the stage of implementation.

In the United States the activities of groups are seen as central in the pluralist theory of democracy, whose foremost exponent is Robert Dahl. Pluralist theory, which Dahl also terms polyarchy, argues that power in Western industrialised societies is widely distributed among different groups. No group is without power to influence decision-making, and equally no group is dominant. Any group can ensure that its political preferences and wishes are adopted if it is sufficiently determined. The importance of pluralist theory is demonstrated by the fact that, implicitly if not always explicitly, its assumptions and arguments now pervade much Anglo-American writing and research on politics, government and the state. There are likewise echoes of the same approach in much of the political science literature in continental Western Europe and Scandinavia. A particularly interesting national variant of pluralist theory is the analysis of 'pillarisation' in Dutch political life emphasising the compromises between the three pillars of Calvinism, Catholicism and secular humanism (Lijphart, 1982).

Dahl's major empirical study was an analysis of power in the town of New Haven, reported in his book *Who Governs?* (Dahl, 1961). What Dahl did in New Haven was to select a number of key political issues and examine who won on those issues. One of the criteria used in identifying key issues was that there should be disagreement among two or more actors about what should be done. An issue was key, in other words, if there was open conflict. After studying a number of such issues, including public education and urban redevelopment, Dahl concludes that no one person or group was dominant in New Haven. Different interests were active on different issues, and there was no consistent pattern of success or failure. Indeed, one of the points Dahl notes is that interests opposed on one issue might join together on another. The only actor consistently involved was the mayor, but he was by no means dominant.

Building on the New Haven case study, Dahl and colleagues such as Nelson Polsby (1963) developed the more general theoretical position known as pluralism. This position does not hold that power is equally distributed. Rather, the theory argues that the sources of power are unequally though widely distributed among individuals and groups within society. Although all groups and interests do not have the same degree of influence, even the least powerful are able to make their voices heard at some stage in the decision-making process. No individual or group is completely powerless, and the pluralist explanation of this is that the sources of power – like money, information, expertise and so on – are distributed non-cumulatively and no one source is dominant. Essentially, then, in a pluralist political system power is fragmented and diffused, and the basic picture presented by the pluralists is of a political marketplace where what a group achieves depends on its resources and its 'decibel rating'.

The idea of politics as a marketplace in which leaders compete for votes is taken forward in the work of Downs (1967) who uses economic theory to analyse political behaviour. This development of pluralism has been regarded by some writers as a separate theory, described as 'public choice' theory or the theory of the state particularly identified with the 'New Right' (see Dunleavy and O'Leary, 1987, who devote a chapter to this kind of 'theory of the state') . We do not feel that it is appropriate to give it this separate treatment, since it is logically merely a development of pluralist theory, but some further comments on it are appropriate. The key argument is that in the political marketplace parties compete to win power, by responding to the demands of pressure groups (see Auster and Silver, 1979; Tullock, 1976; Brittan, 1977). There is a very strong pressure to yield to demands, and thus to enhance the role of the state as a giver of benefits (using that word in its general sense to embrace jobs, contracts, services and tax concessions as well as direct cash benefits). This is not very effectively restrained by the fact that these benefits have to be paid for because of the extent to which these costs can be hidden in the short run (by deficit financing) or spread in ways which lead benefits to be more readily perceived than the mechanisms to pay for them. For example, at the time of writing in Britain a dramatic cut in the impact of an unpopular local tax has been funded by a percentage increase in a sales tax rate (which will have a slight and gradual impact upon prices paid by consumers).

Public choice theorists from the New Right argue (Tullock, Brittan, *op. cit.*) that in this way the state grows in power and importance, and this may be damaging to the working of the capitalist economy. They also suggest that these pluralist (or demand side) pressures for government growth may be reinforced by monopolistic interests on the part of the state suppliers, bureaucrats and professions, in enhancing their 'empires'. At this point public choice theory does diverge from classical pluralist theory in giving a significant role to the state as an autonomous actor. This is an issue to which we will return in Chapter 3.

Another theme emerging from this school of thought has been the notion that there is a 'government business cycle' in which government expenditure, to satisfy demands and curb unemployment, is pushed up before general elections (Nordhaus, 1975; MacRae, 1977). The consequences of this are problems of inflation and adverse trade balances to be dealt with in the post-election period. Hence, it is argued that political behaviour may contribute to the cyclical problems of the modern capitalist state. While it is comparatively easy to find specific examples of behaviour to support this thesis, it is less plausible as a general hypothesis. The empirical data is not conclusive (see Mosley, 1984), the feasibility of this kind of behaviour depends upon electoral systems, fitting political activities to economic trends is a difficult activity, and we have seen attempts to make economic rectitude a political asset (see Dearlove and Saunders, 1991, pp. 66–7).

Let us return, after this brief digression into a particular application of pluralist theory, to the general issue of the way that theory deals with the role of government agencies. While some writers argue that government is neutral and acts essentially as a referee in the struggle between groups (Latham, 1952), the dominant theme in the work of Dahl is that government agencies are one set of pressure groups among many others. According to the latter interpretation, government both pursues its own preferences and responds to demands coming from outside interests. One point to note about modern pluralist analyses is that the state as such is rarely investigated. As Wolfe notes, over time 'political science became the study, not of the state, but of something at a less rarefied level called government' (1977, p. xii). This point is similarly emphasised in Dearlove and Saunders' work on British politics (Dearlove and Saunders, 1991) where they link it to a comparative complacency about democracy.

Elite theory

Elite theory challenges the view that power is distributed in the manner described by the pluralists. Drawing on the work of the classical elite theorists, Pareto and Mosca, later writers such as C. Wright Mills have pointed to the concentration of political power in the hands of a minority of the population. Pareto and Mosca argue that the existence of a political elite is a necessary and indeed inevitable feature of all societies. As Mosca states,

> Among the constant facts and tendencies that are to be found in all political organisms, one is so obvious that it is apparent to the most casual eye. In all societies – from societies that are very meagrely developed and have barely attained the dawnings of civilisation, down to the most advanced and powerful societies – two classes of people appear – a class that rules and a class that is ruled. The first class, always the less numerous, performs all political functions, monopolises power and enjoys the advantages that power brings, whereas the second, the more numerous class, is directed and controlled by the first, in a manner that is now more or less legal, now more or less arbitrary and violent. (1939, p. 50)

The classical elitist thesis maintains that political elites achieve their position in a number of ways: through revolutionary overthrow, military conquest, the control of water power (a key resource in oriental societies; see Wittfogel, 1963), or the command of economic resources. In the modern state, the position of elites is related to the development of large-scale organisations in many areas of life, with the result that there are different kinds of elites, not just those holding formal political power. Bottomore makes a distinction between the political elite which is made up of 'those individuals who actually exercise power in a society at any given time' and which 'will include members of the government and of the high administration, military leaders, and, in some cases, politically influential families of an aristocracy or royal house and leaders of powerful economic enterprises', and the political class, comprising the political elite but also leaders of political parties in opposition, trade union leaders, businessmen and politically active intellectuals (1966, pp. 14–15). Defined in this way, the political elite is composed of bureaucratic, military, aristocratic and business elites, while the political class is composed of the political elite together with elites from other areas of social life. What this suggests is that elite power may be based on a variety of sources: the occupation of formal office, wealth, technical expertise, knowledge and so on. To a certain extent, these resources may be cumulative but power is not solely dependent on any one resource.

In the twentieth century, the growth of large firms, the establishment of trade unions, and the development of political parties – all institutions in which effective power rests with an oligarchic leadership – underlines the significance of organisational control and institutional position as key political resources. Of particular importance in this context was the creation of bureaucratic systems of administration to carry out the increasing responsibilities taken on by the state from the nineteenth century onwards. As Weber notes, bureaucracies have both positive and negative aspects: positive in that they offer an efficient way of organising administration; and negative because they open up the possibility of power being vested in officials who were accountable neither to the public nor politicians (1947). The growth of bureaucracies may, in Weber's view, lead to control of the economy by bureaucrats. In this line of argument, elite theory does, contrary to Nordlinger's contention, draw attention to the need to look at the state itself. These themes are discussed more fully therefore later in the chapter in relation to corporatist theories of the state, and in the following chapter.

C. Wright Mills (1956), in a study of the United States, draws attention to institutional position as a source of power, and suggests that the American political system is dominated by a power elite occupying key positions in government, business corporations and the military. The overlap and connection between the leaders of these institutions helps to create a relatively coherent power elite. The elitist conclusions of Mills were paralleled by studies of local politics in the United States in the 1950s, in particular in the work of Floyd Hunter (1953). Hunter's study of Atlanta, Georgia, which was based on an analysis of the reputation for power of local leaders, uncovered an elite made up mainly of businessmen, bankers and industrialists. However, Hunter's work has been criticised by a number of writers, not least because of doubts about the reliability of the reputational method in identifying power relationships. It was because of these doubts that Dahl, Polsby and other writers in the pluralist tradition undertook their own empirical studies, analysing political activity on key issues rather than focusing on power reputation.

As we have noted, the conclusions of these studies were in conflict with the findings of Hunter. Yet the pluralists have themselves been criticised for ignoring the possibility that power may be exercised other than on key issues. The attack has been led by Bachrach and Baratz (1970), and we will be discussing their important analysis of power and nondecision-making in Chapter 4. The main point to note here is their argument that power may be used to control the political agenda and confine discussion to safe issues. If this is accepted, then the methodology adopted by writers like Dahl, involving the study of who wins in conflicts over key issues, may ignore important aspects of power. One of the implications of Bachrach and Baratz's work, which has been described as the neo-elitist critique, is that the distribution of power may be less pluralistic than Dahl maintains.

The issue which this raises is when does pluralism end and elitism begin? It has been suggested that the existence of elites is not incompatible with pluralist democracy because competition between elites protects democratic government. In other words, regular elections based on competition between the leaders of political parties, together with participation by pressure group elites in between elections, and interaction between these elites and the bureaucratic elites, are the ways in which democracy operates in the modern state. The fact that different elites operate in different issue areas is a protection against domination by one group. According to this interpretation, the structure of power in Western industrialised countries can be described as democratic elitism, involving not only competition between elites but also their circulation and replacement.

Elite theory, in both classical and modern guises, represents an important alternative to pluralism. Yet, while some writers have attempted to reconcile elitism and pluralist democracy, others have used the findings of elitist studies to argue that the power elite is but a ruling class by another name. That is, it is suggested that institutions may well be run by minority groups, but that these groups come from similar social backgrounds and are therefore exercising power in the interests of a dominant group. This is one of the points made by Miliband in his analysis of the role of the state in capitalist society (1969). The similarity in social background between state officials and the bourgeoisie is part of the evidence Miliband invokes to challenge pluralist interpretations of the power structure. In place of these interpretations, Miliband sets out an analysis based on the ideas of Marx. We will now consider the Marxist perspective on the role of the state in more detail.

Before doing that it is important to note that for Marxist theory the dominant *group* is a *class*. Until recently, much of the burden of the argument about the extent to which power is concentrated has been carried by Marxism. This has led to disregard of the extent to which other forms of social stratification, particularly stratification in terms of gender and ethnicity, may be significant for the distribution of power. Now, within both feminist literature and in the analysis of racism, a lively debate has developed about the extent to which these other forms of stratification may operate independently of, or in association with class divisions, to structure and bias the policy process. In this book we have chosen to focus upon the class analysis associated with Marxism, in the absence of a literature which relates these other forms of stratification to the policy process in general (but see Williams, 1989, for an analysis which relates these various stratification issues to social policy).

Marxist theory

Marxism is today seen above all as the ideology which unsuccessfully sustained the collapsed Soviet empire and continues to appear to hold sway in China. But it must be remembered that Marx's original purpose was to analyse the system of economic power dominant within capitalist societies and to show how that system contained the seeds of its own downfall. The fact that it has not fallen in the way predicted by Marx does not invalidate the whole of his analysis, particularly those parts relating to the significance of ownership or control of the means of production for power within the state. Marxist theory is considered here for the contrast it offers to pluralist theory, and for its emphasis upon power concentration which may be taken seriously without necessarily accepting either its predicted or even its prescriptive conclusions.

In his book, *The State in Capitalist Society*, Miliband takes as his starting point not the political process itself but the form of economic organisation or the mode of production. In advanced

Western industrialised societies the capitalist mode of production dominates, giving rise to two major social classes – the bourgeoisie and the proletariat. Miliband's analysis of the distribution of income and wealth, and changes in this distribution over time, demonstrate the continued concentration of wealth in a small section of the population. The question Miliband then asks is whether this economically dominant class exercises decisive political power. In other words, he explores the relationship between economic power and political power.

Taking their cue from Marx, writers like Miliband argue that the state is not a neutral agent, but rather it is an instrument for class domination. Marx expressed this view in the *Communist Manifesto*, where he wrote that 'The executive of the modern State is but a committee for managing the common affairs of the whole bourgeoisie' (quoted in McLellan, 1971, p. 192). Miliband suggests three reasons why the state is an instrument of bourgeois domination in capitalist society. First, there is the similarity in social background between the bourgeoisie and members of the state elite, that is those who occupy senior positions in government, the civil service, the military, the judiciary and other state institutions. Second, there is the power that the bourgeoisie is able to exercise as a pressure group through personal contacts and networks and through the associations representing business and industry. Third, there is the constraint placed on the state by the objective power of capital. Another way of putting this is to say that the freedom of action of state officials is limited, although not eliminated, by their need to assist the process of capital accumulation, which stems from their dependence on a successful economic base for their continued survival in office. In these ways, Miliband contends, the state acts as an instrument which serves the long-term interests of the whole bourgeoisie. As a result his approach has come to be known as 'instrumentalism'.

The argument can be taken a stage further by examining the functions of the state in capitalist society. In broad terms this theory suggests that the capitalist state's main function is to assist the process of capital accumulation. This means creating conditions in which capitalists are able to promote the production of profit. At the same time the state acts to maintain order and control within society. In specific terms, assisting accumulation means providing physical resources such as roads and industrial sites, while maintaining order is carried out both through repressive mechanisms like the police and through agencies such as schools which perform an important legitimation function. The accumulation process is further assisted through state intervention in the provision of services such as housing and health to groups in the working population. One of the functions of these services is to reduce the cost of labour power to capital and to keep the work force healthy.

O'Connor (1973) classifies these different forms of state expenditure as social investment, social consumption and social expenses. Social investment increases labour productivity through the provision, for example, of infrastructure and aid to industry; social consumption lowers the cost of reproducing labour power as, for example, in the provision of social insurance; and social expenses serve to maintain social harmony. In practice, nearly all interventions by the state perform more than one of these functions. O'Connor's typology is valuable in relating state intervention to underlying economic and social processes, but the typology is not by itself intended to provide an answer to the question: whose interests are served by state activity?

O'Connor's own analysis suggests that state expenditure serves the interest of monopoly capital, and that the state is run by a class-conscious political directorate acting on behalf of monopoly capitalist class interests. In a similar vein, Gough (1979) makes use of O'Connor's typology to show how the modern welfare state serves the long-term interests of the capitalist class. Thus O'Connor and Gough are broadly sympathetic to Miliband's perspective on the role of the state. Yet Miliband's thesis has itself been criticised by other Marxists, and it is worthwhile considering some of these criticisms as they have a direct bearing on the question of the relationship between economic power and political power.

Miliband's main protagonist has been Poulantzas, who has maintained that Miliband accepts too readily the concepts and framework of the pluralists. As Poulantzas argues,

> Miliband sometimes allows himself to be unduly influenced by the methodological principles of the adversary. How is this manifested? Very briefly, I would say that it is visible in the difficulties that Miliband has in comprehending social classes and the State as *objective structures*, and their relations as an *objective system of regular connections*, a structure and a system whose agents, 'men', are in the words of Marx, 'bearers' of it – *trager*. (1973a, pp. 294–5)

What Poulantzas seeks to demonstrate is that the class background of state officials is not important. The key is the third set of factors in Miliband's analysis, the structural constraints placed on the state by the objective power of capital. It is these constraints, Poulantzas contends, the 'objective relation' between the bourgeoisie and the state, which explain the political supremacy of the economically dominant class. For Poulantzas, then, the state is not, as we suggested earlier, a collection of institutions and functions, but a relationship between classes in society. In his later analysis in *Marxism and Politics* (1977), Miliband takes forward the discussion in *The State in Capitalist Society*, and goes some way towards meeting Poulantzas's criticisms, placing rather more emphasis on structural constraints. However, he in turn criticises Poulantzas, accusing him of determinism. Miliband contends that the structuralist argument 'deprives "agents" of any freedom of choice and manoeuvre and turns them into the "bearers" of objective forces which they are unable to effect' (1977, p. 73). In contrast to the structuralist approach Miliband wishes to argue that although the state in capitalist societies is a class state, it has some autonomy from the bourgeoisie. This autonomy helps explain why, for instance, the state may carry out reforms in the interests of the proletariat.

This again raises the thorny question of the relationship between economic power and political power. In Marx's work there is explicit acknowledgement that the relationship is not simply deterministic, and that the state may enjoy some independence from the bourgeoisie. His discussion of Bonapartism in France and Bismarck's rule in Germany, and the analysis of the coming to economic power of the bourgeoisie in England while the landed aristocracy retained political power, demonstrate this. Miliband takes up this theme by noting the later growth of Fascism in Italy and Germany, and by pointing to different forms of the capitalist state, including bourgeois democracy and authoritarianism. The key to understanding these developments, argues Miliband, is that all capitalist states have relative autonomy from the bourgeoisie (1977, Ch. 4).

Like Miliband, Poulantzas uses the concept of relative autonomy to explain the disjunction between economic power and political power. One of the points Poulantzas stresses is that the bourgeoisie or capital is divided into different interests, or fractions, and as well as acting in a reformist manner to help the proletariat, the state may also act against the interests of a particular fraction of the bourgeoisie. Thus

> relative autonomy allows the state to intervene not only in order to arrange compromises *vis-à-vis* the dominated classes, which, in the long run, are useful for the actual economic interests of the dominant classes or fractions; but also (depending on the concrete conjuncture) to intervene against the long term economic interests of *one or other* fraction of the dominant class: for such compromises and sacrifices are sometimes necessary for the realisation of their political class interests. (1973b, p. 285)

It should be noted that the concept of relative autonomy presents a number of problems. In particular, although it provides an adequate description of how the state in capitalist society actually operates, it does not furnish a satisfactory explanation of state activities (Saunders, 1981a). To explain the activities of the capitalist state requires the identification of criteria for locating the limits of dependence by the state on the bourgeoisie and the conditions under which state agencies are able to operate autonomously. Neither Poulantzas nor Miliband is able to deal adequately with this issue.

Hence, two developments in neo-Marxist work tend to undermine its special characteristics as a theory which explains the operation of the state. Once it is acknowledged that capitalists are a divided group, who do not necessarily have interests in common, and that the state has a measure of autonomy, it becomes difficult to predict the outcome of the policy process, that is the behaviour of the state, by reference to the interests of capital. The question to be addressed here is whether this has the effect of reducing what we can say about the power of capital to a statement, evident to all but the most naive, that state action will tend to support the existing economic order. Such a sentence sums up over a century's intense debate about the feasibility of democratic socialist change in a banal proposition. Yet it must be acknowledged that there are considerable difficulties in distinguishing some of the positions taken by contemporary neo-Marxist writers from those who subscribe to a version of pluralist theory which stresses group inequalities (see further discussion of this 'convergence' in McLennan, 1989).

Despite their differences, both Miliband and Poulantzas see the capitalist state as one of the main means by which class domination is maintained. In this respect, they represent a radically different approach both to the pluralists – who tend to see government as one set of pressure groups among many others – and to the elitists, who argue that the state elite is powerful but not tied to a particular class within society. For the elitists, the state elite is able to achieve independent power because of its control of organisational and political resources. This argument finds echoes in the fourth theory we consider, corporatism, which gives much greater emphasis to state autonomy and dominance.

Corporatist theory

Winkler has argued that the state in capitalist society has come to adopt a more directive and interventionist stance as a result of a slowing down of the process of capital accumulation (1976). He points to industrial concentration, international competition and declining profitability in the United Kingdom economy as examples of significant changes in the economic system which have prompted the shift towards corporatism. In his writings Winkler stresses the economic aspects of corporatism, seeing it as a system of private ownership of the means of production combined with public control. According to Winkler, examples of corporate involvement by the state in the United Kingdom are provided by the development of policies on prices and incomes and the attempt during the 1970s to develop planning agreements with industry. These policies were worked out by the state in collaboration with business and trade union elites. However, Winkler does not specify precisely the role of the state in a corporate economy, nor does he discuss in detail the sources of state power. What seems clear, though, is that the state is not controlled by any particular economic class or group, but plays an independent and dominant role in its relationship with labour and capital. In this sense, Winkler's thesis has earlier parallels in Weber's arguments about the ability of bureaucracies to exercise power.

The political history of corporatism in Britain has been outlined most fully by Middlemas (1979, 1986). Middlemas argues that a process of corporate bias originated in British politics in the period 1916 to 1926 when trade unions and employer associations were brought into a close relationship with the state for the first time. As a consequence, these groups came to share the state's power, and changed from mere interest groups to become part of the extended state. Effectively, argues Middlemas, unions and employers' groups became 'governing institutions' (1979, p. 372), so closely were they incorporated into the governmental system. By incorporation, Middlemas means the inclusion of major interest groups into the governing process and not their subordination. The effect of incorporation is to maintain harmony and avoid conflict by allowing these groups to share power.

Middlemas's thesis has close parallels in the work of Schmitter, who analyses corporatism as a system of interest representation. Schmitter defines the ideal type of corporatism as

> a system of interest representation in which the constituent units are organised into a limited number of singular, compulsory, non-competitive, hierarchically ordered and functionally differentiated categories, recognised or licensed (if not created) by the state and granted a deliberate representational monopoly within their respective categories in exchange for observing certain controls on their selection of leaders and articulation of demands and supports. (1974, pp. 93–4)

In Schmitter's analysis there are two forms of corporatism: state and societal. State corporatism is authoritarian and anti-liberal and describes the political systems of Fascist Italy and Nazi Germany. In contrast, societal corporatism originated in the decay of pluralism in Western European and North American political systems. Schmitter hypothesises that in the latter systems changes in the institutions of capitalism, including concentration of ownership and competition between national economies, triggered the development of corporatism. The need to secure the conditions for capital accumulation forced the state to intervene more directly and to bargain with political associations. The emerging societal corporatism came to replace pluralism as the predominant form of interest representation. Schmitter sees corporatism as an alternative to pluralism and clearly the pattern of interaction which Middlemas describes bears a close resemblance to Schmitter's definition.

In the United States the relevance of the corporatist thesis has been questioned by observers such as Salisbury (1979) who have argued that Schmitter's model of societal corporatism does not fit the American experience. A different stance is taken by Milward and Francisco (1983) who note important trends towards corporatism in the United States. According to Milward and Francisco, corporatist interest intermediation occurs around policy sectors based on government programmes. In these sectors, state agencies support and rely on pressure groups in the process of policy formulation. The result is not a fully developed corporate state but rather 'corporatism in a disaggregated form'. In Milward and Francisco's view, neither federalism nor the separation of powers has precluded the development of corporatist policies because corporatism is based on policy sectors which cut across both territorial boundaries and different parts of government.

It is apparent even from this brief discussion that corporatism is viewed in different ways by different writers. Theorists such as Winkler define corporatism mainly as an economic system to be compared with syndicalism, socialism and capitalism. In contrast, Schmitter, Middlemas, and Milward and Francisco discuss corporatism as a political system or sub-system. Reviewing these different approaches, Panitch (1980) argues for a limited definition of corporatism. In his view, corporatism is not a total economic system, as Winkler argues, but rather a specific and partial political phenomenon. More concretely, corporatism is a political structure within advanced capitalism which 'integrates organised socioeconomic producer groups through a system of representation and cooperative mutual interaction at the leadership level and mobilisation and social control at the mass level' (p. 173).

Wolfe (1977) is another writer who sees corporatism developing in response to the crises of late capitalism. Noting the tension between the demands of accumulation and the need for legitimation within capitalism, Wolfe argues that political alternatives have been exhausted and that one response to government overload is a corporatist organisation of the state. In Wolfe's analysis this could involve, among other things, the economy being under the domination of monopolies making private investment decisions; the state planning apparatus working closely with these monopolies to further their investment decisions; representatives from trade unions acting as consultants to planning agencies; and the institution of price and wage controls. Both Wolfe and Panitch suggest that corporatist political structures function mainly in relation to economic policy-making and not in other areas of state activity.

This approach bears similarities to the work of Cawson (1978), Saunders (1980) and Cawson and Saunders (1981). These writers maintain that corporate relations tend to characterise the politics of production, while competitive politics dominate the politics of consumption. Interestingly, Cawson and Saunders argue against a single theory of the state. Rather, they suggest that different agencies of the capitalist state are subject to different political influences, and this is important in highlighting the fact that the state may not be a unified set of institutions. In the British context, corporatist policies have developed at national and central levels because of the concentration of economic and productive policy-making activities at these levels. The power of state elites has come to be exercised in collaboration with business and union elites. At local level, competitive or pluralist politics have developed because local agencies of the state are mainly responsible for services and policies concerned with consumption. While economic policies are usually determined through negotiations between representatives of class interests, consumption policies are more generally the product of non-class-based struggles. Here then is an attempt to bring together elements from different theoretical approaches as a way of analysing the operation of the state in capitalist society.

The analysis of Cawson and Saunders has attracted criticism for trying to draw too tight a distinction between the activities of the two levels of government (Dunleavy, in Boddy and Fudge, 1984). It is an approach which is, in any case, too specific to the particular British configuration of central–local relations.

However, it is important not to forget the local dimension of the state. An increasing body of work has examined the operation of the state at the local level, and each of the theories examined here has been applied to both central and local levels. Indeed, many of the most important contributions by political scientists and sociologists to the discussion of the role of the state have their origins in empirical studies of local political systems: Hunter's (1953) work in Atlanta, Dahl's (1961) study of New Haven, and Bachrach and Baratz's (1970) analysis of Baltimore are three American examples; Newton's (1976) case study of Birmingham, Cockburn's (1977) work in Lambeth and Saunders' (1980) study of Croydon are English counterparts. Each of these studies lends support to one or other of the theoretical approaches discussed here.

As far as the corporatist tradition is concerned, it is also useful to consider Pahl's (1975) work on urban managers in the United Kingdom. Pahl's thesis is that the distribution of resources in urban systems is influenced by urban managers, that is, bureaucrats, local politicians and other local elites with control over resource allocation. In its later development (Pahl, 1977), this thesis emphasises also the role of the economy in influencing resource distribution, seeing the urban managers as performing a mediating function between the central state and the local population and between public and private sectors. As such, the urban managerialist thesis is almost indistinguishable from corporatism, and indeed Pahl collaborated with Winkler in developing the idea of the corporate economy. Pahl's work, and that of Saunders, suggests that it is important to examine in specific terms the operation of the state at the local level rather than to assume that the local state will function in the same way as the national state.

The corporatist thesis has been criticised by Marxists who have taken Winkler and others to task for failing to develop an adequate theory of the state. Thus, Westergaard argues that in Winkler's analysis the state 'figures in a curiously disembodied form' and 'its ability to put the powers which it has acquired to uses of its own is only asserted, not demonstrated' (1977, p. 177). Westergaard goes on to maintain that the principles which guide corporatism are merely those of capitalism, and that corporatism is not a distinctive economic system. For his part, Winkler does not argue that corporatism favours redistribution or equality, nor does he quarrel with the view that the state acts to restore private profitability and to enhance capital accumulation. Where Winkler and other writers in the corporatist tradition take issue with the Marxists is in their analysis of the role of the state and its autonomy. The corporatist thesis is that the state has moved from a position of supporting the process of capital accumulation to directing that process. In making this shift, new patterns of relationships have developed between the state and the major economic interest groups, and the state, although constrained by these interests, has autonomy deriving from its command of legal, organisational and other resources. It is this autonomy which enables the state to act in the interests of capital, labour and other interests as appropriate. To return to O'Connor's typology of state expenditures, it can be suggested, following Saunders (1981b), that social investment operates mainly to support capital while social consumption functions in the interests of other sections of the population.

The eleven-year rule of Mrs Thatcher led some British writers to dismiss corporatist theory as merely a description of a passing phase (see, for example, Gamble, 1988). During this period the trade unions were dismissed from the 'triangular' relationship, and at times even the role of business seemed to be downgraded. But this evidence surely only discredits those who proclaimed, borrowing Marxist historicism, that we entered, in the 1970s, the 'age of corporatism'. Corporatism remained in other countries, and may return in Britain, as a way in which the state may 'manage' its relations with key economic actors. Indeed, for some writers it is seen as the best way of managing the conflict between the needs of the economy and the demands of consumers, highlighted as a problem for democracy by public choice theory (see Mishra, 1984). Such a view is also embodied in those cautious formulations of corporatist theory which talk about the existence of 'iron triangles' embracing state and both sides of industry and operating in specific industrial sectors and not necessarily across the economy as a whole (Jordan, 1986). In this formulation it is a strategy the state may choose in relation to all or some of the policy system, or, as in the case of the governments of Mrs Thatcher, reject. In some cases the power of the interest groups involved may make it expedient for the state to choose such a strategy, but there is nothing preordained about corporatist arrangements.

The state as a key actor

What is, therefore, for us, important about the corporatist contribution to the debate about power is its emphasis on the state itself as a key actor. This point is also emphasised by Nordlinger. As we noted earlier in the chapter, Nordlinger maintains that state-centred explanations of public policy need to be given greater prominence. His thesis is that

> the preferences of the state are at least as important as those of civil society in accounting for what the democratic state does and does not do; the democratic state is not only frequently autonomous insofar as it regularly acts upon its preferences, but also markedly autonomous in doing so even when its preferences diverge from the demands of the most powerful groups in civil society. (1981, p. 1)

Nordlinger develops this thesis by identifying three types of state autonomy. Type 1 autonomy exists when the state acts on its own preferences when they diverge from societal preferences; type 2 autonomy obtains when state and societal preferences diverge and public officials act to bring about a change in societal preferences; type 3 autonomy describes the situation in which state and societal preferences are non-divergent and it is just as plausible to argue that state preferences influenced societal preferences to produce convergence as vice versa.

Nordlinger's analysis is valuable in making the case for the state and public officials to be given a more prominent place in explanations of government action. Of course, as Evans, Rueschemeyer and Skocpol (1985) have emphasised, he is not alone among American political scientists in identifying recently the comparative neglect of the state. Moreover, it must be questioned whether other theoretical perspectives down-grade the role of the state to the extent that he argues. As we have noted, pluralism tends to see government agencies as one set of pressure groups among many others; elitism points to the power of public bureaucracies alongside other elites; Marxism notes the relative autonomy of the state and its ability to act against the wishes of the bourgeoisie; and corporatism highlights the increasing independence of the state. Nordlinger recognises these arguments, but maintains that each theory is predominantly society-centred. We would dispute this, noting that corporatism in particular recognises the importance of state action.

Once we accept the idea of the state as an independent actor, we also need to recognise that it is not necessarily more unitary in its nature than the other participants in the policy process. Two other writers who have given considerable attention to the state as a partially autonomous creator of policies, Ashford (1982, 1986) and Heclo (1974) have, through comparative studies, drawn attention to the wide range of questions which need to be addressed about specific interest groups within the state, if policy outputs are to be satisfactorarily explained. This is a theme which will receive further attention at various places throughout the rest of this book.

Conclusion

In this chapter we have reviewed four main theoretical approaches to understanding the role of the state. In reality, of course, each approach carries within itself a number of contradictions and alternatives, as, for example, in the debate between Miliband and Poulantzas in the Marxist school. We agree with Saunders (and his co-writers, Cawson, 1981, and Dearlove, 1991, pp. 10–11) that to search for a single theory of the state is less useful than adopting a more eclectic approach which draws on the strengths of different theories. As Alford has noted, the difficulty with single bodies of theory, or single paradigms, is that 'Each paradigm has a tendency to claim more explanatory power than it possesses and to extend the domain of its concepts to answer those questions it is actually unable to deal with' (1975b, p. 152; see also Alford and Friedland, 1985).

In conclusion, then, let us spell out the key points we wish to draw from each theory. The strength of Marxist analysis is in focusing attention on the economic context of political activity. By reminding us that the state in Western industrialised societies functions in a capitalist economy in which the goal of capital accumulation is fundamental, Marxist theory avoids the trap of analysing political behaviour in isolation from factors which have a significant influence on that behaviour. However, the major difficulty with Marxist approaches is their treatment of the relationship between economic power and political power. While it is clear that the state in capitalist society is not completely independent of economic interests, it is equally apparent that the capitalist state is not merely an instrument of class domination and that it can and sometimes does serve non-bourgeois interests. Marxist theory fails to provide an adequate explanation of independent action by the state, and it gives insufficient attention to the way in which political power may derive other than from economic power. In particular, there is a need to bear in mind the way in which power relations within the family, and power derived from forms of ethnic and religious domination may reinforce, and accordingly be reinforced by, political power.

In any case, it is not necessary to subscribe to Marxist theory in order to be able to recognise the influence of the so-called 'bourgeoisie'. Lindblom's (1977) analysis of the privileged position occupied by business corporations in the capitalist state is an excellent example of a study in the non-Marxist tradition which is able to challenge the dominance of pluralist assumptions in much contemporary political science. Lindblom argues that business corporations enjoy a privileged position because government officials regard the functions performed by businesses as indispensable. It is this that gives businesses an advantage over trade unions and other interests. Accordingly, fundamental issues are never raised, and those issues that are contested cover a relatively narrow range.

There are clear echoes here of corporatist and elitist theories. The particular value of corporatism is in explaining the role of the state and the form of interest intermediation in relation to the economy and issues of production. The value of elitism is in arguing that political power may derive from a variety of sources, and that in all political systems a minority of the population is likely to exercise that power. The central role played by elites – bureaucratic, business, trade union, intellectual, professional and so on – is apparent not just in the area of economic policy-making, but also in respect of welfare services and consumption policies. On issues of consumption a more pluralistic pattern of political activity exists with the leaders of interest groups negotiating policies with bureaucratic elites in a system which may be described as democratic elitism or biased pluralism (see, for example, Newton, 1976; and Simmie, 1981). Moreover, it is necessary to go beyond this production/consumption dichotomy, to recognise how different issues bring into play different interest groups. The politics of economic management is very different, for example, from the politics of abortion.

One of the important points this discussion draws attention to is the relationship between elites and non-elites, and the impact of the state on individual citizens. This point is taken up in the work of Jessop (1982) who, in an extensive review of contemporary Marxist theories of the state, maintains that the state must be analysed as a set of institutions involving conflicts between a range of interests, not just social classes. Jessop draws particular attention to the relationship between state officials and citizens as a source of potential conflict. These relationships may take a number of forms, for example as between taxpayer and tax collector, tenant and housing official, and pensioner and social insurance officer. While Jessop points to the role of the state in mediating class relations, he argues that an adequate theory of the state needs to consider non-class-based struggles. This is a view we would endorse, and we return to consider these issues in later chapters.

CHAPTER 3

BUREAUCRACY AND THE STATE

Introduction

In order to explore further the nature of the state and its role in the policy process we need to give attention to questions about the role of the state apparatus or bureaucracy. Alongside, and connecting with it to various degrees, the debate about the nature of the state is a debate about the nature of bureaucracy. The different theories of the state take, or imply, different positions on the role of bureaucracies in capitalist societies. Pluralists tend to see bureaucracies as agencies which both pursue their own interests and respond to pressure placed on them by outside groups and individuals. Elitists argue that bureaucracies are an important source of power alongside other large-scale organisations. Marxists view bureaucracies mainly as a means by which dominant class interests are maintained, although recent Marxist theory does recognise the scope for independent bureaucratic action through the notion of relative autonomy. Corporatists hold that bureaucracies play a dominant role in the policy process in modern capitalist societies. Among these theorists there is an important distinction between the elitists and corporatists who in essence derive their inspiration from Max Weber and who point to the increasing importance of bureaucracies, and Marxists who argue that bureaucracies are principally instruments of class domination. Marxists maintain that in capitalist societies the institutions of the state will to a large extent be controlled by the bourgeoisie, and many of the earlier Marxists argued that administration would be unproblematical in socialist societies as the state would simply 'wither away'.

In contrast to both of these positions, the liberal pluralist tradition in political science has often implicitly assumed that there will be no difficulty in securing a civil service that carries out the will of its political masters without question. Albrow has shown how, in the nineteenth century, the development of a representative democratic system of government was seen as ensuring that the European 'disease' of bureaucracy did not occur in England. He quotes Carlyle as saying, 'I can see no risk or possibility in England. Democracy is hot enough here' (1970, p. 21). It may be taken as a common view at that time that England had democratic government, while Germany had bureaucratic administration because she had not yet acquired a fully representative system of government. The dangers of bureaucratic government were recognised by English students of government like Mill and Bagehot, but they saw the political system as supplying sufficient protection against them.

For Marx and Engels, as we showed in Chapter 2, this 'representative government' provides no more than a vehicle for the reinforcement of the power of the bourgeoisie. To them the debate about the relations between democracy and bureaucracy is irrelevant, and the presence in central Europe of autocratic administrative systems was simply a survival from the precapitalistic era. They argue that 'all struggles within the state, the struggle between democracy, aristocracy and monarchy, the struggle for the franchise etc. etc., are merely the illusory forms in which the real struggles of the different classes are fought out among one another' (Marx and Engels in Feuer, 1959, p. 296).

Notwithstanding their aloof position in regard to the liberal concern with the relations between state power and democracy, Marx and Engels recognise the coercive nature of the state, and regard it as one of the evils of capitalist society, an instrument to ensure bourgeois domination. Accordingly, for them, the eventual revolution, the eventual overthrow of the bourgeoisie by the proletariat, will take care of the state too. In the words of Engels (1958):

> The state, then, has not existed from all eternity. There have been societies that did without it, that had no conception of the state and state power. At a certain stage of economic development, which was necessarily bound up with the cleavage of society into classes, the state becomes a necessity owing to this cleavage. We are now rapidly approaching a stage in the development of production at

which the existence of these classes not only will have ceased to be a necessity but will become a positive hindrance to production. They will fall as inevitably as they arose at an earlier stage. Along with them the state will inevitably fall. The society that will organise production on the basis of a free and equal association of the producers will put the whole machinery of state where it will then belong; into the Museum of Antiquities by the side of the spinning wheel and the bronze axe. (p. 322)

The main assault upon the positions taken by both Marxists and liberals developed between the last years of the nineteenth century and the First World War, as a number of writers produced evidence of the growing importance of the administrative, or bureaucratic, machinery in industrialised societies and argued from that evidence that the bureaucracy represented a social and political force of increasing importance.

The most important of these writers was Max Weber (1947). Weber's discussion of bureaucracy is associated with his analysis of types of authority. He postulates three basic authority types: charismatic, traditional and rational-legal. Charismatic authority is based upon 'devotion to the specific and exceptional sanctity, heroism or exemplary character of an individual person' (p. 328). It is a transitory phenomenon associated with periods of social turmoil; the essentially personal nature of the relationship between leader and follower makes the development of permanent institutions impossible and accordingly it succumbs to processes of 'routinisation' which transform it into one of the other types of authority. Traditional authority on the other hand rests upon 'an established belief in the sanctity of immemorial traditions and the legitimacy of the status of those exercising authority under them' (*ibid.*). While charismatic authority's weakness lies in its instability, the weakness of traditional authority is its static nature. It is thus the case that the rational-legal type of authority is superior to either of the other two types.

Weber states that rational-legal authority rests upon 'a belief in the legality of patterns of normative rules, and the right of those elevated to authority under such rules to issue commands' (*ibid.*). The maintenance of such a system of authority rests upon the development of a bureaucratic system of administration in which permanent officials administer, and are bound by, rules.

Weber regards the development of bureaucratic administration as intimately associated with the evolution of modern industrialised society. Bureaucratisation is seen as a consequence of the development of a complex economic and political system, and also a phenomenon that has helped to make these developments possible. Therefore in his view it is a phenomenon with which exponents of theories of representative government must learn to come to terms.

Students of Weber have differed in the extent to which they regard him as a theorist who believed that bureaucracy can be subjected to democratic control. The view that he was doubtful of the capacity of the liberal ideal to survive, as well as being a critic of the Marxist position, is expressed by Bendix (1960), who draws attention to Weber's observation that:

> bureaucracy had turned from an ally into an enemy of capitalism. At the time of the absolute monarchies the bureaucratisation of government has made possible a 'wider range of capitalist activity'. But today one can expect 'as an *effect* of bureaucratisation a policy that meets the petty bourgeois interest in a secure traditional "subsistence", or even a state socialist party that strangles opportunities for private profit'. Along these lines, Weber anticipated some kind of reversion to patrimonialism. The dictatorship potential implicit in mass appeals added to the desire for a secure subsistence which would result in a centralised bureaucracy under a dictator, a vast army of state pensioners, and an array of monopolistic privileges. (quoted in Gerth and Mills, 1948, p. 49)

Clearly, then, Weber stresses the importance of the authority system, where Marx is concerned mainly with the system of production, to explain political relations in the capitalist state. Moreover, Weber implies that the bureaucracy gives the state power to shake itself free of bourgeois control. But he goes further to express scepticism about the Marxist claim that the state will 'wither away' under socialism. According to Weber, say Gerth and Mills, 'Socialisation of the means of production would merely subject an as yet relatively autonomous economic life to the bureaucratic management of the state' (p. 49).

After Weber: the pluralist reaction to the evidence of the growth of bureaucracy

Part of Weber's thesis about the growing power of bureaucratic officials is illustrated with reference to one specific political area by

Roberto Michels. In his book *Political Parties* (1915), Michels sets out to show that power in democratic mass parties becomes concentrated in a few hands. A key part of his argument is that full-time officials in socialist parties and trade unions are in a very strong position as 'professionals' relative to the 'amateurs' who may challenge them from the ranks of their supporters. A logical extension of this argument is to point out that permanent civil servants are in a similar strong position relative to politicians. Moreover, Michels argues that radical and socialist politicians tend to become conservative, compromised by the bourgeois comfort of their own positions. They enjoy a situation in which they are at least partially accepted by the established order which they were elected to challenge, and inevitably many of them identify with one-time 'class enemies' rather than with their own mass supporters. In such cases they are ill-equipped to offer an effective challenge to civil servants who do not share their political commitments.

The primary target for Michels' attack was the democratic socialists, aspiring to achieve peaceful social change through control of the state by a mass political party, but his argument does hint indirectly at the problems that face the proletariat in controlling their own political apparatus in the Marxist post-revolutionary situation. Mosca (1939), on the other hand, is concerned to show much more directly that a socialist state will inevitably centralise power, and that mass democratic institutions are unable to control those at the centre of the political system. His argument implies either that permanent bureaucrats will enjoy a powerful position relative to politicians or that politicians will become, in effect, bureaucrats rather than servants of the people. While the actual institutional structure may vary, the ultimate tendency will be for politicians and bureaucrats to become indistinguishable, and as far as democracy is concerned it will matter little whether what has happened has been the 'bureaucratisation of the politicians', or the 'politicisation of the bureaucrats'. To avoid this it is necessary to prevent the monopolisation of political power. The development of a powerful central bureaucracy must be checked by other independent institutions providing a source of countervailing power. What this seems to involve in particular, is the continued existence of economic power outside the control of the state. Mosca is one of the first theorists, therefore, to argue that pluralism must be sustained to protect democracy from bureaucrats. His theory was taken up in the 1930s by Burnham who is best known for his argument that managers are replacing owners as the dominant group in capitalist society. But Burnham (1942) also widens his argument to suggest that members of the 'managerial class' he claims to identify are beginning to dominate the state bureaucracy in all advanced industrial societies. He argues that the extension of state activities has helped to accelerate this trend, by widely extending the power of administrative bureaux. Burnham's position represents probably the most extreme of all the 'pessimistic' arguments about bureaucratic inevitability. He pays little attention to the possibility that bureaucracies may differ in kind and may be dominated by different kinds of people. As Gerth and Mills (1963) argue,

> much of the cogency that Burnham's thesis has is due to the simple fact that the form of organisation all over the world is, perhaps increasingly, bureaucratic. But the ends to which these structures will be used, who will be at their tops, how they might be overthrown, and what movements will grow up into such structures – these are not considered; they are swallowed in the consideration of the *form* of organisation, the demiurge of history, the 'managerial world current'. (p. 65)

While Burnham is little read today the burden of Mosca's attack on bureaucratic power has been taken up by the public choice theorists who suggest that many distribution issues in the modern state are better settled by markets than by bureaucracies. The analysis that has been developed has close links with the development of the economic theory of democracy discussed in the last chapter. In that discussion it was pointed out that the argument about the impact of demand upon state behaviour is reinforced by a 'supply side' argument which is concerned with the consequences of the fact that public bureaucracies tend to be monopoly providers of goods and services. This perspective then draws upon economic theory on monopoly which stresses the absence of constraints upon costs when these can be passed on to consumers and the extent to which in the absence of market limitations a monopolist will tend to over-supply commodities. It is argued therefore that bureaucrats will tend, like monopolists, to enlarge their enterprises and to use resources extravagantly (Niskanen, 1971; Tullock, 1967; and Buchanan and Tullock, 1962). Thus Tullock argues: 'As a general rule, a bureaucrat will find that his possibilities for promotion increase, his power, influence and public respect improve, and even the physical conditions of his office improve, if the bureaucracy in which he works expands' (1976, p. 29).

This theory has an intuitive plausibility, but comparatively little empirical evidence has been produced to support it. It is not necessarily the case that bureaucratic success is measured by bureau enlargement. Smith (1988, p. 167) points out how some of the most powerful and highly paid roles in civil services, in central finance departments for example, are in small organisations. Self has observed that 'Bureaucratic self-interest takes many different forms, depending on the different career patterns and normative constraints found in different public services' (Smith, *ibid.*, paraphrasing Self, 1985). Indeed, the political attack on big government has led to situations in which civil servants have been rewarded for their skills at cutting budgets, privatising public services and so on.

The use of such an economic model to theorise about public bureaucracy does however help us to analyse such organisations. It has led to a diligent search for situations in which 'perverse incentives' may be built into the day-to-day work of public organisations (see, for example, an influential examination of this issue in relation to the British National Health Service in Enthoven, 1985).

The model has also provoked a radical counterblast, cast in its own terms. Where market considerations apply organisations are likely to try to externalise costs. Without the constraints imposed by markets, bureaucracies may also, Dunleavy has suggested (Dunleavy, 1985, 1986, 1991), internalise costs. Examples of this include: exemplary employment practices (in relation to wages, equal opportunities, employee welfare, etc.), responsiveness to clients' needs and interests (appeals procedures, opportunities for participation on policy issues, etc.) and indeed general openness to political intervention. Demands that bureaucracies operate as if they were private firms directly challenge a variety of 'benefits' (that is, the costs which have been internalised), therefore, that have been often taken for granted as characteristics of the public service. Privatisation of such organisations, Dunleavy argues (1986) may both undermine the provision of these benefits and create situations in which there are incentives to externalise costs (pollution, needs arising out of low-wage policies, health consequences of employment practices, etc.).

Dunleavy accepts that bureaucrats will tend to engage in self-interested activities which are directed towards maximising their own welfare; but he shows that whether or not this will involve maximising the size of their organisation will depend upon the task of the organisation, the external (including political) pressures upon it and upon their own roles within the organisation. He describes their strategies as 'bureau shaping'. He sums up his position as follows:

> Rational bureaucrats therefore concentrate on developing bureau-shaping strategies designed to bring their agency into line with an ideal configuration conferring high status and agreeable work tasks, within a budgetary constraint contingent on the existing and potential shape of the agency's activities. (Dunleavy, 1991, p. 209)

Hence public choice theory has *both* provided a set of arguments to support an attack on public bureaucracy *and* stimulated thinking about how we analyse organisational outputs. The attack on the public sector has taken the forms of both outright privatisation and efforts to create competition between or within bureaucracies (see Olson, 1965 and 1982 for the development of a rationale for this). Nevertheless, in both this theory and Dunleavy's alternative to it, readers must note that the emphasis, as in classical economic theory, is upon what will be expected of an individual acting upon 'rational' self-interest. There remains a need to test whether actual behaviour is determined in this way.

Bureaucracy in twentieth-century Marxist theory

Marxist theorists were slow to take into account the implications of arguments about the growth of bureaucracy for their perspective. While Lenin's main preoccupation was to defend the Marxist position from the gradualist social-democratic theorists, rather than to deal with the views of writers like Weber and Mosca, he introduced a significant amplification of the doctrine that the state would wither away after the overthrow of capitalism by arguing that in the aftermath of revolution:

> The proletariat needs state power, the centralised organisation of force, the organisation of violence, both to crush the resistance of the exploiters and to *lead* the enormous mass of the population – the peasantry, the petty bourgeoisie, the semi-proletarians – in the work of organising the socialist economy. (1917, p. 41)

Thus, in this restatement of Marxist theory, the 'withering away of the state' accompanies the completion of the work of social transformation. In this way Lenin opened a gate that Stalin drove a cart and horses through, when he espoused the doctrine of 'revolution in one country' to explain the fact that the state did not wither away on account of its encirclement by bourgeois powers, and the consequent fact that the final attainment of socialism had to await world revolution. As realistic revolutionaries, Lenin and Stalin both found it necessary to acknowledge to some degree bureaucratic realities and to repudiate the anarchist tinge to the theories of Marx and Engels.

Of course the Leninist and Stalinist position on the state still involves no suggestion that there might be a split between the proletariat as executive – and hence nominal controllers of the state – and their officials as administrators, and thus perhaps the real controllers of the state. The role given in both pre- and post-revolutionary society to the 'party' by Lenin and Stalin, and their adoption of the notion of 'democratic centralism' as an organising principle, led the communist movement in such a direction, in a way which they obviously were not prepared to acknowledge. It was left to a Yugoslav communist 'renegade', Djilas (1957), to spell out what was really happening to the power structure of communist societies in his book, *The New Class*.

Djilas argued that the party ran communist society by means of a bureaucratic structure which elevated party officials into the position of a new ruling class. While it is possible to quarrel with Djilas' use of the concept of class, it has proved more difficult to find fault with his general analysis of the way in which power was distributed in communist societies. The eventual collapse of all the European versions of the communist model now, of course, undermines even the claims that this was a necessary stage in the effective transformation of capitalism.

Within Western Marxist ranks a more extensive debate developed about the independence of the state apparatus. One approach has been to argue that the evidence does not support the view that bureaucrats are a new class. This is found, for example, in Bottomore's book, *Elites and Society* (1966). Bottomore's argument with regard to civil servants is primarily based upon evidence from studies which show that recruits to the higher branches of civil services are largely drawn from the upper-middle classes, and have educational backgrounds that suggest that they will identify themselves closely with bourgeois interests. The evidence is not as unambiguous as Bottomore seems to imply, the main drawback of this kind of argument being that social origin does not necessarily determine current identification, interest or commitment.

However, to supplement the necessarily rather weak argument from social origins, Miliband (1969) argues that civil servants tend to be selected from people who are considered to have values lying within an ideologically safe spectrum, that civil service neutrality must involve an implicit commitment to the *status quo* and that, as the operators of the bureaucratic machine, civil servants become intrinsically suspicious of innovation. As was shown in our earlier discussions of his work, Miliband's Marxist position is naturally sustained primarily by a more general analysis of the social structures of Western societies. His argument about civil servants is that, even if they are in a position of potential power, they are constrained by the need to support the process of capital accumulation. The main elements in this argument have already been explored in Chapter 2.

Bureaucracy in elitist and corporatist theory

Contemporary elitist and corporatist theory regards the attempts of both the pluralists and the Marxists to come to terms with the growth of bureaucracy as unsatisfactory. The pluralists are seen as still either giving insufficient attention to the growth of bureaucratic power or determinedly holding on to an obsession about competition and a belief that devices to preserve it can be sustained and strengthened. The Marxists are regarded as still too concerned with economic power to give adequate consideration to state power. The attempt by some Marxists to account for the increasing power of the state through the concept of relative autonomy is, as we noted in Chapter 2, beset by difficulties.

Perhaps the most powerful attack on both the pluralist and the Marxist positions has come from C. Wright Mills:

> Liberalism has been concerned with freedom and reason as supreme facts about the individual; Marxism with supreme facts about man's role in the political making of history. But what has been happening in the world makes evident, I believe, why the ideas of freedom and

reason now so often seem so ambiguous in both the capitalist and the communist societies of our time; why Marxism has so often become a dreary rhetoric of bureaucratic defence and political abuse; and liberalism, a trivial and irrelevant way of masking social reality. The major developments of our time can be adequately understood in terms of neither the liberal nor the Marxian interpretation of politics and culture. (1963, p. 237)

Mills goes on to argue that this irrelevance is particularly a result of the development of bureaucracies, which neither kind of political theory adequately deals with, and so he claims:

Great and rational organisations – in brief, bureaucracies – have indeed increased, but the substantive reason of the individual at large has not. Caught in the limited milieux of their everyday lives, ordinary men often cannot reason about the great structures – rational and irrational – of which their milieux are subordinate parts. Accordingly they often carry out series of apparently rational actions without any ideas of the ends they serve, and there is increasing suspicion that those at the top as well – like Tolstoy's generals – only pretend they know. (pp. 237–8)

Mills argued that the only hope of preventing the massive bureaucracies of the United States and Soviet Union from racing on to the point where they destroy us all to lie in the fact that centralised decision-making was possible within them. Accordingly he argued that, paradoxically, these juggernauts, which are currently being run 'without reflection' by 'cheerful robots', can be brought under control. He thus asserted:

In the polarised world of our time, international as well as national means of history-making are being centralised. Is it not thus clear that the scope and the chance for conscious human agency in history-making are just now uniquely available? Elites of power in charge of these means do now make history – to be sure under circumstances 'not of their own choosing' – but compared to other men and other epochs these circumstances do not appear to be overwhelming. (1963, p. 244)

So Mills calls upon the 'intellectuals, the scholars, the ministers, the scientists of the rich societies' (1963, p. 246) to assume political responsibility and control their bureaucracies. Was this what happened in the Soviet Union?

It is easy to deride Mills' faith in the reason of intellectuals; as Bachrach (1969) argues, it is hard to see how the intellectuals can avoid being bought off, as Mills himself acknowledges they are now, or how they can reach a value consensus that will enable them to act concertedly to influence events (p. 59). Mills' argument focuses upon the fact that centralised decisions are taken in bureaucratised systems of government, and it is his view therefore that there are key decision points which are open to influence. The conclusion this suggests is that before rushing to any of the available macro-sociological conclusions about the role and control of bureaucracy in modern society it is necessary to study precisely how decisions are taken, and to what extent there are really key positions of power. It is also necessary to ask questions about the kinds of people in powerful roles, about who is able to influence them, and about who benefits from their decisions. This takes the argument from high-level theorising down to some quite detailed questions about the exercise of power. As Lipset (1950) argues: 'The justified concern with the dangers of oligarchic or bureaucratic domination has . . . led many persons to ignore the fact that it does make a difference to society which set of bureaucrats controls its destiny' (p. 271).

This points to the need to examine the characteristics and affiliations of public officials. We have already noted the arguments advanced by Bottomore and Miliband about the social origins of officials, and comparable views are also discussed by Kingsley (1944) and Lipset (1950). Kingsley shows that the British civil service was transformed from an aristocratic into a bourgeois organisation during that period in the nineteenth century when the commercial middle class were becoming politically dominant. The British bureaucracy was thus made representative of the dominant political class, but not of course of the people as a whole. To work effectively the democratic state requires a 'representative bureaucracy', Kingsley argues, thus taking up the theme, developed also by Friedrich (1940), that the power of the civil service is such that formal constitutional controls upon its activities are insufficient. Kingsley sees the recruitment of the civil service from all sectors of the population as one means of ensuring that it is a 'responsible bureaucracy'. Kingsley's is a Jacksonian doctrine updated to fit a bureaucratic age. Again, as in Chapter 2, it is important to point out that this issue has traditionally been explored very much in class terms (for a more recent comparative exploration of this issue along the same lines see Aberbach, Putman and Rockman, 1981). This has meant a disregard of the equally important issues about gender and about ethnic, regional or religious origins or background.

Lipset's treatment of this issue can be found in his study of the Saskatchewan socialist party, the Co-operative Commonwealth Federation, where he analyses the difficulties the party found in implementing their policies once they acquired power. Lipset supplements Kingsley's argument about the social backgrounds of civil servants by pointing out that previous experience of serving more conservative governments will also have an impact upon the behaviour of civil servants called upon to implement markedly different policies. With reference to Saskatchewan he says:

> Trained in the traditions of a *laissez-faire* government and belonging to conservative social groups, the civil service contributes significantly to the social inertia which blunts the changes a new radical government can make. Delay in initiating reform means that the new government becomes absorbed in the process of operating the old institutions. The longer a new government delays in making changes, the more responsible it becomes for the old practices and the harder it is to make the changes it originally desired to institute (p. 272).

This approach to the problem squares much better with the classical theory of bureaucracy than either the legalistic approach which treats civil service impartiality as an unalterable fact or the conspiratorial view that portrays civil servants as persons naturally committed to undermining a government of the Left. Civil servants are recruited from certain kinds of social backgrounds, given certain kinds of training, and become accustomed to working for certain kinds of people and dealing with certain kinds of problems; any new group of political masters who want to turn their attentions to new issues and problems are bound to find that they cannot easily reorient the civil servants. Indeed it is interesting that, while in Britain the higher civil service remains as biased in its social origins as ever (despite efforts to change this in the late 1960s), some representatives of the comparatively radical Right conservative government which came to power in 1979 did precisely hint at this kind of concern. There has subsequently been some controversy about the extent to which Mrs Thatcher directly intervened in appointments to deal with this 'problem' (see Young, 1989, for this claim, and Hennessy, 1989, for arguments to the contrary).

This suggests that it is misleading to present the issue here simply as a conflict between individuals with differing formal political affiliations or loyalties. Those writers who attack arguments about the power of public officials by stressing the detachment of officials from party politics largely miss the point. Chapman (1970) brings this out very clearly in showing the strong reservations civil servants in Britain have about party politics while at the same time possessing commitments to particular policies. He argues:

> However favourable to one party a civil servant is in his early years, because he works so closely with politicians, he soon becomes aware of the ineptitude of any party. After a time, it seems, he learns to think more in terms of policies and their workability, he focuses his political interests on the merits and demerits of particular policies, and since all political parties tend to have a mixture of policies, the parties are seen in a distinctly neutral light. (p. 120)

The implication is that public officials find changes in their political masters easy to adjust to so long as they do not involve violent ideological shifts. Officials can operate most easily in a situation of political consensus. Where consensus does not exist, however, their role may become one of trying to create it. Graham Wallas (1948) sums this up most neatly:

> The real 'Second Chamber', the real 'constitutional check' in England, is provided, not by the House of Lords or the Monarchy, but by the existence of a permanent Civil Service, appointed on a system independent of the opinion or desires of any politician and holding office during good behaviour. (p. 262)

This approach sees bureaucrats as a comparatively independent element in the political system. Similar arguments are advanced about the professional element in the public services. For example, Rex and Tomlinson (1979), in their study of race relations in an English city, argue:

> the existence of professional traditions and the relative independence with which professionals and bureaucrats sometimes operate, means that we should by no means treat these professionals and bureaucrats simply as the agents of prejudice and oppression or, as popular Marxist jargon now has it, as part of the repressive or the ideological state apparatus. (p. 66)

Rex and Tomlinson go on to take a stance very like C. Wright Mills on the relationship between these public officials and academics,

voicing explicitly a perspective which is implicit in the political behaviour of many committed intellectuals:

> There is much scope for communication between academics and
> professionals, and, whatever convictions one might have about our
> governmental agencies being subjected to political control, there
> is always a fruitful possibility of an expert's paper coming up
> through the bureaucracy, and, by its technical expertise, blinding a
> hapless politician who has to translate it into action with 'science'.
> (*ibid.*)

This kind of assertion does in some respects belong with the
traditional liberal case against both bureaucratic pessimism and
Marxist theory. It rarely emerges in the academic literature on
bureaucracy, yet policy studies such as, for example, Banting's
(1979) analysis of social policy developments in Britain in the sixties, pay tribute both to the power of ideas and the influence of
intellectuals. This is, however, very different from the liberalism of
democratic theory since this kind of influence may owe little to
popular support. Moreover, while Rex and Tomlinson are clearly
drawing attention to this influence as a benign force combating
racism, to claim that groups of this kind have power should not
imply any assumptions about the direction of that influence. This
has been a weakness in some of the social democratic theorising
about the welfare state. As Room (1979) argues: 'There is a certain
naivety over the accountability and beneficence of bureaucratised
welfare professionals, taking for granted their promotion of citizens' interests' (p. 256). Room's point is taken further by Gould
(1981) who sees the 'salaried middle class' of managerial and professional workers, many of them in state employment, as the dominant force in – and the main beneficiaries from – the welfare state.
Gould links his argument with corporatist theories, arguing that
the development of corporatism has shifted the balance of power
within the state from the bourgeoisie to the salaried middle class.
If, as Winkler maintains, corporatism is a system of private ownership of the means of production combined with public control,
then control rests largely with the salaried middle class, who, it can
be argued, have gained most from the welfare state. In this context,
Gould takes issue with Marxist approaches, arguing that state welfare may well be functional for capital but that bureaucracies on
the scale of those that exist in contemporary capitalist societies are
not in the interests of the bourgeoisie. It should be noted that some

of these arguments about the role of bureaucracies examine 'who governs' while others consider 'who benefits'. This is a theme to which we will return in the next chapter.

Reference here to professionals reminds us that in the whole of this debate there are dangers in treating public servants as a unitary group or class. Some of the issues about differences between bureaucrats and professionals will be explored further in Chapter 8. But we should also not lose sight of the fact that there will be differences of interests, experience and culture within a vast state bureaucracy, and in particular differences between the personnel of different departments (see Hennessy, 1989, especially Ch. 10). There are also groups of state employees to whom we have given little attention – such as the military, the police and the security services staff – who are radically different from most career administrators.

Alongside the concern to analyse the role of central state officials, a related interest has developed in the analysis of the management of the local state and of cities. The intense concern with community power, which has done much to advance the study of power in general, has had inevitably to embrace consideration of the roles of local bureaucrats. Pahl (1975) has written of these bureaucrats as urban managers with some degree of autonomy, but working in close cooperation with private sector elites (property developers, estate agents, architects, etc.). Others have seen local elites as essentially subordinate to the pattern of power and class relations in the national state (Cockburn, 1977). This issue, which was examined in Chapter 2, is relevant both to theories of the state and to studies of the role of bureaucracies. In our view, it is necessary to recognise that bureaucrats, whether at central or local levels, play an important part in policy-making, not least in mediating social and economic influences. In this sense, our position is closer to that of Pahl and corporatist theories than to Cockburn and Marxist analyses.

Conclusion

The analyses of the impact of bureaucracy upon political power examined in this chapter have been concerned mainly with relatively high-level theorising about the impact of public sector organisations in capitalist society. Our emphasis towards the end of the chapter on the need for more careful attention to be given to the specific manifestations of power and power relationships leads us in two directions. First, it suggests the importance, as we have indicated, of focusing on the role of different groups, including professions, within organisations. We take up this theme in Chapter 8. Second, it indicates the need to examine another body of theory concerned with bureaucracies, that which analyses in a more detailed way how organisations work. We take up this theme in Chapter 7.

CHAPTER 4

POWER AND DECISION-MAKING

Introduction

In examining the concept of power, the debate between the elitists and pluralists provides a good starting point. This is so because elitists and pluralists differ not only in the conclusions they draw about the distribution of power in contemporary society, but also in the methods they use to reach these conclusions and the definitions on which their analyses are built. Indeed, the methodological and definitional debates have at times threatened to overwhelm the substantive questions about the nature of the power structure that originally interested researchers in this field. In practice, of course, it is difficult to discuss methodological and substantive questions about power separately, and in this chapter we will examine both together, where appropriate referring back to the discussion of power and the state contained in Chapter 2.

The decisional approach

In an article published in 1958 Robert Dahl argues that 'the evidence for a ruling elite, either in the United States or in any specific community, has not yet been properly examined so far as I know' (p. 469). Dahl's article and the criticisms it contains were aimed explicitly at two studies which had claimed to find a ruling elite in the United States. The first study, by Floyd Hunter (1953), examined the distribution of power in Atlanta, Georgia. By analysing the reputation for power of local leaders, Hunter concluded that control rested with a small group of key individuals. The second study, by C. Wright Mills (1956), focused on the United States as a whole, and argued that a power elite drawn from the military, business corporations and state agencies governed American society. In his article, Dahl contends that the research methods used by Hunter and Mills were not sufficiently rigorous to justify their conclusions. In particular, Hunter's approach of examining the *reputation* for power of local leaders, and Mills' strategy of identifying those in key *positions* in large-scale organisations, did not meet the test Dahl proposes should be required of those claiming to find a ruling elite. In Dahl's view, there is a need for researchers interested in the power structure to examine neither power reputation nor organisational position, but rather to focus on *actual decisions* and to explore whether the preferences of the hypothetical ruling elite are adopted over those of other groups. Only in this way is it possible to test the assertion that a ruling elite exists. As neither Hunter nor Mills had adopted this test, Dahl maintains that the ruling elite model has not been examined properly.

Underpinning Dahl's critique is a definition of power that is spelt out more fully in his other writings. According to this definition, 'A has power over B to the extent that he can get B to do something that B would not otherwise do' (1957, p. 203). This draws attention to the fact that power involves a relationship between political actors. These actors may be individuals, groups or other human aggregates, and Dahl emphasises that power must be studied in cases where there are differences of preferences between actors. Actors whose preferences prevail in conflicts over key political issues are those who exercise power in a political system. It follows that the student of power needs to analyse concrete decisions involving actors pursuing different preferences. Careful study of these decisions is required before the distribution of power can be described adequately.

This is the method Dahl used in his own empirical study of New Haven (1961). In asking *Who Governs?* in New Haven, Dahl examined a number of more specific questions, including whether inequalities in resources of power were cumulative or noncumulative, how important decisions were made, and if the pattern of leadership was oligarchic or pluralistic. He concluded that in the period from the 1780s to the 1950s New Haven had gradually changed from oligarchy to pluralism. Analysis of the handling of three key political issues in the 1950s – urban redevelopment, public education and political nominations – revealed a situation in which power was not concentrated in a single group as the ruling elite theorists had hypothesised. Rather, because the resources which contributed to power were widely dispersed in the population, power itself was fragmented between different actors. And while only a few people had direct influence over key decisions, most had indirect influence through the power of the vote.

Nondecision-making

Dahl's work in New Haven, far from resolving the disagreements between the elitists and their critics, marked the beginning of a new phase in the debate about power. Specifically, Dahl came under attack from Bachrach and Baratz who, in an article published in 1962, argue that power does not simply involve examining key decisions and actual behaviour. Bachrach and Baratz assert that 'power is also exercised when A devotes his energies to creating or reinforcing social and political values and institutional practices that limit the scope of the political process to public consideration of only those issues which are comparatively innocuous to A' (1962, p. 948). Borrowing a term from Schattschneider, Bachrach and Baratz describe this as 'the mobilisation of bias' (Schattschneider, 1960, p. 71), a process which confines decision-making to safe issues. What this suggests is the existence of two faces of power: one operating, as Dahl indicates, at the level of overt conflicts over key issues; the other operating, through a process which Bachrach and Baratz term nondecision-making, to suppress conflicts and to prevent them from entering the political process. The implication of Bachrach and Baratz's analysis is that the methodology adopted by researchers such as Dahl is inadequate, or at least partial. A more complete analysis needs to examine what does not happen as well as what does happen, and to unravel the means by which the mobilisation of bias operates to limit the scope of debate.

But what does nondecision-making actually involve? In a second article published in 1963, Bachrach and Baratz define nondecision-making as 'the practice of limiting the scope of actual decision-making to "safe" issues by manipulating the dominant community values, myths, and political institutions and procedures' (p. 632). Bachrach and Baratz argue that a nondecision-making situation can be said to exist 'when the dominant values, the accepted rules of the game, the existing power relations among groups, and the instruments of force, singly or in combination, effectively prevent certain grievances from developing into full-fledged issues which call for decisions' (p. 642). In this respect Bachrach and Baratz distinguish nondecision-making from negative aspects of decision-making such as deciding not to act and deciding not to decide. In their view, nondecision-making differs from these other phenomena in that when nondecision-making occurs issues do not even become matters for decision. That is, issues remain latent and fail to enter the decision-making process because of the impact of the mobilisation of bias.

It is relevant to note the parallels which exist between Bachrach and Baratz's work and that of Easton. Easton's (1965a) systems model of political life discusses how gate-keepers help to regulate the flow of demands into the political arena. As such, systems theory recognises the significance of the second face of power. Yet whereas Easton is principally concerned with the way in which demand regulation helps to preserve the stability of political systems, Bachrach and Baratz emphasise the means by which vested interests are protected by nondecision-making. In their model of the political process, Bachrach and Baratz argue that demand regulation is not a neutral activity, but rather operates to the disadvantage of persons and groups seeking a reallocation of values. As we noted in Chapter 2, one of the implications of Bachrach and Baratz's analysis is that the distribution of power may be less equal than Dahl and the pluralists maintain.

The pluralists responded to Bachrach and Baratz's critique by claiming that nondecision-making was unresearchable (Merelman, 1968; Wolfinger, 1971). How, they asked, could nondecisions be studied? On what basis could social scientists investigate issues that did not arise and conflicts that did not emerge? Bachrach and Baratz replied by amplifying and to some extent modifying their position. In their book, *Power and Poverty*, published in 1970, they maintain that the second face of power operates to keep grievances covert. A nondecision – defined as 'a decision that results in suppression or thwarting of a latent or manifest challenge to the values or interests of the decision-maker' (1970, p. 44) – can be investigated through the identification of covert grievances and the existence of conflicts that do not enter the political arena. If no grievances or conflicts can be discovered, then a consensus exists and nondecision-making has not occurred.

Bachrach and Baratz go on to give a series of examples of the different forms that nondecision-making can take. First, there is the use of force to prevent demands from entering the political process. An example is the terrorisation by whites of civil rights workers in the southern United States. Second, there are various ways in which power can be used to deter the emergence of issues. The cooptation of groups into decision-making procedures is an illustration. Third, rules or procedures may be invoked to deflect unwelcome challenges. Referring issues to committees or commissions for detailed study is one example; labelling demands as unpatriotic or immoral is another. Fourth, existing rules and procedures may be reshaped as a way of blocking challenges. To these examples, Bachrach and Baratz add the point that power may be exercised by anticipated reactions. That is, an actor, A, may be deterred from pursuing his or her preferences because he or she anticipates an unfavourable reaction by another actor, B. Anticipated reactions may operate when a community group fails to mobilise because it anticipates an unfavourable response by decision-makers, or when decision-makers themselves do not act because they expect opposition from key political actors. Although these examples involve an exercise of power, Bachrach and Baratz note that this 'is not nondecision-making in the strict sense' (p. 46).

The value of the nondecision-making perspective has been demonstrated in a study of air-pollution policies in the United States. The study, which was carried out by Matthew Crenson (1971), compares two cities with respect to action taken to control dirty air. The cities, Gary and East Chicago in Indiana, are adjacent steel towns. While East Chicago passed a law controlling air pollution in 1949, Gary did not act until 1962. Crenson explains the differences between the two cities in terms of the existence in East Chicago of many different steel companies and the domination of Gary by a single corporation, US Steel. The delay in legislating in Gary resulted, Crenson suggests, from the power reputation of US Steel. Although not politically active, the economic power of US

Steel, which was exercised through anticipated reactions, was decisive. Thus, indirect influence was important, with political leaders anticipating that US Steel might move from Gary and adversely affect its prosperity if restrictive legislation were passed. In contrast, in East Chicago the fragmentation of the steel industry meant that it was easier for those seeking to control pollution to secure favourable action.

As Crenson notes, Dahl's empirical work recognises that power may operate in this way, as when Dahl attributes indirect influence to the community in New Haven. Crenson observes 'if indirect influence can work for ordinary community residents, then there is no reason why it cannot work for US Steel or General Motors or bank presidents or members of families in the Social Register' (p. 108). On this basis, Crenson supports Bachrach and Baratz's critique of the pluralists, and he maintains that observable action provides an incomplete guide to the distribution of political power. There can be little doubt that Crenson's study lends significant empirical support to the nondecision-making thesis. The comparative method used in the study, and the operation of indirect influence through anticipated reactions, illustrates the way in which the thesis can be tested.

The third dimension of power

The debate about power was taken a stage further by Lukes (1974), who argued that power must be studied on three dimensions. First, there is the exercise of power which occurs in observable overt conflicts between actors over key issues: the pluralists' approach. Second, there is the exercise of power which occurs in covert conflicts between actors over issues or potential issues: Bachrach and Baratz's method. Third, there is the dimension of power which Lukes adds, involving the exercise of power to shape people's preferences so that neither overt nor covert conflicts exist. In other words, when the third dimension of power operates, there is *latent* conflict.

Lukes states that latent conflict exists when there would be a conflict of wants or preferences between those exercising power and those subject to it were the latter to become aware of their interests. In this context, the definition of power employed by Lukes is that 'A exercises power over B when A affects B in a manner contrary to B's interests' (p. 27). In Lukes' view the existence of a consensus does not indicate that power is not being exercised, for as he argues

> is it not the supreme and most insidious exercise of power to prevent people, to whatever degree, from having grievances by shaping their perceptions, cognitions and preferences in such a way that they accept their role in the existing order of things, either because they can see or imagine no alternative to it, or because they see it as natural and unchangeable, or because they value it as divinely ordained and beneficial? To assume that the absence of grievance equals genuine consensus is simply to rule out the possibility of false or manipulated consensus by definitional fiat. (p. 24)

In large part, Lukes' argument that power should be studied on three dimensions is a response to the weaknesses he perceives in the writings of both the pluralists and Bachrach and Baratz. While accepting Bachrach and Baratz's critique of the pluralists, and the superiority of the nondecision-making thesis over the decisional approach, Lukes maintains that the idea of nondecision-making is itself inadequate because it does not admit the possibility that power can be used to prevent even covert conflict and potential issues emerging. Bachrach and Baratz had seemed to recognise that power might be used in this way in their early writings, but, as we have noted, they were forced to modify their position because of the criticism that grievances and issues that did not exist could not be researched. As a result they came close to advocating the very methodology they originally found wanting. This has been noted by Polsby (1980) who argues that

> Insofar as studying the mobilisation of bias entails studying the anticipated reactions of significant community actors, familiar methods – interviews and observations – are available to cope with the problem, and there is no reason to suppose that pluralists are any less able to deal with it than anyone else (p. 205).

Polsby also notes, in commenting on Bachrach and Baratz's reformulation of the concept of nondecision-making, that 'to define "nondecision" as a certain sort of "decision" is to revive the very pluralist approach that these authors earlier deplored' (p. 211). This is also part of Lukes' objection to Bachrach and Baratz's approach, and in his own analysis Lukes seeks to retain the more radical strand which was implicit in the original statement of the nondecision-making thesis.

The relevance of Lukes' ideas has been explored by Walsh and his colleagues in an analysis of power within organisations. Walsh *et al.* (1981) argue the need to examine not only overt conflicts in organisations but also, following Clegg (1975), the system of domination. By this they mean the way in which 'the prevailing set of values . . . works, systematically through its expression in the organisation, to the advantage of some individuals or groups rather than others' (1981, p. 136). Walsh *et al.* maintain that those who gain in an organisation do not necessarily do so through fighting battles. Drawing on the insights of Bachrach and Baratz as well as Lukes, they argue that those who win advantage benefit from the dominant values which 'act as yardsticks or criteria for the operation of an organisation' (p. 137). Similarly, one of the authors' studies of health policy has demonstrated how the dominant value system in the health field favours the medical profession (Ham, 1982). In the health field the pre-eminence of the medical model of health and illness helps to maintain the powerful position of doctors. Other values and models of health do exist but take second place to the medical model. As Alford (1975a) argues, the medical profession is the dominant structural interest in the health field. Other groups are either challenging or repressed, and the fact of medical dominance means that issues are defined in a way which favours doctors. Alternative definitions are either not perceived or are so weakly articulated that they represent no serious challenge. Hence, power is being exercised, even though overt conflicts may not occur. It is at this point, where the second dimension of power begins to merge with the third, that Lukes departs from Bachrach and Baratz. In other words, the proposition that power may be used to manipulate people's interests and preferences divides writers like Bachrach and Baratz from writers such as Lukes. This suggests a need to examine the relationship between power and interests and the stance taken by different writers in analysing interests.

Power and interests

Pluralist theory is based on a liberal conception of interests which equates people's interests with expressed preferences. That is, pluralists argue that people's interests are what they say they are,

and the nature of these interests may be inferred through observation of political action and inaction. This conception of interests
poses at least two difficulties. First, occasions arise when people
appear to act or not act in a way which is against their interests. An
example taken from the community power literature, would be
retailers who fail to oppose urban redevelopment plans that would
put them out of business (Polsby, 1980, p. 226). In a case such as
this, it could be argued that the retailers' real interests were not
reflected in their political behaviour. Even more problematic is the
second objection to the liberal conception of interests, namely that
it does not admit the possibility that a false consensus may exist. In
other words, if interests are equated with expressed preferences
and a consensus exists, then the assumption must be that the consensus is genuine. Writers who find this conception of interests
untenable have sought ways of distinguishing subjective interests
from objective or real interests. As a consequence,

> the search for a means to describe interests as something other than
> the revealed preferences or expressed desires of actors becomes an
> integral part of an argument about the adequacy of one or another
> description or generalisation about the configuration of power in
> local communities. (Polsby, 1980, p. 221)

In examining this argument, it may be helpful to return to an
early statement of the pluralist position by Robert Dahl. In his
critique of the ruling elite theorists, Dahl recognises that the test
he proposes for discovering a ruling elite (examining cases involving key decisions in which elite preferences run counter to those of
other groups) may not be appropriate in totalitarian dictatorships.
The reason for this is that in these dictatorships 'the control of the
elite over the expression of opinion is so great that overtly there is
no disagreement' (1958, p. 468). Dahl goes on to concede that,
even in the United States,

> a ruling elite might be so influential over ideas, attitudes, and opin-
> ions that a kind of false consensus will exist – not the phoney con-
> sensus of a terroristic totalitarian dictatorship but the manipulated
> and superficially self-imposed adherence to the norms and goals of
> the elite by broad sections of a community. (*ibid.*)

However, Dahl argues that either the consensus is perpetual, in
which case there is no way of determining who is ruler and who is
ruled, or it is not, in which case concrete issues can be examined to

discover which groups are successful in getting their preferences adopted.

Thus, Dahl recognises the possibility that an elite may be able to control opinion, and in his empirical work in New Haven he acknowledges that 'leaders do not merely respond to the preferences of constituents; leaders also shape preferences' (1961, p. 164). It is precisely this point that Lukes seizes on in articulating the third dimension of power. Lukes argues that a false or manipulated consensus may exist and may be maintained through domination by a powerful group. Arguing that 'the most effective and insidious use of power is to prevent . . . conflict from arising in the first place' (p. 23), Lukes contends that people's wants are formed by the society in which they live and these wants may not be the same as their real interests. The question this raises is do people have interests which differ from their expressed preferences, and if so how can the nature of these interests be established?

As we have noted, the pluralists would deny the existence of interests which are different from expressed preferences. The behaviourist research methods used by the pluralists do not provide grounds for establishing the existence of a false consensus except through the investigation of what happens when the consensus breaks down. The pluralist position is well represented by Polsby, who points to the danger of observers claiming to know the real interests of citizens who do not acknowledge the existence of such interests (1980, p. 224). In Polsby's view, researchers need to be extremely cautious in going beyond people's expressed preferences in analysing power relationships, although he does accept that there may be situations in which people do not act to maximise their values or their interests. Against this position, Lukes maintains that people's expressed preferences are shaped by socialisation, education and the mass media, and their real interests can only be established by examining what they would choose when exercising choice relatively free of these constraints. Put another way, Lukes argues that real interests can only be identified in conditions of *relative autonomy*. The difficulty with this is how to create such conditions.

A slightly different approach to the question of interests is provided by Saunders. Like Lukes, Saunders maintains that people's preferences are constrained from birth and therefore cannot be taken as an indication of real interests. Further, he argues that ideological mechanisms shape the way in which people interpret the world, and serve to perpetuate and transmit a system of values and beliefs about that world. These mechanisms may be the result of domination by particular groups, and they may serve the interests of these groups, but 'dominant ideologies reflect (to some extent) the life experiences of all classes, and they make sense only because they are grounded in the form of life of the society as a whole' (1980, pp. 55–6). It is this, rather than conscious manipulation, which makes ideology such a powerful force and which presumably lies behind Dahl's reference to the adherence by the community to a superficially self-imposed set of norms and goals. Within a dominant ideology, Saunders argues that real interests can be identified by estimating the costs and benefits accruing to various groups from particular social arrangements. This involves 'a definition of interests which, while necessarily ultimately contestable, nevertheless rests on the assumption that real interests refer to the achievement of benefits and the avoidance of costs in a particular situation' (p. 45). Thus, according to this formulation, examining who gains and who loses in a specified community or society indicates those whose real interests are and are not met.

Saunders is here echoing Bachrach and Baratz who have argued that who benefits must be the central question in community power research. The pluralists' objection to this approach is voiced by Polsby, who argues that who benefits is an interesting and fruitful question for research, but it is a different question from who governs. The problem posed by Polsby is that

> Even if we can show that a given *status quo* benefits some people disproportionately (as I think we can for any real world *status quo*), such a demonstration falls short of showing that these beneficiaries created the *status quo*, act in any meaningful way to maintain it, or could, in the future, act effectively to deter changes in it. (1980, p. 208)

Polsby's warning is a useful reminder that individuals or groups may benefit from policy-making processes unintentionally. What this suggests is a need to establish clear links between the distribution of benefits and the way in which issues are resolved. Crenson's air-pollution case study is one attempt to do this, and, as we have noted, the particular value of his work is in showing how a pattern of benefits may be maintained through the operation of anticipated reactions and indirect influence in the policy-making process. In a similar vein, Saunders points to the effect which political routines may have on political activity. Drawing on the work of Parry and Morriss (1974), Saunders argues that access to power operates in a way which favours some sections of the population against others. A number of studies lend support to this argument, demonstrating how certain groups find it much easier to penetrate decision-making processes than others (for example, Dearlove, 1973, and Newton, 1976). Effectively, then, the rules of access reinforce the position of powerful groups and work to the disadvantage of the relatively powerless. On the basis of empirical work in the south London borough of Croydon, Saunders maintains that the failure to mobilise among working-class groups is often the result of fatalism about the likely success of political action rather than an inability to recognise grievances. Equally, he demonstrates how business interests enjoyed close contacts with local political leaders, even though these interests did not directly control Croydon Council. Businesses were able to benefit from the decisions of the council because:

> In their clubs, committees and boards, as well as in their more formal consultative meetings, the various representatives of Croydon's business community interact regularly with political leaders who generally believe what they believe, think what they think, and want what they want. No pressure group, no matter how well-organised or how well-connected, enjoys a relationship like this, for in such a fertile context, opinions, suggestions and modes of thought pass almost imperceptibly, like osmosis, from businessmen to politicians, and from politicians to businessmen. In the relationship between the town's political and business leaders, political partnership has reached its highest and most sublimated form. (Saunders, 1980, p. 324)

On the basis of these findings, Saunders argues that routines and rules of access may be just as significant as the dominant ideology in accounting for patterns of political behaviour.

Another approach to this issue is provided in Blowers' study of a British pollution issue, the nuisance caused by brickworks in Bedfordshire (Blowers, 1984). Here a change over time when a community problem off the political agenda shifted on to the agenda is explored in terms of a comparison between pluralist, elitist and structuralist perspectives. The latter term refers to a theoretical position close to that of the modern neo-Marxists who see the dominance of economic interests as of determining importance.

These are seen, as in the case analysed by Crenson, as explaining the failure of the issue to emerge on the political agenda for a considerable period. Then, there were changes in the economic climate which reduced the power of the brick-making companies to determine the agenda. One of the authors was involved in a study of the emergence of an agricultural pollution issue on the political agenda (Hill, Aaronovitch and Baldock, 1989) which similarly suggested that the structural analysis used by Blowers offered an approach to explanation. The interesting difference in this case was evidence that the changing British relationship to the European Economic Community was undermining the power of agricultural interests to keep their polluting behaviour off the political agenda.

Blowers describes the structuralist perspective as deriving from the Marxist analysis of power (as discussed above in Chapter 2). Yet, he acknowledges that this tends in practice to boil down to a form of economic determinism which does not help to explain the detailed events. But surely the interesting thing about both of these cases is that the determinism is conditional on a particular set of economic and political circumstances which did not remain constant over time. This is a long way from the simplistic determinism of classical Marxism.

A number of these points are reiterated in the work of Offe who seeks to provide a general explanation of political activity and the selective attention given to issues in contemporary capitalist societies. Drawing on both Easton's systems analysis and Bachrach and Baratz's non-decision-making thesis, Offe maintains that 'In advanced systems of state-regulated capitalism, political stability can be more reliably ensured through the systematic exclusion and suppression of needs which if articulated would endanger the system' (1976, p. 397). According to Offe various exclusion rules which are an intrinsic part of the institutions and structures of capitalism operate to select certain issues for attention and omit others. Selection mechanisms include those discussed by Saunders – ideological and procedural – as well as repressive and structural mechanisms. The former comprise the application or threat of acts of repression by the police, armed forces and judiciary, while the latter include formal and informal limits as to what matters can be dealt with by the state. These mechanisms act as 'a system of filters' (1974, p. 39), narrowing the scope of political events and

screening out non-capitalist demands. Offe contends that the difficulty in researching these mechanisms and in demonstrating a consistent pattern of bias in the filtering which occurs results from the
fact that the capitalist state has to deny its class character and claim
neutrality as a condition for its survival. Nevertheless, he argues
that the state does intervene to support capitalist interests, and in
this sense there is a systematic bias in what the state does. At the
same time, echoing the views of corporatist theories, Offe points
out that autonomous action is increasingly a feature of state intervention under conditions of late capitalism.

Conclusion

In this chapter we have explored some of the areas of disagreement between writers who have examined the concept of power
and methods of researching the power structure. The conclusion
indicated by our survey of the literature is that a decisional
approach, although valuable, provides only a starting point for
understanding the complexities of power relationships. Conflicts
over key issues furnish some evidence about the nature and distribution of power, but this evidence needs to be supplemented by
analysis of nondecision-making processes. In many cases, nondecisions take the form of decisions, and can be investigated using the
methodology employed by the pluralists. This applies, for example,
to the forcible suppression of demands, referring issues for study
by committees and commissions, and the cooptation of challenging
groups. Equally, the way in which political routines produce or
reinforce bias, and most instances of how decision-making is
affected by anticipated reactions, can be investigated using conventional research methods. More problematic is how to study
power when it is exercised to shape people's preferences. This, the
third dimension of power, is at once the most important and the
most difficult aspect of power to research, yet we would argue that
despite the problems the effort is worth making, and we have
pointed to some ways in which this might be done.

 This is an area of study where there are advantages to be gained
by applying the approach recommended in Chapter 1, deriving
from the work of Graham Allison, of exploring the extent to which
the concurrent use of apparently conflicting theories provides com-

plementary insights. Blowers' use of such an approach in his pollution study influenced one of the authors to try something similar (Hill, Aaronovitch and Baldock, 1989). Blowers' observations on the method are instructive:

> it is clear that different perspectives illuminate different aspects of power conflict, and that each is flawed. Pluralist theories are particularly strong in the analysis of the active phase of the conflict, and there is evidence to support the idea of widespread participation, responsiveness and the role of actors. The neo-elitist critique is to an extent complementary . . . But structuralism takes the analysis further with its emphasis on the class nature of interests, the stress on underlying economic forces and its denial of the importance of individual action to the outcomes of the conflict. (Blowers, 1984, pp. 250–1)

Yet, as has been shown above, the structural perspective does not necessarily put 'class interests' and 'economic forces' as the only kinds of determining agents. Implicit in the concept of structure is a system which gives dominance to a range of powerful groups (see Degeling and Colebatch, 1984, for a discussion of the relevance of this sociological theory for public administration). Such groups will include professional and bureaucratic elites; males; specific ethnic, religious, linguistic groups and so on. This dominance is given structural form by customary practices and modes of organisation. It may well be built into language, and manifested symbolically in a variety of ways.

But structures like constitutions (see references on pages 16 and 24) are not fixed and immutable. They are changed by action, and some actions may be specifically directed at trying to change structure. The prevailing order is continually being renegotiated. This is clearly not an easy process, but in addressing the determinants of decision-making, it is one which must not be entirely disregarded (this sort of approach to the relationship between structure and action is explored in the sociological writings of Giddens; see Bryant and Jary, 1991, for a discussion of this). These are themes to which we will return in the last chapter.

CHAPTER 5

RATIONALITY AND DECISION-MAKING

Writers on decision-making may be divided, broadly and roughly, into two schools: those who focus on the relationship between power and decision-making and those who examine the relationship between rationality and decision-making. The literature on power and decision-making was discussed at some length in the previous chapter. In this chapter we turn our attention to the analysis of rationality and decision-making, concentrating in particular on the debate between writers who analyse decision-making by reference to rational models and writers who portray decision-making as an incremental process. Unlike some commentators we do not accept that this is an artificial debate (Smith and May, 1980). It is correct to observe that rational models usually serve prescriptive purposes, and incremental models are often intended to be descriptive. Yet, here we have an important point at which analysis *of* policy and analysis *for* policy come together. There is a continuing search for prescriptive models which suffer from neither the unrealism of the ideal-type rational model nor the incompleteness of incremental approaches. It is this search, and the debate between the writers who have been engaged in it, which is the central concern of this chapter. The chapter proceeds through an examination of the ideal-type rational model, to a consideration of incrementalism and an analysis of middle ways between these two approaches. The strengths and weaknesses of each model are assessed, and at the end of the chapter an attempt is made to establish links between the discussion of rationality and decision-making and the analysis of the role of the state and of power contained in earlier chapters.

Rational models

Herbert Simon's *Administrative Behaviour*, first published in 1945, constitutes an important early contribution to thinking about decision-making within organisations. In his book Simon argues that theories of administration must take decision-making as a central focus. In contrast to previous writers, who concentrated on ways of securing effective action within organisations, Simon seeks to examine in some detail the processes leading up to action. In his view, a theory of administration has to be concerned with 'the processes of decision as well as with the processes of action' (Simon, 1945, p. 1), and to this end Simon attempts to specify exactly what is involved in decision-making.

Beginning with a definition of a decision as a choice between alternatives, Simon states that rational choice, which involves selecting alternatives 'which are conducive to the achievement of goals or objectives within organisations', is of fundamental importance in giving meaning to administrative behaviour. That is, administrative behaviour is purposive if it is guided by goals. In any organisation there might be a number of ways of reaching goals, and when faced with the need to make a choice between alternatives the rational decision-maker should choose the alternative most likely to achieve the desired outcome. In essence, then, rational decision-making involves the selection of the alternative which will maximise the decision-maker's values, the selection being made following a comprehensive analysis of alternatives and their consequences.

Simon acknowledges that there are several difficulties with this approach. The first is: whose values and objectives are to be used in the decision-making process? Clearly, organisations are not homogeneous entities, and the values of the organisation as a whole may differ from those of individuals within the organisation. Simon's response to this point is to argue that 'a decision is "organisationally" rational if it is oriented to the organisation's goals; it is "personally" rational if it is oriented to the individual's goals' (pp. 76–7).

This leads on to a second difficulty with Simon's approach, namely that it may not make sense to refer to the goals of an organisation. A similar problem arises here as in the discussion of policy (see Chapter 1), namely that general statements of intention within organisations are implemented by individuals and groups who often have discretion in interpreting these statements. If, as we argue in the next chapter, policy is to some extent made, or at least reformulated, as it is implemented, then it may be less useful to refer to an organisation's goals than to the goals of the individuals and groups who make up the organisation.

The third major difficulty with Simon's model of rationality is that in practice decision-making rarely proceeds in such a logical, comprehensive and purposive manner. Among the reasons for this are that it is almost impossible to consider all alternatives during the process of decision; knowledge of the consequences of the various alternatives is necessarily incomplete; and evaluating these consequences involves considerable uncertainties. It is precisely because of these limits to human rationality, maintains Simon, that administrative theory is needed. As he observes in *Administrative Behaviour*,

> The need for an administrative theory resides in the fact that there are practical limits to human rationality, and that these limits are not static, but depend upon the organisational environment in which the individual's decision takes place. The task of administration is so to design this environment that the individual will approach as close as practicable to rationality (judged in terms of the organisation's goals) in his decisions. (p. 241)

What Simon is arguing, then, is the need to explore ways of enhancing organisational rationality.

There is a fourth difficulty in achieving this, namely how to separate facts and values, and means and ends, in the decision-making process. The ideal rational model postulates the prior specification of ends by the administrator and the identification of means of reaching these ends. Simon notes a number of problems with the means–ends schema, including that of separating facts and values. As he argues, the means of achieving ends are not devoid of values, and a way of coping with this has to be found in decision-making. Simon's proposed solution is 'A theory of decisions in terms of alternative behaviour possibilities and their consequences' (p. 66) in which 'The task of decision involves three steps: (1) the listing of all the alternative strategies; (2) the determination of all the consequences that follow upon each of these strategies; (3) the comparative evaluation of these sets of consequences' (p. 67). Rationality has a place in this model in that 'The task of rational

Rational-comprehensive (root)		Successive limited comparisons (branch)	
1a	Clarification of values or objectives distinct from and usually prerequisite to empirical analysis of alternative policies	1b	Selection of value goals and empirical analysis of the needed action are not distinct from one another but are closely intertwined
2a	Policy-formulation is therefore approached through means–end analysis: first the ends are isolated, then the means to achieve them are sought	2b	Since means and ends are not distinct, means–end analysis is often inappropriate or limited
3a	The test of a 'good' policy is that it can be shown to be the most appropriate means to desired ends	3b	The test of a 'good' policy is typically that various analysts find themselves directly agreeing on a policy (without their agreeing that it is the most appropriate means to an agreed objective)
4a	Analysis is comprehensive; every important relevant factor is taken into account	4b	Analysis is drastically limited: i) Important possible outcomes are neglected ii) Important alternative potential policies are neglected iii) Important affected values are neglected
5a	Theory is often heavily relied upon	5b	A succession of comparisons greatly reduces or eliminates reliance on theory

Figure 5.1 Models of decision-making (Source: Lindblom, 1959)

decision is to select that one of the strategies which is followed by the preferred set of consequences' (*ibid.*).

It follows that the means–ends rational model is, as Simon always intended, an idealised view of decision-making in organisa-tions. However, it is by no means clear that the theory of alterna-tive behaviour possibilities is any less idealistic. Simon recognises this, and he notes various ways in which actual behaviour departs from the theory. Accordingly, in his later work Simon elaborates the idea of 'bounded rationality' (1957, p. xxiv) to describe decision-making in practice. Bounded rationality involves the decision-maker choosing an alternative intended not to maximise his values but to be satisfactory or good enough. The term 'satisficing' describes this process, and bounded rationality enables the administrator faced with a decision to simplify by not examining all possible alternatives. Rather, rules of thumb are adopted, and as a result important options and consequences may be ignored. In this way the exacting demands of the rational-comprehensive model are avoided and replaced with a more realistic set of criteria. Simon argues that both common sense and computer simulation of human behaviour in decision-making serve to verify bounded rationality as a correct description of decision-making 'in its main features' (1957, p. xxvii).

Incrementalism

Simon's espousal of bounded rationality finds many echoes in the work of Charles Lindblom (1959). Like Simon, Lindblom is critical of the rational-comprehensive method of decision-making. In its place, Lindblom sets out an approach termed 'successive limited comparisons'. The rational-comprehensive approach is characterised as the root method, starting with basic issues on each occasion and building from the ground up; the successive limited comparisons approach is characterised as the branch method, starting from the existing situation and changing incrementally. The two approaches are compared in Figure 5.1.

In describing decision-making by successive limited comparisons, Lindblom reiterates many of Simon's reservations about the rational model. These reservations are listed most fully in Lindblom's later work where he notes eight failures of adaptation of the rational-comprehensive model, which is also referred to as the synoptic ideal. According to Lindblom, the synoptic ideal is

1. Not adapted to man's limited problem-solving capacities.
2. Not adapted to inadequacy of information.
3. Not adapted to the costliness of analysis.
4. Not adapted to failures in constructing a satisfactory evaluative method.

5. Not adapted to the closeness of observed relationships between fact and value in policy-making.
6. Not adapted to the openness of the system of variables with which it contends.
7. Not adapted to the analyst's need for strategic sequences of analytical moves.
8. Not adapted to the diverse forms in which policy problems actually arise (Braybrooke and Lindblom, 1963).

Consequently, decision-making in practice proceeds by successive limited comparisons. This achieves simplification not only through limiting the number of alternatives considered to those that differ in small degrees from existing policies, but also by ignoring consequences of possible policies. Further, deciding through successive limited comparisons involves simultaneous analysis of facts and values, and means and ends. As Lindblom states, 'one chooses among values and among policies at one and the same time' (1959, p. 82). That is, instead of specifying objectives and then assessing what policies would fulfil these objectives, the decision-maker reaches decisions by comparing specific policies and the extent to which these policies will result in the attainment of objectives. For Lindblom, the test of a good policy is not, as the rational-comprehensive model posits, that the policy maximises the decision-maker's values. Rather it is whether the policy secures agreement of the interests involved.

This theme has been taken up again very forcefully by Gregory (1989), taking issue with a restatement of the 'rationalism' case by Goodin (1982), questioning the value of adopting an 'ideal' approach which flies in the face of political realities. Indeed, inasmuch as this is the case we would question the use of the very word 'rationalism', a point to which we will return.

Lindblom argues that incrementalism is both a good description of how policies are actually made, and a model for how decisions should be made. Prescriptively, one of the claimed advantages of muddling through is that serious mistakes can be avoided if only incremental changes are made. By testing the water the decision-maker can assess the wisdom of the moves he or she is undertaking and can decide whether to make further progress or to change direction. Lindblom emphasises that successive limited comparisons is a method. Despite its acknowledged shortcomings, the method is to be preferred to 'a futile attempt at superhuman comprehensiveness' (1959, p. 88). Given the rough process which is usually involved in making decisions, Lindblom maintains that the best that can be hoped for is to muddle through more effectively.

These points are developed at some length in Lindblom's later writings. In *A Strategy of Decision*, a book he co-authored with David Braybrooke (1963), Lindblom describes in detail the strategy of disjointed incrementalism, which is a refinement of the successive limited comparisons method. Disjointed incrementalism involves examining policies which differ from each other incrementally, and which differ incrementally from the *status quo*. Analysis is not comprehensive but is limited to comparisons of marginal differences in expected consequences. Using disjointed incrementalism, the decision-maker keeps on returning to problems, and attempts to ameliorate those problems rather than to achieve some ideal future state. What is more, decision-makers adjust objectives to available means instead of striving for a fixed set of objectives. Braybrooke and Lindblom note that disjointed incrementalism is characteristic of the United States where 'policy-making proceeds through a series of approximations. A policy is directed at a problem; it is tried, altered, tried in its altered form, altered again, and so forth' (p. 73). There are similarities here with the writings of Wildavsky (1979) who argues that problems are not so much solved as succeeded and replaced by other problems, and who is equally critical of the rational model. Braybrooke and Lindblom describe the strategy as disjointed incrementalism because policies and problems are analysed at different points without apparent coordination.

This theme of coordination is taken up in Lindblom's book, *The Intelligence of Democracy* (1965). The problem addressed in that book is of how to achieve coordination between people in the absence of a central coordinator. Partisan mutual adjustment is the concept Lindblom develops to describe how coordination can be achieved in such a situation. Partisan mutual adjustment is the process by which independent decision-makers coordinate their behaviour. It involves adaptive adjustments 'in which a decision-maker simply adapts to decisions around him' and manipulated adjustments 'in which he seeks to enlist a response desired from the other decision-maker' (1965, p. 33). Each of these forms of adjustment is further divided into a variety of more specific behaviour, including negotiation and bargaining. In a later article, Lindblom (1979) notes that although there is no necessary connection between partisan mutual adjustment and political change by small steps, in practice the two are usually closely linked. This has been shown, by Harrison, Hunter and Pollitt (1990, pp. 8–13), to be a weakness in Lindblom's argument since a sequence of essentially incremental changes may well occur in a context in which certain parties are dominating and therefore 'mutual adjustment' is not occurring. This they contend has been characteristic of change in British health policy, where medical interests have dominated. We will see, at the end of this chapter, that this is an issue on which Lindblom himself has had second thoughts. Taken together, nevertheless, partisan mutual adjustment, disjointed incrementalism and successive iimited comparisons have formed the key concepts in the incrementalist model of decision-making.

There is a large measure of agreement in the literature on decision-making that disjointed incrementalism is a good description of how decisions are actually made in organisations. Yet the rational-comprehensive model remains important because it continues to influence attempts to improve the machinery of government in various countries. In the British context, this can be seen in the development of the Public Expenditure Survey Committee (PESC) system for planning public expenditure, and the subsequent introduction of programme budgeting, programme analysis and review, and the Central Policy Review Staff (Blackstone and Plowden, 1988). Again, the planning system introduced into the National Health Service in 1976 was presented as a process involving taking stock of services, setting objectives, defining strategy, developing a plan and monitoring implementation. These examples, many of which have their roots in American experience, suggest that the ideal of rational-comprehensiveness is still powerful.

Nevertheless, the experience of a number of these innovations bears out Lindblom's objections to the synoptic approach. An extensive literature has developed on the contribution of research to government (see, in particular Bulmer, 1987 and Booth, 1988) which is generally pessimistic about the extent to which it makes a direct contribution, compatible with the rational model. Rather, the best that can be expected is that it contributes indirectly to decision-making, performing an 'enlightenment' function (Weiss, 1977; Thomas, 1985). Similarly, a study of PESC, for example, came to the conclusion that far from enhancing rationality, PESC ended up strengthening incrementalism (Heclo and Wildavsky, 1981). Similarly, researchers who analysed the operation of the NHS planning system noted the failure of health planners to live up to the synoptic ideal (Barnard *et al.*, 1980, p. 263). Studies of policy-making in organisations are replete with examples which demonstrate the failure of rational-comprehensiveness and the prevalence of incrementalism. This is not to say that incrementalism is the only way in which decisions are made in practice for there is evidence that other approaches are sometimes adopted (Vickers, 1965; Ham, 1981). The question this raises is what *prescriptive* stance should be adopted in view of the less than satisfactory experience of the rational ideal? Of the many attempts to address this question, two in particular stand out: Dror's (1964) discussion of a normative optimum model, and Etzioni's (1967) work on mixed scanning. We will consider each of the models in turn.

Optimal methods and mixed scanning

While Dror finds much to admire in Lindblom's work, he is critical of the conservative bias he detects in incrementalism. The problem identified by Dror is that Lindblom's favoured strategy of muddling through more skilfully acts 'as an ideological reinforcement of the pro-inertia and anti-innovation forces' (1964, p. 153). According to Dror this strategy is only acceptable if existing policies are in the main satisfactory, there is a high degree of continuity in the nature of problems and there is a high degree of continuity in the means available for dealing with problems. These criteria may be met when there is a large measure of social stability, and Dror argues that incrementalism may be appropriate in many policy areas in the United States. But where the conditions do not prevail, and where a society is seeking to bring about significant social changes, then incrementalism will not be appropriate.

The alternative to muddling through, suggests Dror, is not the rational-comprehensive model but a normative optimum model which is able to 'combine realism and idealism' (p. 157). In broad outline, such a model involves attempts to increase both the rational and extra-rational elements in decision-making. The extra-rational elements comprise the use of judgements, creative invention, brainstorming and other approaches. The rational elements involve not a comprehensive examination of alternatives and their consequences and the complete clarification of values and objectives but a selective review of options and some explication of goals. What this implies is a decision-making method somewhere between the rational-comprehensive and incremental methods. Thus, while Dror is prepared to accept the validity of incrementalism as a descriptive theory, he argues for an optimal method as a means of strengthening and improving decision-making. One of the features of the method is the stress placed on meta-policy-making, that is 'policy-making on how to make policy' (1968, p. 160). In Dror's analysis, there is a need to invest resources in designing procedures for making policies in order to produce better decisions.

Lindblom's response to Dror is to argue that in a political democracy like the United States and also in relatively stable dictatorships the conditions necessary for incrementalism are met (Lindblom, 1964). Further, Lindblom expresses scepticism about the criticism that muddling through has a conservative bias. He maintains that significant changes can be achieved through a succession of small steps as well as through infrequent large steps.

This point is taken up by Etzioni who, like Dror, seeks a middle way between rationality and incrementalism. Etzioni accepts the force of the argument that a series of small steps could produce significant change, but adds that 'there is nothing in this approach to guide the accumulation; the steps may be circular – leading back to where they started, or dispersed – leading in many directions at once but leading nowhere' (1967, p. 387). In place of incrementalism, Etzioni outlines the mixed scanning model of decision-making, a model he suggests is both a good description of how decisions are made in a number of fields and a strategy which can guide decision-making.

Mixed scanning rests on the distinction between fundamental decisions and incremental or bit decisions. Etzioni suggests that fundamental decisions, such as the declaration of war and the initiation of the space programme, are recognised by the incrementalists but are not given sufficient emphasis. In Etzioni's view, fundamental decisions are important because they 'set basic directions' (p. 388) and provide the context for incremental decisions. Mixed scanning is an appropriate method for arriving at fundamental decisions because it enables a range of alternatives to be explored. Essentially, mixed scanning involves the decision-maker undertaking a broad review of the field of decision without engaging in the detailed exploration of options suggested by the rational model. This broad review enables longer-run alternatives to be examined and leads to fundamental decisions. In turn, incremental decisions lead up to and follow on from fundamental decisions and involve more detailed analysis of specific options. According to Etzioni,

> each of the two elements in mixed scanning helps to reduce the effects of the particular shortcomings of the other; incrementalism reduces the unrealistic aspects of rationalism by limiting the details required in fundamental decisions, and contextuating rationalism helps to overcome the conservative slant of incrementalism by exploring longer-run alternatives. (p. 390)

Despite Etzioni's claim that his strategy is an adequate description of decision-making in various fields, the importance of mixed scanning and also of Dror's optimal model is mainly that they are attempts to meet widely held reservations about incrementalism as a prescriptive approach. What then are the strengths and weaknesses of mixed scanning and the optimal model? Taking Dror's work first, it is clear that in many respects he shares the assumptions and the aspirations of the rational-comprehensive model. Wary of the potential dangers of inertia and conservatism, Dror seeks to provide guidelines for those attempting to improve policy-making. In his book, *Public Policymaking Re-examined* (1968), Dror details eighteen phases of optimal policy-making, ranging from the meta-policy-making stage of designing policy-making systems, through the policy-making stage of examining alternatives and making decisions, and on to the post-policy-making and feedback stages. There is no doubt that Dror offers one of the most considered attempts to devise a prescriptive policy-making model and, in our view, a particular strength of Dror's work is its recognition of the extra-rational elements in the process of decision-making.

As the writings of experienced policy-makers like Vickers (1965) attest, judgement, hunch and intuition do play a part in the mind of the decision-maker. It is paradoxical, then, that at the same time as incorporating extra-rational aspects, the optimal model emphasises many of the key features of the rational-comprehensive model. As Smith and May (1980) note, Dror recapitulates various stages in the model, but adds caveats in order to avoid the charge of unrealism. What is more, it is not clear what criteria are to be employed when the decision-maker is advised by Dror to undertake 'some clarification of values, objectives, and decision-criteria' and a 'preliminary estimation of expected pay-offs'. For these reasons, it is difficult to see how the optimal model can be successfully operationalised.

Turning to Etzioni, one of the questions which needs to be raised about mixed scanning is whether fundamental decisions are as significant as he suggests. While in some situations fundamental decisions are important in setting broad directions, in other situations decision-making proceeds in a much less structured way. In many organisations and policy areas, action is justified because 'things have always been done this way', rather than through reference to fundamental decisions which serve as a context for action. When this occurs, unplanned drift rather than conscious design characterises the policy process, and unplanned drift may be more common than Etzioni assumes.

A further difficulty with mixed scanning is how to distinguish fundamental decisions and incremental decisions. As Smith and May note, 'fundamental decisions in one context are incremental in another and vice versa' (p. 153). Etzioni's example of declaration of war seems an obvious enough *fundamental* decision, yet wars have emerged from a succession of incremental decisions, made with a minimum of open debate (Vietnam!). It would therefore seem important to specify criteria for distinguishing the two types of decision and Etzioni does not do this. Despite these criticisms, a number of writers have pointed to the virtues of mixed scanning as a prescriptive model (Gershuny, 1978; Wiseman, 1978 and 1979). Particularly in the planning context, it is suggested that decision-makers may find the twin strategies of overall scanning followed by a more detailed exploration of specific problems and alternative ways of tackling these problems to be a useful and realistic way of proceeding. The longer time scale usually associated with planning decisions offers the possibility of overcoming some of the constraints which ordinarily preclude any more than incremental analysis. Often these may be the sorts of fundamental or contextualising decisions discussed by Etzioni. While there will no doubt be continuing disputes over the distinction between fundamental and incremental decisions, in many cases it is not difficult to identify fundamental decisions. As Braybrooke and

Lindblom argue, 'in any society there develops a strong tendency towards convergence in estimates of what changes are important and unimportant' (1963, p. 62). Some examples include: whether to undertake a programme of building nuclear reactors to provide energy; whether to undertake a programme of space exploration; whether to develop supersonic passenger aircraft; and whether to rely on nuclear or non-nuclear armed forces. On these kinds of issues it may be possible to use a strategy which combines features of bounded rationality, mixed scanning and Lindblom's later elaboration of incrementalism, which we now consider.

Incrementalism revisited

Bounded rationality, it will be recalled, involves the decision-maker in choosing an alternative which is good enough. Satisficing in this way enables the decision-maker to stop his search for alternatives long before all possible alternatives and their consequences have been examined. This approach, originally outlined by Simon, is seen by a number of writers as having merit. Vickers, for example, argues that satisficing is the way in which most decisions are made in practice. As Vickers comments, 'Only if nothing "good enough" is found . . . are other possibilities seriously considered' (1965, p. 91). Bounded rationality also receives favourable comment from Lindblom. In an article published in 1979 reviewing the debate surrounding incrementalism, Lindblom argues that the limitations on rationality are such that bounded rationality is the best that can be achieved. Lindblom introduces the term strategic analysis to describe a form of incrementalism which appears to be similar to bounded rationality. What is significant in Lindblom's 1979 article is that strategic analysis emerges as only one form of incrementalism. According to Lindblom we need to distinguish simple incremental analysis, disjointed incrementalism and strategic analysis. *Simple incremental analysis* involves analysis limited to consideration of alternatives which are only incrementally different from the *status quo*. *Disjointed incrementalism* involves limiting analysis to a few familiar alternatives, an intertwining of goals and values with the empirical aspects of the problem, a greater preoccupation with the problem than the goals to be sought, a sequence of trials, errors and revised trials, analysis that explores only

Ill-considered, often bumbling incompleteness in analysis	seat-of-pants semi-strategies	seat-of-pants plus studied strategies	Strategic analysis: informed and thoughtful choice of methods of problem simplification
	Most of us are in this broad range: some here towards the right (we ought to be in this range)		

Figure 5.2   Incremental and strategic analysis (Source: Lindblom, 1979)

some consequences of an alternative and fragmentation of analytical work to many participants. *Strategic analysis* involves analysis limited to any calculated or thoughtfully chosen set of stratagems to simplify complex policy problems. Simple incremental analysis is one element in disjointed incrementalism, and disjointed incrementalism is one form of strategic analysis. Lindblom argues that strategic analysis is a preferable ideal to synoptic analysis. Figure 5.2 illustrates the range of options discussed by Lindblom.

A further refinement introduced into the discussion is the distinction between the various forms of incremental analysis, as outlined above, and incremental politics. Incremental politics involves political change by small steps, and may or may not result from incremental analysis. The distinction, then, is between the process of decision – incremental analysis – and the scale of the change brought about by the decision. What characterises incremental politics is that only small changes result from decisions, although Lindblom reminds us there is no reason in principle why large changes cannot result from a succession of small steps.

Commenting on Lindblom's discussion, Gunn and Hogwood argue that the ideal of strategic analysis represents a significant departure from Lindblom's early writings. 'Surely', they argue, 'this . . . all adds up to a form of modified rationality rather than Lindblom's early attempts to stand rationality on its head?' (1982, p. 21). There is sufficient ambiguity in Lindblom's writings to leave room for doubt on this point. Nevertheless it does seem that simple incremental analysis or muddling through is no longer sufficient, even though it is necessary. This does not mean aspiring to synoptic analysis, which Lindblom still considers an impossible ideal. Instead, what is proposed is 'the supplementation of incremental analysis by broad ranging, often highly speculative, and sometimes utopian thinking about possible futures, near and far in time' (Lindblom, 1979, p. 522). It is as a result of statements like this that it seems possible to argue that Lindblom has moved towards the middle ground and indeed comes close to the bounded rationality and mixed scanning models which command considerable support as prescriptive models in the decision-making literature.

Lindblom's reformulation of the incrementalist thesis also links in with Dror's argument for the use of extra-rational approaches in decision-making. Dror maintains that rational-comprehensiveness, bounded rationality, mixed scanning and incrementalism all have their roots in ideas about rationality, the main difference between rational-comprehensiveness and the other models being that the latter 'are presented as realistic second bests to the unachievable ideal, pure rationality' (1964, p. 149). According to Dror the only real alternative to all of these models is an extra-rational approach. It is relevant to note that Lindblom in his later writings also appears to be in sympathy with the need for different kinds of contributions to decision-making processes. This much is indicated by his advocacy of 'methods that liberate us from the synoptic and incremental methods of analysis' (1979, p. 522). Ultimately, this amounts to an argument for strategic analysis on appropriate issues to be joined with various forms of creative problem-solving. It is in this direction that a new form of rationality may emerge.

Conclusion: rationality and power

One of the issues underlying the debate about models of decision-making is the relationship between the way decisions are made and the distribution of power in contemporary society. Lindblom's early work provides an important link between incrementalism and pluralism. He argues that, in a society like the United States, groups are able to defend the interests of different sections of society and in this way no interests are entirely ignored. Through a process of mutual adjustment issues are resolved and a system of dispersed power centres enables more values to be protected than a system of centralised coordination. It was this that led Etzioni to argue that disjointed incrementalism 'is presented as the typical decision-making process of pluralistic societies, as contrasted with the master planning of totalitarian societies' (1967, p. 387). In Etzioni's view this interpretation needs to be challenged, for two reasons: first, because mutual adjustment will favour the well-organised partisans and work against the underprivileged (note here the earlier comment from Harrison *et al.* that partisan adjustment is not necessarily 'mutual'); and second, because incrementalism will neglect basic innovations and fundamental questions. A third reason why the association of incrementalism with pluralistic societies and comprehensive planning with totalitarian societies needs to be questioned is that empirical studies suggest that incrementalism may be prevalent even in totalitarian societies, Indeed, that whole preoccupation with the relationship between decision-making and democratic processes has now a rather dated ring, reminiscent of Popper's attack (1966) on the holistic planning he saw as characteristic of socialist systems. We now see that socialists have seldom engaged in holistic planning, despite their claims and rhetoric, rather they have tended to lock themselves in to bureaucratic allocation systems which are hard to change. On the other 'wing', however, ideologues of the 'liberal' right seem prepared to disregard Popper's endorsement of the desirability of 'piecemeal social engineering' in their endeavours to eliminate the collectivist state or to enforce their concept of the ideal family. This reminds us that underlying the whole debate is not merely the relationship between analysis *of* policy and analysis *for* policy but also a philosophical issue about what rationalism really entails in a democratic society. It is perhaps unfortunate that one side in the debate we have reviewed here has attempted to adopt this ambiguous word to give value to its own theory, disregarding in particular the complex relationship between rationality in respect of *ends* and rationality with regard to the means adopted to try to reach those ends (see Albrow, 1990, on Max Weber's difficulties with this concept).

Lindblom recognises the strength of Etzioni's points. As far as the first is concerned, in *Politics and Markets* (1977), Lindblom accepts that pluralism is biased in favour of certain groups, particularly businesses and corporations. Yet he resists the argument that centralised planning would be a preferable means of making decisions. Rather, Lindblom argues that the veto powers so prevalent in the US political system, and which prevent even incremental change occurring in some policy areas, need to be challenged through a restructuring of mutual adjustment. Specifically, he proposes that planners should be brought into policy-making to give absentees a voice. The overall aim should be 'greatly improved strategic policy-making, both analytical and inter-active' (1977, p. 346).

On the second point, Lindblom accepts that partisan mutual adjustment is only active on ordinary questions of policy. Certain grand issues such as the existence of private enterprise and private property and the distribution of income and wealth are not resolved through adjustment. Rather, because of 'a high degree of homogeneity of opinion' (1979, p. 523) grand issues are not included on the agenda. Lindblom adds that this homogeneity of opinion is heavily indoctrinated, and in *Politics and Markets* he explores the operation of what, in the previous chapter, we have referred to as ideology. Lindblom's argument is that in any stable society there is a unifying set of beliefs which are communicated to the population through the Church, the media, the schools and other mechanisms (1977, Ch. 15). These beliefs appear to be spontaneous because they are so much taken for granted, but in Lindblom's analysis they are seen as favouring and to some extent emanating from dominant social groups.

Is there an inconsistency here between Lindblom's early and later work? Lindblom argues not, reiterating that the pluralism which results from partisan mutual adjustment is heavily lopsided, at the same time arguing that the key task is to muddle through more skilfully and to strengthen strategic analysis. Nevertheless, it does seem that the optimistic tone of the original incrementalist thesis has been replaced by a more critical and pessimistic analysis. It may not be going too far to suggest that in his early writings Lindblom was content to endorse incrementalism because of his interpretation of the US power structure in pluralistic terms. In contrast, in his later writings, Lindblom, reflecting the changing political conditions of the United States, and the accompanying challenge to pluralism within political science, explicitly acknowledges the limitations of pluralism, and is less sanguine about incrementalism. In short, it would seem that his call for improved strategic analysis follows on from a recognition that the distribution of power is less equal than he once assumed.

CHAPTER 6

TOWARDS IMPLEMENTATION THEORY?

Introduction

In the United States in the early 1970s and in Europe later in that decade there emerged a wave of studies examining the implementation of public policy. Their rationale was that there had been, in the study of public policy, a 'missing link' (Hargrove, 1975) between the concern with policy-making and the evaluation of policy outcomes. While the absence of theory and literature on implementation before Pressman and Wildavsky's seminal work (1973) on that topic has been exaggerated, for example many organisational studies are *de facto* concerned with this phenomenon, there was perhaps a gap in the literature, particularly in political science. As Gunn (1978) argues 'Academics have often seemed obsessed with policy formation while leaving the "practical details" of policy implementation to administrators' (p. 1).

Hence, the explosion of implementation studies represents an important advance in policy analysis. Yet, like so many paradigm shifts in the social sciences, this new intellectual development has come to be seen to have its own limitations. Its very strength in stressing the importance of the implementation process as distinguishable from the policy-making process, and deserving of study in its own right, has tended to lead to the weakness of over-emphasising the distinctiveness of the two processes. There has been a tendency to treat policies as clear-cut, uncontroversial entities, whose implementation can be quite separately studied. This has raised both methodological problems and problems about the extent to which the very practical concerns of implementation studies may involve, explicitly or implicitly, identification with some actors' views of what should happen. An attack has been made on the 'top-down' character of the kinds of implementation studies influenced by Pressman and Wildavsky's work, and an alternative 'bottom-up' approach has been developed.

This chapter will, therefore, look at the contribution made to the study of the policy process by the 'discovery' of the importance of implementation. It will outline some of the ideas that have emerged from the top-down work on this theme. It will then go on to examine the criticisms which have developed of that work, which suggests some overall limitations to the case for implementation studies as a distinctive branch of policy analysis.

The top-down model for the study of implementation

In a number of public policy studies textbooks a distinction is made between policy-making, policy implementation and the evaluation of policy outcomes. A model is often drawn which bears some relationship to Easton's (1965a) portrait of the political process, which we discussed in Chapter 1, of inputs going into a decision system and producing outputs. Those who use models of this kind stress, quite rightly, the need to try to disaggregate the decision system so that it is not so much of a black box. Usually this involves making a distinction between policy-making and implementation.

For many who make that distinction, implementation is defined in terms of a relationship to policy. Hence, Van Meter and Van Horn (1975) define the implementation process as 'Those actions by public or private individuals (or groups) that are directed at the achievement of objectives set forth in prior policy decisions' (p. 445). In a similar vein, Pressman and Wildavsky (1973) say 'A verb like "implement" must have an object like "policy" ' (p. xiv). The pioneering implementation studies therefore argue that the process of putting policy into action is deserving of study, that it is wrong to take it for granted that this process will be smooth and straightforward. Indeed, we may go further and suggest that in many ways these studies are concerned with the discovery that many things go wrong between policy formulation and output.

Hence, Pressman and Wildavsky subtitle their book 'How great expectations in Washington are dashed in Oakland; or why it's amazing that federal programs work at all, this being a saga of the economic development administration as told by two sympathetic observers who seek to build morals on a foundation of ruined hopes'.

One senses here some of the frustration felt by many Americans about the failures, or limited successes, of the War on Poverty and Great Society programmes of the late 1960s. Pressman and Wild-avsky were not the first observers of this apparent gap between federal aspirations and local reality. There was a similar body of literature on the limitations of Roosevelt's reformist interventions in American society (see, in particular, Selznick, 1949). Clearly, an important preoccupation in this work is the concern with the problem of intervention from the top of a federal system; it comes through similarly in other analyses of American social policy with less of an emphasis on implementation *per se* (see Marris and Rein, 1967; Moynihan, 1969).

However, the concern with American federalism does not destroy the value of this approach for the study of implementation in other societies. Indeed, if analysed in this manner, it raises important questions about the ways in which policy transmission occurs, or fails to occur, through multi-government systems. Certainly a great deal of the analysis in Pressman and Wildavsky's book is concerned with the extent to which successful implementation depends upon linkages between different organisations and departments at the local level. They argue that if action depends upon a number of links in an implementation chain, then the degree of cooperation between agencies required to make those links has to be very close to 100 per cent if a situation is not to occur in which a number of small deficits cumulatively create a large shortfall. They thus introduce the idea of implementation deficit and suggest that implementation may be analysed mathematically in this way.

This notion of cumulative deficit, if cooperation is less than perfect, has similarities to the approach to the study of administration developed in Britain by Christopher Hood (1976). He suggests

One way of analyzing implementation problems is to begin by thinking about what 'perfect administration' would be like, comparable to the way in which economists employ the model of perfect competition. Perfect administration could be defined as a condition in which 'external' elements of resource availability and political acceptability combine with 'administration' to produce perfect policy implementation. (p. 6)

Hood goes on to develop an argument about the 'limits of administration' (his book title) which focuses not so much on the political processes that occur within the administrative system as on the inherent limits to control in complex systems. This is similarly the concern of a two-volume contribution to the subject by another British writer, Andrew Dunsire (1978, a and b). Hood and Dunsire, although they use examples from real situations, are concerned to link organisation theory with the study of implementation to provide an abstract model of the problems to be faced by persons attempting top-down control over the administrative system. The results are very complex, and seem likely to be hard to operationalise in actual empirical studies.

A rather less elaborate and more explicitly practice-related version of the top-down approach is provided in a short article by Gunn (1978), subsequently elaborated in Hogwood and Gunn (1984), in which ten preconditions necessary to achieve perfect implementation are set out. These are:

1. That circumstances external to the implementing agency do not impose crippling constraints.
2. That adequate time and sufficient resources are made available to the programme.
3. That not only are there no constraints in terms of overall resources but also that, at each stage in the implementation process, the required combination of resources is actually available.
4. That the policy to be implemented is based upon a valid theory of cause and effect.
5. That the relationship between cause and effect is direct and that there are few, if any, intervening links.
6. That there is a single implementing agency which need not depend upon other agencies for success or, if other agencies must be involved, that the dependency relationships are minimal in number and importance.
7. That there is complete understanding of, and agreement upon, the objectives to be achieved; and that these conditions persist throughout the implementation process.

8. That in moving towards agreed objectives it is possible to specify, in complete detail and perfect sequence, the tasks to be performed by each participant.
9. That there is perfect communication among, and coordination of, the various elements involved in the programme.
10. That those in authority can demand and obtain perfect obedience.

Gunn's list epitomises the top-down approach to implementation. It takes as its central purpose the provision of advice to those at the top on how to minimise implementation deficit. Similar work has been produced in the United States (notably by Sabatier and Mazmanian (1979)). Policy is taken to be the property of policy-makers at the 'top'. The issues to be tackled are as follows:

1. The nature of policy – see that it is unambiguous.
2. The implementation structure – keep links in the chain to a minimum.
3. The prevention of outside interference.
4. Control over implementing actors.

Developments of these notions have been many and varied. There has been a concern to examine how the nature of policy may have an impact, with attempts to develop Lowi's (1972) typology of policies as 'distributive', 'redistributive' and 'regulatory' to explore how this may influence the implementation process. Hargrove (1983) argues: 'It is assumed that it is possible to classify types of policies so that the categories can be used as a basis for predicting the implementation process within each category.' He goes on to amplify this: 'The plausibility of using a typology as a point of departure follows from the idea that different kinds of policy issues will evoke different sets of participants and levels of intensity according to the stakes presented by the issue.'

Implicitly this suggests that underlying the question of whether some kinds of policy may be harder to implement than others lie issues about the probability of outside interference. Significantly, Hargrove suggests that redistributive policies are harder to implement than distributive ones, while the success of regulatory policies may often rest upon the extent to which they have redistributive consequences.

Mountjoy and O'Toole (1979) have linked the theme of policy specificity with the notion that inter-organisational linkages create hazards for successful implementation. They identify some policies which avoid these hazards because of the clarity of their mandates and the security of their resources. Nixon (1980), looking at the handing down of policies from central to local level in Britain, has stressed the role of communication, perhaps a related notion to Mountjoy and O'Toole's mandate. Nixon emphasises the importance of clarity and consistency in the communication of policy. Both the notion of clear communication and the idea of mandate highlight the significance of an absence of ambiguity and compromise at the policy-making stage. This may be easier to achieve when conflict of interests is minimal than when disagreement exists among the various groups affected by a decision.

The work discussed above provides a variety of examples of the way the agenda for implementation studies has been established, principally by writers who accept some variant of the top-down approach. The examination of the implementation process must be concerned with the nature of policy, the inter- and intra-organisational context within which it is implemented and the external world on which it is expected to impact. What has, however, proved more controversial has been the way in which writers of the top-down school of thought handle both the concept of policy and the policy-implementation relationship. There are, in their approaches, some crucial unanswered questions about how clarity may be achieved at the policy-making stage, why it is often not, and how interest conflict may be successfully negotiated at the implementation stage.

Problems with the top-down model

The argument in this section will be complicated, since there are a number of different kinds of criticisms of the top-down approach which apply differently to different representatives of that school of thought. Broadly, the arguments separate out in the way suggested above, into those about the nature of policy, those about the interrelationship between policy-making and the implementation process and those about the normative stance adopted by students of implementation (particularly when this is implicit rather than explicit).

Pressman and Wildavsky were quoted earlier as approaching their definition of implementation by asserting that implement is a verb that must have an object, policy. In arguing in this way they surely ran the risk of catching themselves in a linguistic trap of their own making. As Wildavsky subsequently recognised, it is dangerous to regard it as self-evident that implementers are working with a recognisable entity that may be called a policy. In Chapter 1 we showed that policy is indeed an extremely slippery concept. It may really only emerge through an elaborate process that is likely to include those stages which are conventionally described as implementation.

The definitions quoted in Chapter 1 (see page 11) referred to the different characteristics of policy which make it difficult to work within implementation studies. Friend's (Friend *et al.*, 1974) is the simplest definition in seeing policy as a stance, but it is the way in which that stance contributes to a policy context which influences decisions which creates difficulties. Phenomena which are typically described as policy-making rather than implementation are involved in translating a stance – a commitment to cutting public expenditure, or extending support for some specific group, for example – into action. For this reason it is perhaps better to use a definition which identifies policy at a stage where it has been made more concrete. This entails using the concept of policy for what is articulated at the end of a legislative process, and is enshrined in new laws, regulations or executive directives.

The two rather different approaches to identifying policy, however, both entail problems for implementation studies, problems which are, in a sense, mirror images of each other. Policies as defined by Friend may be relatively clear-cut, political commitments to specific action. The difficulty is that they are made much more complex as they are translated into action. Policies as defined in more concrete terms are, as the definitions of Easton (1953) and Jenkins (1978) cited in Chapter 1 suggest, often so complex that we are unlikely to be able to identify simple goals within them. Friend's definition is really closer to the concept of policy as used in everyday speech. It refers to the goals embodied in the Queen's Speeches or the President's Messages to Congress, not to the complex phenomena which emerge at the end of the legislative process. Yet it is surely the latter with which students of implementation work.

Recognisably this is the case with the major American implementation studies. They deal with specific programmes, with their own specific budgetary allocations, as laid down by Congress. One of the problems they raise is the way in which such programmes interact, and perhaps conflict, with other programmes. But that is a different problem for implementation studies, not one stemming from problems with the concept of policy *per se*. However, if attempts are made to translate the same approach to the British context we have to grapple with a more unified system of government in which (a) new initiatives generally also entail modifications of older initiatives with which they might conflict; (b) most (though not all) policy areas are dominated by single agencies which take intra-organisational decisions about how to make new programmes compatible with older ones; and (c) the executive dominates the governmental system and legislates in a multiplicity of ways, only some of which are made manifest in specific Acts of Parliament, and thus practises legislative fine tuning continuously in subtle and often ambiguous ways.

The argument so far has been that implementation studies face problems in identifying what is being implemented because policies are complex phenomena. We want now to go a stage further and suggest that perhaps they are quite deliberately made complex, obscure, ambiguous or even meaningless. As was suggested in Chapter 1 with particular reference to the work of Edelman, in the most extreme case the policies which are the concern of politicians may be no more than symbolic, formulated without any intention to secure implementation. To what extent do politicians want to be seen as in favour of certain ideals or goals while actually doing nothing about them? Any system in which policy-making and implementation are clearly separated, either by a division between legislature and executive (as in the United States) or by a division between levels of government (present in most systems but most clear in federal ones), provides opportunities for the promulgation of symbolic policies. In Britain, for example, many regulatory policies require parliamentary enactment but local authority implementation. The former may relatively easily pass laws allowing the control of certain activities or the provision of certain services whilst not providing the resources to make action possible.

Even when policies are not simply symbolic it is important to recognise that the phenomena upon which action must be based are products of negotiation and compromise. Hence, as Barrett and Hill (1981) argue:

(a) many policies represent compromises between conflicting values;
(b) many policies involve compromises with key interests within the implementation structure;
(c) many policies involve compromises with key interests upon whom implementation will have an impact;
(d) many policies are framed without attention being given to the way in which underlying forces (particularly economic ones) will undermine them. (p. 89)

It must then be recognised first that this compromise is not a once and for all process but one that may continue on throughout the history of the translation of that policy into action, and second that the initial 'policy-makers' may be happy to let this occur as it enables them to evade decision problems. If, then, the implementers are distanced from the original policy framing process, and indeed perhaps even in separate 'subordinate' agencies, they may be perceived as responsible for problems and inconsistencies and for unpopular resolutions of these. Thus, one of the authors has shown how, in Britain, local authorities have been given responsibilities for support for the rents of low income people where the central government has failed to resolve a conflict between its desire to deregulate the housing market and the pressure that puts upon social security costs, which it wishes to curb, because means tested support is available towards low income people's housing costs (Hill, 1990).

A further complication for the analysis of policies is that many government actions do not involve, as a reading of most of the American empirical studies of implementation would seem to suggest, the promulgation of explicit programmes requiring new activities. They involve adjustments to the way existing activities are to be carried out. The most common and obvious interventions of this kind are increases or decreases in the resources for specific activities. In this way programmes are stimulated or allowed to wither away. What, however, makes implementation studies even more complex is that the relationship between resource adjustment and substantive programmes may be an indirect one. This is particularly a feature of British central–local relations where, generally, central government does not explicitly fund programmes but makes resources available to multi-purpose authorities.

Indirect funding means that the study of the relationship between policy and implementation is by no means straightforward. Bramley and Stewart have shown how varied was the actual effect of public expenditure cuts in Britain in the late 1970s (in Barrett and Fudge, 1981). A study by Webb and Wistow (1982) looks at personal social services policy and demonstrates apparent implementation deficit because local authorities chose to disregard central guidelines and preserve social services expenditure, letting the impact of a reduction of central grants fall on other services. They refer to the central government minister subsequently boasting of his success in protecting social services from cuts. Yet their way of presenting these events, with its deference to the top-down approach, makes this appear more inconsistent than it really is since they treat the initial cutting decisions as rational top-down policy-making. The reality is of a government committed to cutting public expenditure, a bargaining process in which different spending ministers were forced to deliver specific shares in the cuts, and a cash supply control process in which lower level actors (the local authorities) were able to do their own separate priority exercises. The ministry at the top did not have a *policy for social services spending*, in any very substantive sense.

Adjustments to the context in which decisions are made do not only come in the form of resource change, they may also come in the form of structure change. These structure changes may or may not carry implications for substantive outputs. Hence services may be transferred from one agency to another, new rules may be made on how services are to be administered, or new arrangements may be made for policy delivery. These 'meta-policy' (see page 16) adjustments or changes to the 'programme shell' (Knoepfel and Weidner, 1982; Whitmore, 1984) are common top-down interventions in public policy, but the analysis of their effects must rest upon an elaborate study of the way in which the balance of power is changed within the implementation system. In purposive language they are concerned with *means* not *ends* and therefore explicit goals cannot be identified, yet they may be of fundamental importance for outcomes and may embody implicit goals. The developments in Britain and elsewhere which are transforming the way policies are delivered – replacing large bureaucratic departments by hived-off agencies, units that are placed in a quasi-market situation or even private organisations operating as contractors for public services – must be seen not merely as restructuring the policy delivery system but also as often transforming the policies themselves. As suggested in Chapter 1, changing the rules of the game may change the outcome of the game.

When we contrasted the 'stance' definition of policy with the 'interrelated decisions' definition (see page 103) we suggested that there is a process of concretising which goes on. We also implied that there may be a difficulty about determining where policy-making stops and implementation begins. That point should be further emphasised. Elsewhere one of the authors has argued:

> to say that some policies are easier to implement than others one has to be able to identify the point at which they are packaged up ready for implementation. We may be able to say some commitments in party manifestos are easier to implement than others. We may equally be able to say that some Acts of Parliament are easier to implement than others. But in both cases such generalisation may be heavily dependent upon the extent to which aspirations have been concretised. (Hill, in Barrett and Fudge, 1981, p. 208)

We are confronted with a process in which the concretisation of policy continues way beyond the legislative process. There is something of a seamless web here, though it may be, as we suggested in the previous chapter, that it is possible to identify some decisions which are more fundamental for determining the major (policy?) issues than others. There is, however, no reason why we should always expect to find such decisions, nor is it the case that these decisions, when they exist, are invariably taken during what we conventionally define as the policy-making process. There are, on the contrary, a number of reasons why they may be left to the implementation process, of which the following is by no means an exhaustive list:

- Because conflicts cannot be resolved during the policy-making stage.
- Because it is regarded as necessary to let key decisions be made when all the facts are available to implementers.
- Because it is believed that implementers (professionals, for example) are better equipped to make the key decisions than anyone else.

- Because little is known in advance about the actual impact of the new measures.
- Because it is recognised that day-to-day decisions will have to involve negotiation and compromise with powerful groups.
- Because it is considered politically inexpedient to try to resolve the conflicts.

Considerations of this kind must lead us to regard the policy-making process as something which often continues during the so-called implementation phase. It may involve continuing flexibility, it may involve the concretisation of policy in action, or it may involve a process of movement back and forth between policy and action. Barrett and Fudge (1981) have stressed the need, therefore, 'to consider implementation as a policy/action continuum in which an interactive and negotiative process is taking place over time between those seeking to put policy into effect and those upon whom action depends' (p. 25).

Lane highlights some of the key issues here in a paper in which, among a variety of approaches to implementation, he identifies 'implementation as evolution' (Lane, 1987, p. 532; see also Majone and Wildavsky, 1978), 'implementation as learning' (Lane, 1987, p. 534; see also Browne and Wildavsky, 1984), 'implementation as coalition' (Lane, 1987, p. 539, with important references to the essentially collaborative implementation implicit in corporatist relationships, see Chapter 3), and 'implementation as responsibility and trust' (Lane, p. 541, this is a theme which we will explore further in Chapters 8 and 9). All of these imply a system in which a close collaborative relationship characterises relations within the policy system allowing policy to emerge in action. It is perhaps appropriate to comment that Lane is Swedish and that the system of central–local government relations in his country has been one in which the latter have substantial constitutional autonomy but accept a substantial measure of policy 'steering' from the centre (Gustafsson, 1991).

These arguments lead us to the view that a model of the policy-implementation relationship in which the policy-making process can be seen as setting 'goals', the extent of whose realisation in action can be measured, provides an insufficient foundation for studies of implementation. It is this that has led various contemporary students of implementation to argue for a bottom-up rather than top-down stance for the study of implementation. Elmore has coined the term 'backward mapping' which he defines as:

'backward reasoning' from the individual and organisational choices that are the hub of the problem to which policy is addressed, to the rules, procedures and structures that have the closest proximity to those choices, to the policy instruments available to affect those things, and hence to feasible policy objectives. (Elmore, 1981, p. 1; see also Elmore, 1980)

Focusing on individual actions as a starting point enables actions to be seen as responses to problems or issues in the form of choices between alternatives. One of Elmore's justifications for this approach derives not so much from our concern about the difficulty in separating policy-making and implementation, as from a recognition that in many policy areas in the United States (youth-employment policy is Elmore's particular interest) implementation actors are forced to make choices between programmes which conflict or interact with each other.

The proponents of this approach argue that it is, by comparison with the top-down model, relatively free of predetermining assumptions. It is less likely to imply assumptions about cause and effect, about hierarchical or any other structural relations between actors and agencies, or about what should be going on between them.

The approach is expounded even more forcefully by Hjern and his associates (Hjern and Porter, 1981; Hjern and Hull, 1982) who argue for a methodology in which researchers construct empirically the networks within which field-level decision-making actors carry out their activities without predetermining assumptions about the structures within which these occur. One of the authors, in his work with Susan Barrett, has added his own support to the methodological argument for this perspective, arguing as follows:

> to understand the policy–action relationship we must get away from a single perspective of the process that reflects a normative administrative or managerial view of how the process should be, and try to find a conceptualisation that reflects better the empirical evidence of the complexity and dynamics of the interactions between individuals and groups seeking to put policy into effect, those upon whom action depends and those whose interests are affected when change is proposed. To do this, we have argued for an alternative perspective to be adopted – one that focuses on the actors and agencies themselves and their interactions, and for an action-centred or 'bottom-up' mode of analysis as a method of identifying more clearly who seems to be influencing what, how and why. (Barrett and Hill, 1981, p. 19)

What, in many respects, is being emphasised in this more action-centred mode of analysis is that the very things which Gunn urges must be controlled are the elements which are difficult to bring under control. The reality, therefore, is not of imperfect control but of action as a continuous process of interaction with a *changing and changeable policy*, a *complex interaction structure*, an *outside world which must interfere* with implementation because government action is, and is designed to, impinge upon it, and implementing actors who are *inherently difficult to control*. Analysis is best focused upon the levels at which this is occurring, since it is not so much creating implementation deficiency as recreating policy.

This emphasis, in the bottom-up critique, upon the complexities in the concept of policy and in the way it is made also suggests that implementation may itself be an ambiguous concept. Lane has argued that there is some confusion in the implementation literature between 'implementation or successful implementation as an outcome, and the implementation process or how implementation comes about' (Lane, 1987). The classical top-down studies are principally concerned with explaining why a successful outcome does or does not occur; to do this they need clear goal statements to work with. These may be supplied by the policy-makers or imputed by the researchers. Without such yardsticks we may still study processes, but our activity is rather different. Sabatier, in an attempt to fuse the best ideas from both the top-down and the bottom-up process rightly suggests that the presence or absence of a 'dominant piece of legislation structuring the situation'(Sabatier, 1986, p. 37) may help to determine which approach is appropriate. However, that may involve starting with a question-begging assumption that this structuring has in fact occurred. Obviously one can treat a piece of legislation as dominant. However, if you do so the problems for *explanation*, in cases of implementation failure, tend to be either what others have done to subvert it, or what is wrong with it. Both of these may be over-simplified questions about both policy and its implementation context, and particularly about the relationship between the two.

Our stance is neither to side with one or other argument, nor to believe with Sabatier (and Elmore in a 1985 contribution to the debate) that one can readily integrate the approaches. Rather, this is another example from the social sciences where looking at an issue from alternative perspectives illuminates the complexity of human interaction. Choice of approach partly depends upon the issue, partly upon what we want to understand about a policy process and partly upon a value choice. This last issue is the subject of the next section.

Implementation studies – descriptive or prescriptive?

A characteristic of the top-down approach to the study of implementation has been a concern to give advice to top actors about how they should secure effective implementation. The propositions from Gunn are framed in these terms (see pages 100–1). Sabatier and Mazmanian (1979) are even more explicit in their article 'The Conditions of Effective Implementation: A Guide to Accomplishing Policy Objectives'. There they set out five conditions to be satisfied if *implementation is to be effective*. Here, then, is a prescriptive approach to policy analysis which embodies two cherished values: a liberal-democratic view that policy should be made by the elected representatives of the people and implemented in a subordinate manner by public officials, and a view that rationality in public policy involves goal setting followed by activities in pursuit of those goals which may be systematically monitored.

Conversely there is in some of the work of the bottom-up school of thought an opposite position that rationality in policy action can only occur 'close to the ground' and at that level real 'accountability' to the 'people' can be achieved (see particularly Hjern and Hull, 1982). We find some difficulty with this notion. The danger is that traditional top-down accountability to the public through the political process, albeit an ideal difficult to attain and often violated in practice, is abandoned too readily here. The result may easily be not accountability to the public but policy domination by the officials and professionals responsible for its implementation (another theme to which we will return in Chapters 8 and 9). It is obviously a view made more attractive if it is linked with the enhancement of local and grass-roots democracy. There is no doubt that some of the passion which has gone into the top-down bottom-up debate, particularly in Britain, is linked to arguments about the respective roles of central and local government in the determination of policy.

However, setting on one side conflict over where democratic policy-making should occur, we seem, nevertheless, to have a conflict between the desirability of a prescriptive approach and the reality of the need to recognise that implementation involves a continuation of the complex processes of bargaining, negotiation and interaction which characterise the policy-making process. Elmore (1978) puts the dilemma like this:

> The rationalist critique of the conflict and bargaining model is that it elevates confusion and mindless drift to the level of principle, that it provides an easy excuse for acquiescing in results that satisfy no one, and that it provides no basis for improving the implementation process. These criticisms are difficult to counter, except by observing that a failure to understand intricacies of bargaining is sometimes more costly than a failure to agree on an objective measure of success. (p. 226)

We seem to have here, as we showed to be the case in the discussion on decision-making in Chapter 5, a situation in which the demands of good descriptive analysis conflict with a key prescriptive concern. Indeed, there are many parallels with the concerns of that chapter, where it was recognised that acknowledging that decision processes tend to be incremental needs to be distinguished from arguments that they should be so. However, in this case, the simple statement of democratic theory above is not sufficient to resolve the normative argument. To take it for granted, for example, that interventions in social policy from central government are motivated by a concern to advance equality, as seems to have been the case with some American analyses of federal programmes, may not merely be building a misleading assumption into analysis, it may also be begging the question as to whether in fact such interventions are the best way to advance equality. American analyses of implementation are to a considerable extent still dominated by a special American liberal assumption that can be most graphically described in terms of the view that 'if the Feds had not intervened they would still be lynching blacks in Alabama'. European discussions of central–local relations do not necessarily entail the same assumptions about the extent to which the moral cards are held by the centre.

It was suggested early in this chapter that Pressman and Wildavsky's emphasis 'on the dashing of Washington's great expectations' is characteristic of the normative concern of many of the pioneers of implementation studies. While arguing that implementation rarely involves the direct translation of policy goals into action, the authors do not wish to reject the normative concern about rational goal achievement embodied in the work of Pressman and Wildavsky, Sabatier and Mazmanian or Gunn. Nor would they want to deny the importance of the value questions raised by many of the researchers who have used the top-down approach to explore how, in the implementation process, the advancement of ideal goals such as the enhancement of equality or the reduction of pollution have been retarded. What they do suggest is that there is a danger that the top-down approach takes it for granted that such goals are embodied in policy, and that in using notions like implementation deficit it offers only one kind of solution to deficient public sector performance, namely that the top should get a better grip on the situation.

Conclusions

The latter part of this chapter has been concerned with the arguments between top-down and bottom-up approaches to the study of implementation. While we have pointed out the limitations of the school of implementation studies initiated by Pressman and Wildavsky, we want to stress again their role in opening up the analysis of an important, and previously rather neglected, part of the policy process.

We should not rule out the possibility of discovering situations in which implementation studies may involve some quite explicitly goal-directed activities, and it may be justifiable to work with notions such as implementation deficit. This might be particularly the case where a quantifiable output is available and explicit inputs can be measured. The British experience with the Thatcher governments has been of a number of examples where government goals have been very clear. There have been cases of very determined top-down pursuit of clearly specified objectives (the sale of local authority-owned homes to their occupiers – see Forrest and Murie, 1988), cases where clear evidence of implementation problems ahead has pulled government back (the strange case of an identity cards scheme to prevent football hooliganism) and a dramatic case of implementation difficulty leading to yet further policy innovation (the rise and fall of the 'poll tax', a local taxation 'reform').

Yet many events in the policy process do not involve such clarity. Examples can be taken, even from the Thatcher years in Britain, of complex and confusing cases where central goals are not nearly so clear, or where central goal statements should be received with great scepticism – in fields like community care, employment policy, urban renewal, or the prevention of crime, for example. Yet if this is true of unified, centralised, one-party-dominated Britain how much more true is it of societies where politics is dominated by compromises between federal units or coalition governments.

In focusing attention on the advance in implementation studies stimulated by Pressman and Wildavsky, and in looking at the critique of their approach which has now developed, this chapter has perhaps neglected, as Pressman and Wildavsky did, the many contributions to the study of this part of the policy process made by others who, generally speaking, did not describe their work as concerned with implementation.

Chapter 3 has already made some reference to sociologists' interest in the study of bureaucracy. It is perhaps more fruitful to continue to deepen the emphasis upon explaining the outputs of the policy process which come from the examination of the policy-making and implementation organisations (or the bureaucracy, in an alternative terminology) than to concentrate on developing a special branch of policy analysis called implementation studies. A similar case can be made for developing a growing concern about explaining the way the public sector impacts upon people. This has developed in Britain as the study of social policy has developed as an academic enterprise. It has also been associated in both Britain and the United States with a concern about explaining how the law is operationalised with particular reference to the phenomenon of discretion. Good work on the study of implementation must embrace all these other academic developments, and not seek to confine attention to a narrowly conceived theory which separates it from the study of policy-making. Accordingly, further chapters will consider some of these other themes – the contribution of the study of organisations to policy analysis, the consideration which needs to be given to the roles of public officials at points where they interface with the public and the significance of the discretionary element in much public policy.

As a final comment we may note that any attempt to develop implementation theory must face the difficulty – once it moves away from the attempt to develop checklists of pitfalls for the implementation process in the way described and criticised above – of becoming involved with the wide range of questions which have been raised in relation to policy-making and in the study of organisations. If we substitute the word 'doing' for implementation we see how we are confronted by an attempt to develop a 'theory of doing' – or of action. Perhaps, therefore, that is not a very helpful way to proceed. Rather, as Susan Barrett and Michael Hill have suggested, it is hard to go beyond the identification of the key elements which must be analysed in the study of implementation, and the recognition of the overwhelming importance of the negotiation and bargaining which occur *throughout* the policy process. Barrett and Hill (1981) argue:

> many so-called implementation problems arise precisely because there is a tension between the normative assumptions of government – what ought to be done and how it should happen – and the struggle and conflict between interests – the need to bargain and compromise – that represent the reality of the process by which power/influence is gained and held in order to pursue ideological goals. (p. 145)

The next three chapters will take up that theme in a variety of different ways.

CHAPTER 7

THE CONTRIBUTION OF THE
STUDY OF ORGANISATIONS TO
THE STUDY OF THE POLICY PROCESS

Introduction

The case for the discussion of the study of organisations within a book of this kind has been pithily made by Elmore (1978): 'Since virtually all public policies are executed by large public organisations . . . only by understanding how organisations work can we understand how policies are shaped in the process of implementation' (p. 187).

As was pointed out at the end of the last chapter, many of the major contributions to this subject were made by writers who did not see themselves as concerned with the study of policy implementation. Indeed, some of the significant advances in organisation theory which will be discussed in this chapter came from writers who were not concerned about public organisations at all. Nevertheless their contributions significantly further the understanding of phenomena which need to be explored if the role of organisations in the policy process is to be comprehended.

The contribution of Max Weber

Chapter 3 has already outlined Max Weber's role in the development of theory about bureaucracy in the modern state. Here we need to go more deeply into his concern with the inner working of organisations. The strength of the bureaucratic form of administration, according to Weber, rests upon its formal rationality, a notion

116

which a number of modern students of organisations have equated with efficiency. This translation of Weber's concept has led to some useful discussions of the relationship between formalism and efficiency but has also given currency to a rather unsubtle characterisation of Weber's theory. Albrow (1970) shows how this confusion arose and provides the following clarification of Weber's position:

> The real relation between formal rationality and efficiency can best be understood by considering the means by which efficiency is commonly measured, through the calculation of cost in money terms, or in time, or in energy expended. Such calculations are formal procedures which do not in themselves guarantee efficiency, but are among the conditions for determining what level of efficiency has been reached. At the heart of Weber's idea of formal rationality was the idea of correct calculation, in either numerical terms, as with the accountant, or in logical terms, as with the lawyer. This was normally a necessary though not sufficient condition for the attainment of goals; it could even conflict with material rationality. (p. 65)

Weber's theory is seen as providing a number of simple propositions about the formal structure of organisations, a misconception that has contributed to his usefulness to students of organisations but which does not do justice to the depth of his understanding of the critical issues in organisational sociology. As he outlines the characteristics of an organisational type that is important in complex societies because of its formal rationality, he naturally stresses the strength of that type rather than its weakness. In contrast, many of his nineteenth-century predecessors emphasise its weakness and use the term 'bureaucracy' in a purely derogatory sense (see Albrow, 1970). Weber's aim is to define a widespread kind of organisation and explain why it is growing in importance, offering thereby sociological analysis rather than political polemic.

Weber lists a number of characteristics which, taken together, define bureaucracy. These characteristics are as follows:

1. A continuous organisation with a specified function, or functions, its operation bound by rules. Continuity and consistency within the organisation are ensured by the use of writing to record acts, decisions and rules.
2. The organisation of personnel is on the basis of hierarchy. The scope of authority within the hierarchy is clearly defined, and the rights and duties of the officials at each level are specified.

3. The staff are separated from ownership of the means of administration or production. They are personally free, 'subject to
   authority only with respect to their impersonal official
   obligations'.
4. Staff are appointed, not elected, on the basis of impersonal
   qualifications, and are promoted on the basis of merit.
5. Staff are paid fixed salaries and have fixed terms of employment.
   The salary scale is normally graded according to rank in the
   hierarchy. Employment is permanent with a certain security of
   tenure, and pensions are usually paid on retirement. (1947, pp.
   329–41)

While Weber does not see these characteristics as prescriptions
for organisation, many subsequent writers have seized upon their
similarity to the model prescribed by others who were searching
for the best way to organise. Pundits like Fayol (1916), a French-
man writing around the time of the First World War, and Urwick,
an Englishman who was influential in both private and public organisations in the inter-war period, seek to set out rules and max-
ims for successful administration.

But perhaps the most influential figure in the search for principles of organisation before the First World War was F.W. Taylor
(1911). He was an American who tried to develop scientific principles for industrial management, based upon a series of generalisations which he claimed to be of universal application. His
importance for this account is that he has been widely seen as the
leading exponent of methods of organisation which rest upon
treating human beings as units of labour to be used efficiently
without regard to their attitudes and emotions. Hence a great deal
of the subsequent concern about human relations in organisations
emerged from the exposure of the limitations of 'Taylorism'. Despite that exposure the influence of Taylorism lives on. Pollitt
(1990) has described much modern managerialism in the public
services as 'neo-Taylorism'. He argues:

> Taylorism was centrally concerned with the 'processes of determin-
> ing and fixing effort levels' and can be seen as 'the bureaucratization
> of the structure of control but *not* the employment relationship'
> (Littler, 1978, pp. 199 and 185 respectively). It proceeded on the
> basis that . . . the work process could and should be measured by
> management, and then used as a basis for rewarding and controlling
> effort . . . This is not far, in principle, from the recent epidemic of

electronically-mediated public-service systems of performance in-dicators, individual performance review and merit pay. (p.16)

Mayo and the development of the study of organisational life

In the 1920s and 1930s management theory gradually began to move away from a concern with the development of formal pre-scriptions for organisational structure towards a better under-standing of organisational life. This development, while still firmly preoccupied by a concern with control over subordinates within the industrial enterprise, nevertheless eventually contributed to a transformation of the way organisations were understood. This is the reason we devote some space to describing it here.

The work carried out under Elton Mayo at the Hawthorne Works in Chicago during the late 1920s and early 1930s is often credited with effecting this revolution in industrial sociology (Roethlisberger and Dickson, 1939). This is an over-simplified view. The Hawthorne researchers were influenced by research on morale carried out during the First World War. They were also well aware of the progress being made in social psychology be-tween the wars, and in particular they were influenced by the more sophisticated approach to human motivation that Freudian psy-chology helped to produce. The development of a more complex approach to social structure at this time, by sociologists and an-thropologists under the influence of Pareto, Simmel, Durkheim and the 'Functionalists', also had an impact on their work. In some ways, too, their thinking had been foreshadowed by the writings of Mary Parker Follett (1941) on management. For these reasons it makes more sense to say that the Hawthorne researches represent the most significant single advance in the understanding of human behaviour in a work context. The Hawthorne researches have had a colossal impact upon subsequent workers in this field, and it is only natural that the process of the simplification of the history of ideas has led to their being accorded a significance out of propor-tion to their true contribution.

We have not the space here to discuss in detail the findings of the Hawthorne researches but their main importance lies in the way they shifted the emphasis in organisation theory from a mechanical concern to discover the *one best way* to organise work tasks to a recognition of the importance of human relationships for organisational performance. Their early research draws attention to the relevance of managerial interest in workers' activities for motivation and morale, while their later work throws light upon relationships within the work group.

The Hawthorne researches demonstrate the need to analyse organisations as living social structures. They indicate that, just as to discover that there are such and such a number of farmers, shopkeepers and labourers living in a village and that 'x' works for 'y' and so on is not to find out a great deal of significance about the social structure of that village, so to regard an organisation as merely a pattern of formal roles is likely to make it impossible to understand fully the determinants of behaviour, even formally prescribed behaviour, within that organisation.

Although these findings relate to the shop floor, to the lowest level in an organisation's hierarchy, subsequent research has demonstrated the validity of these findings for all levels. Interpersonal relationships within groups of office workers or within management have equally been found to determine work behaviour in a way that formal organisational rules in no way anticipate.

As the social sciences began to grow in importance in the United States in the 1940s and 1950s, two developments in organisation theory – one stimulated by the work of Max Weber, the other influenced by the more obviously relevant findings of Mayo and his associates – began to come together. Sociologists, using Weber's work (or their understanding of it) as their starting point, set out to show the importance of patterns of informal relationships alongside the formal ones. Social psychologists on the other hand sought to explore the conflict between human needs and the apparent requirements of formal organisations. Drawing on this work, administrative theorists sought to update the old formal prescriptive models with more flexible propositions based upon this new understanding of organisational life. It is not possible in this short account to do justice to the full richness of the flowering of this work on organisations. In the following pages some comments will be made about those developments which still seem very important.

The contribution of the sociology of organisations

Once Weber's work became available to sociologists in the United States in the 1940s and 1950s it was applied to organisational studies as a kind of model against which real situations might be measured. By treating it in this way sociologists began to identify problems about the rational model of bureaucracy, often unjustly alleging that Weber had not been aware of them but nevertheless usefully advancing organisational theory.

In some of this work it is suggested that there is likely to be a conflict within the bureaucratic organisation between the principle of hierarchy and the need to maximise the use of expertise. Gouldner (1954) makes this point in the following way: 'Weber, then, thought of bureaucracy as a Janus-faced organisation, looking two ways at once. On the one side, it was administration based on expertise: while on the other, it was administration based on discipline' (p. 22).

Bureaucratic organisation is founded upon the need to make the maximum use of the division of labour. Such division is based upon the need to subdivide a task either because of its size or because it is impossible for a single individual to master all its aspects. In fact, in most cases both these reasons apply. The principle of hierarchy rests upon the notion of the delegation of responsibility to subordinates. If the superior could perform the whole of the task which is delegated, there would be no need to have subordinates. He or she will delegate part of the task either because of a lack of time to do it alone, or because he or she has neither the time nor the knowledge to perform certain parts of the task. Inasmuch as the latter is the case, it is obvious that in respect of at least part of the task the superior is less expert than the subordinate. But even in the former case this may also be true, since, particularly as far as tasks that require decision-making are concerned, the subordinate will be in possession of detailed information which, in delegating responsibility, the superior has chosen not to receive.

It is for these reasons that, as far as detailed parts of an organisation's functions are concerned, it must be recognised that expertise resides primarily in the lower ranks of a hierarchy. And it is for these reasons that it is inevitable that there tends to be conflict between authority based upon expertise and authority based upon hierarchy in bureaucratic organisations.

This apparent inconsistency in Weber's theory has helped to provoke several valuable studies of conflict between experts and administrators within organisations. An allied topic that has also been explored is the conflict that exists for experts between professional orientation and organisational orientation in their attitudes to their work (Gouldner, 1957–8; Reissman, 1949).

A second important theme deriving from Weber's work, although based upon a misunderstanding of his approach to the issue, concerns the relationship between rationality and rigidity. One of the earliest essays on this theme was Merton's (1957) discussion of bureaucratic structure and personality. He argues as follows:

1. An effective bureaucracy demands reliability of response and strict devotion to regulations.
2. Such devotion to the rules leads to their transformation into absolutes; they are no longer conceived as relative to a set of purposes.
3. This interferes with ready adaption under special conditions not clearly envisaged by those who drew up the general rules.
4. Thus, the very elements which conduce towards efficiency in general produce inefficiency in specific instances. (p. 200)

This emphasis fits with the arguments about expertise within organisations. Its implications for the behaviour of bureaucratic employees will be explored further in the next chapter.

Merton's work led to an exploration of the relationship between organisational structure and organisational tasks. Thus, the question raised was whether the 'rational' structure may not be well-adapted to some tasks but ill-adapted to others. Two British researchers, Burns and Stalker (1961), made one of the most important contributions on this theme. They drew a distinction between 'mechanistic' and 'organic' management systems. The former, involving structures broadly comparable to the Weberian model, are, their research suggests, most suitable for stable, unchanging tasks. The latter, by contrast, are best

> adapted to unstable conditions, when problems and requirements for action arise which cannot be broken down and distributed among specialist roles within a clearly defined hierarchy. Individuals have to perform their special tasks in the light of their knowledge of the tasks of the firm as a whole. Jobs lose much of their formal definition in terms of methods, duties, and powers, which have to be

Conceptual framework summary

Contingent variables		Structural variables
Size		Differentiation
Environment, i.e.		committees
population density		departments
socio-economic		functional-
structure wealth		specialists
Interdependence		Integration
Political structure, i.e.		coordinating
party composition	Organisation filters	committees
electoral-	Ideas	central-
volatility	corporate planning	departments
Ideologies	administrative	chief executive
corporate planning	efficiency	officer
administrative	democracy	management team
efficiency		
democracy	Occupational cultures	
Type of authority	professionalism	
	departmentalism	

Figure 7.1 Contingency theory

redefined continually by interaction with others participating in a task. Interaction runs laterally as much as vertically. Communication between people of different ranks tends to resemble lateral consultation rather than vertical command. Omniscience can no longer be imputed to the head of the concern. (pp. 5–6)

Burns and Stalker base their dichotomy on experience of research into two contrasting industrial situations. Other sociologists began, however, to raise wider questions about the fit between organisational task and structure, by examining a wide range of work situations. Some other British research played a seminal role in this development. First, Woodward developed a typology of industrial organisations based upon differences in technology. Then, later sociologists, notably a group working together at Aston University, began to argue for the recognition of the multi-dimensional nature of the determinants of organisation structure. Hence by 1975 researchers working in this tradition, which had become known as 'contingency theory', could suggest, for a study of British local authorities, a complex interaction between contingent variables and structural variables as shown in Figure 7.1 (Greenwood, Hinings and Ranson, 1975, p. 5).

If you examine the range of 'contingent' variables set out in Figure 7.1 you find much more than the technologically determining variables present in Burns and Stalker or Woodward. You find variables which are external to the organisation in its 'environment', you find variables determined by the power structure in which it operates and you find variables which will depend upon 'ideology' or what Child (1972) has described as 'strategic choice'. Some brief comments are essential about how the analysis of organisations has been elaborated in relation to these three issues.

Organisations have been recognised as being power systems in which structural features interact with and are affected by factors which make some participants within them more powerful than others. This has been called 'strategic contingencies theory'. It owes a great deal to a research report by Crozier (1964) which stresses the way in which particular participants in an organisation can dominate, and influence structure, by their indispensability. His main example concerns the role of maintenance workers whose contributions were essential whenever an otherwise highly routinised plant broke down. Developments of this theory have stressed the way it explains 'differential sub-unit power by dependence on contingencies ensuing from varying combinations of coping with uncertainty, substitutability, and centrality' (Hickson *et al.*, 1971, p. 229).

Yet even this approach tends to take internal contingencies as determinants of the power structure. There is a need to turn it the other way round too, accepting that contingencies and structures determine power but also asking whether these should be taken for granted. It is important to ask to what extent they themselves reflect a pre-existing or external power structure, and to what extent organisations have been designed to reflect and reinforce this. Hence various writers, notably Salaman (1979), Clegg and Dunkerley (both separately, and together: 1977, 1979, 1980, 1989, 1990) and Benson (1977) have taken this emphasis upon the importance of organisational power much further, making, in what may be described as radical organisation theory, links with theories of power in society. Hence Salaman argues:

> What occurs within organisations, the ways in which work is designed, control applied, rewards and deprivations distributed, decisions made, must be seen in terms of a constant conflict of interests, now apparent, now disguised, now overt, often implicit, which lies

behind, and informs, the nature of work organisations within capitalist societies. (1979, p. 216)

In the same way Cousins (1987) has shown that power within organisations reflects gender inequalities in the wider society.

The internal and the external

Clearly it is important to make connections between issues about internal organisational power and the external context. While the modern radical theorists are right to emphasise the neglect of this theme in much organisation theory, it has never been absent from discussions of organisations. Our earlier examination of bureaucracy and the state made this clear. Moreover, within organisation theory the concern with environments or external relations of organisations has roots in earlier work.

Selznick, much of whose significant work was done in the 1940s and 1950s, remains one of the most sophisticated exponents of the dependence of organisations upon their environments. He emphasises the need to study organisations as institutions:

> The term 'organisation' thus suggests a certain bareness, a lean no-nonsense system of consciously coordinated activities. It refers to an expendable tool, a rational instrument engineered to do a job. An 'institution' on the other hand, is more nearly a natural product of social needs and pressures – a responsive adaptive organism. (1957, p. 5)

In this way Selznick relates organisations both to their external environment and to the informal social systems that develop within them. But he goes an important step further, to relate external environment directly to the internal social system. Individuals within an administrative organisation bring with them certain social commitments and attachments. Then, in the course of their administrative duties they have to take actions that affect the public. Their particular public may be single individuals or powerful organisations. The reactions of the public to any administrative actions must be taken into account, particularly if they have any bargaining power. In the course of time a pattern of complex relationships may grow up between an individual and those people and organisations who constitute his public. At the same time the individual will be involved in a similar network of relationships with colleagues, who will also be likely to be involved in a series of external relationships of the same kind.

Selznick has been criticised by Gouldner (1955) and by Perrow (1972) for too deterministic an approach to the study of organisations. Nevertheless it would be foolish to underestimate the extent to which the environment, however much it too is manipulable, also places constraints upon organisational action. The following quotation from Selznick's classic, *TVA and the Grass Roots* (1949), expresses this most clearly:

> All formal organizations are moulded by forces tangential to their rationally ordered structures and stated goals. Every formal organization – trade union, political party, army, corporation etc. – attempts to mobilize human and technical resources as means for the achievement of its ends. However, the individuals within the system tend to resist being treated as means. They interact as wholes, bringing to bear their own special problems and purposes; moreover the organization is embedded in an institutional matrix and is therefore subject to pressure upon it from its environment, to which some general adjustment must be made. As a result, the organization may be significantly viewed as an adaptive social structure, facing problems which arise simply because it exists as an organization in an institutional environment, independently of the special (economic, military, political) goals which called it into being. (p. 251)

This concern with organisations and their environments raises questions about the extent to which inter-organisational relationships influence individual organisational action. Hence, there has been a considerable interest in inter-organisational bargaining and negotiation (Friend, Power and Yewlett, 1974; Aldrich, 1979; Pfeffer and Salancik, 1978). The importance of this for the public sector is considerable in view of the extent to which governmental activities involve sets of organisations rather than single entities. In this sense Benson (1983) has written of policy sectors. But, as inter-organisational relationships are analysed, it is inevitable that discourse shifts back to a more macro-level in which it is the place of those relationships in the wider social structure that becomes important. Hence we find strands of both corporatist (Winkler, 1976) and neo-Marxist theory (Benson, 1983; Offe, 1975) which strive to link inter-organisational analysis with some of the arguments about the relationship between bureaucracy and the social structure. Some important questions remain, and these are discussed further in Chapter 10.

In the study of the non-governmental sector attempts have been made to apply an ecological, Social Darwinist approach to the analysis of the extent to which organisations are adapted to their environment (Hannan and Freeman, 1977). While this theory attempts to generalise beyond profit-making ventures its thinking has been influenced by studies of the rise and decline of firms and of the ways in which enterprises have adapted to the market by organisational changes and particularly by absorbing smaller companies upon whom they have become dependent (Chandler, 1977, 1984).

Perhaps the most influential development of this kind of theory has been in the work of Williamson (1975, 1981) which applies ideas from economics to the analysis of organisations. It is important to bear in mind that for Williamson inter-organisational relationships are best determined by markets. His starting point is what is an idealised past in which enterprises were small and related to each other through contracts – with, for example, companies assembling large entities trading with suppliers of smaller parts. Then, as Chandler (1977) has shown, these market relations were gradually transformed into 'hierarchies' as peripheral suppliers were absorbed by enlarging enterprises. Williamson is then concerned to know why this occurred, since for him 'markets' are economically superior to 'hierarchies'. His explanation rests upon an analysis of 'market failure' in which limits to human rationality led to, for him, irrational decisions.

This work is generalised into forms of contingency theory (Donaldson, 1985, 1987) and has been challenged by writers who see issues of power and of control over environmental uncertainties as of greater explanatory value than Williamson's original approach (see, for example, Minzberg, 1983).

Reference has been made to Williamson's theory here because of its parallels with the theory of bureaucratic inefficiency developed by Niskanen (see Chapter 3). For a long while thinking about public bureaucracies was dominated by a perspective that saw the large Weberian organisation as inevitable. From such a perspective the idea that a public organisation might need to be adapted to its environment made sense only as an issue about public accountability. Now, however, there is a search for ways of making public organisations smaller and more adaptable, engaging in contractual relations with each other (or with private organisations) and accountable to the public as 'customers'. Whilst this is still largely uncharted territory, it offers new challenges to the students of public sector organisations to use theories and concepts from studies of the private sector.

Participants within organisations

What makes the study of organisations so complex is that just as some bodies of theory have shifted attention outwards to their environments so others have emphasised the need to give attention to relationships between organisations and individual participants in their activities.

The work of social psychologists on the fit, or lack of it, between people and organisations can naturally be said to have its roots in the critique of Taylorism developed by Mayo (1933). The concern has been with the conflict between basic human needs and the requirements of work tasks in formal organisations. Maslow (1954), for example, suggests that there is a hierarchy of human needs from basic physiological needs to self-actualisation. The lower-order needs must be satisfied but, once they are, then higher-order needs become more significant. Hence, employment in routine tasks leaves individuals unsatisfied. As Argyris (1960) argues, therefore:

> administrators of complex organisations are faced with one of the most difficult human problems ever to challenge them. On the other hand, it becomes easy for both the administrator and the employee to de-emphasise human values and to operate on a *quid pro quo* basis of money, job security and benefits. As long as a minimum standard of human relationships is maintained, the 'rational man relationship' could well flourish. But . . . such a theory will produce and reward apathy, indifference, alienation, and non involvement. (p. 235)

McGregor (1960) adopts a similar position in an influential book, *The Human Side of Enterprise*, contrasting Theory X which assumes that employees are typically indolent, passive and so on and must be organised, directed and motivated by economic rewards with Theory Y, which emphasises self-actualisation and sees management's tasks as to encourage this and organise so that people can achieve their own goals best by directing their own efforts towards organisational objectives.

Paralleling this work on human motivation are studies of leadership. But while the work of Maslow, Argyris and McGregor has its roots in post-Freudian theorising about the character of human growth and development, the leadership studies involve detailed empirical work in small group situations. They show that it is wrong to search for leadership traits which will hold for all situations. Instead, as Gibb (1954) argues:

> The traits of leadership are any or all of those personality traits which in any particular situation, enable an individual to (i) contribute significantly to group locomotion in the direction of a recognised goal, and (ii) be perceived as doing so by fellow group members . . . Different people want different things of leadership. Patterns of behaviour which constitute effective leader behaviour in one group may not be effective in another. As group goals change, leadership needs change and different forms of leader behaviour are demanded. (p. 889)

There are several different points that need to be disentangled here. First, there are differences in task. Cartwright and Zander (1968) refer to an attempt by Krech and Crutchfield to list different functions of leadership in which fourteen such functions are suggested. They propose that a leader serves to some degree as an executive, planner, policy-maker, expert, external group representative, controller of internal relationships, arbitrator, exemplar, group symbol, surrogate for individual responsibility, ideologist, father figure or scapegoat.

Second, there are differences between groups. There are markedly different definitions of leader and follower roles in different cultures. Moreover, even within one culture there may be subcultural variations in response to authority situations. The personality structures of group members may also be relevant.

Third, as Etzioni (1961) has suggested, individuals may expect a very different kind of leadership according to whether their orientation to the organisation is 'calculative' or 'moral', and may also require both 'instrumental' and 'expressive' leadership – very different kinds of leadership which it may be impossible to find combined in the same person. Somewhat similarly, individuals may more effectively be led by authoritarian leaders when faced with what they recognise as serious and ambiguous problems, yet be less ready to accept this sort of leadership style in other situations.

Both the self-actualisation theorists and the students of leadership have come under attack. One of the main ingredients of that attack is, of course, obvious. People with power and authority have been reluctant to adopt forms of organisation or patterns of behaviour which undermine their prerogatives. However, some of the arguments they have used cannot be so lightly dismissed. One of the dilemmas implicit in Weber's emphasis upon rationality is that organisational success, yielding high productivity and thus high monetary rewards for participation, has often rested upon the adoption of hierarchies and authoritarian organisational patterns. Another problem of particular relevance to public organisations is that hierarchical control implies the subservience of bureaucrats to their political, and perhaps democratic, masters.

Hence, the organisational world has adapted in limited ways to the strictures of the human-relations theorists. Very often this adaptation takes the form of fringe benefits – better working environments, social facilities after work, pensions and sick-pay schemes and so on – rather than any diminution of control over the work task. Some sociologists who have studied worker motivation have suggested that many individuals participate only for financial rewards and are not particularly interested in job enlargement or participation in management (Goldthorpe *et al.*, 1968).

However, perhaps the most fundamental attack on the human-relations school of thought comes from Marxists who point out that writers like Argyris have borrowed and misused Marx's concept of alienation, so that they emphasise job enlargement and control over the day-to-day work task without considering the wider issue within which this is embedded, the ownership of the means of production (see Salaman, 1979). Even those readers who find Marxist theory unacceptable should consider whether the problems Argyris and McGregor identify in work situations can be easily solved without attention being given to the wider social context within which remunerative work takes place.

Sociological studies of the individual in organisations have been rather less concerned than the social psychologists with motivation and leadership but rather more concerned with informal behaviour within formal structures. The importance of informal work group structures had, as was shown earlier, been identified by Mayo and his associates in the 1930s. The sociologists of the post-war period developed this line of work, relating it to Weber's typology. Blau (1955) shows how organisational participants may disregard rules in order to carry out their tasks more effectively, or in order to ensure that they maximise some objectives while disregarding others they perceive to be in conflict with them. Dalton (1959) shows how cliques and patterns of clientism develop in organisations which create a separate informal structure alongside the formal one. Gouldner (1954) demonstrates that rules will be manipulated in the internal power conflict within an organisation, becoming themselves weapons in battles which may equally be used by high- or low-level personnel. Selznick (1957) summarises the resulting picture of organisations which emerge when the informal is taken into account:

> An organisation is a group of living human beings. The formal or official design for living never completely accounts for what the participants do. It is always supplemented by what is called the 'informal structure', which arises as the individual brings into play his own personality, his special problems and interests . . .
> The formal, technical system is therefore never more than a part of the living enterprise we deal with in action. The persons and groups who make it up are not content to be treated as manipulable or expendable. As human beings and not mere tools they have their own needs for self-protection and self-fulfilment – needs that may either sustain the formal system or undermine it. (pp. 7–8)

However, to discuss the formal–informal distinction in this way may still be to attribute too much importance to the formal. It tends to involve the assumption that the former is somehow fixed and readily identifiable while the latter is a grey, hazy development underneath it. In practice the two concepts should not be dichotomised, they continually adapt, interacting with each other. Moreover, more recent sociologists have warned against treating the formal structure as the real structure, when it is no more than the portrait of the organisation certain powerful actors within it would like the researchers to accept as real (see Silverman, 1975). It may be that individual actors construct their view of their world of work in ways which pay little attention to rules and structures but rather to a network of relationships. Within that network people outside the organisation may be as important as people inside. Hence we come back, by way of a discussion of the individual *in* the organisation, to issues about the organisation in its *environment*. The implication of this perspective is, as Degeling and Colebatch (1984) argue, that managers of organisations need to be aware:

> how prevailing organizational arrangements and practices have different meanings and significance for those who are subject to them as well as for those responsible for their operation. They need an understanding of how frameworks of meaning, and consequent modes of discourse, are developed and propagated, and how in their use, these modes of discourse shape the terms under which organizational relationships are conducted. (p. 323)

Once we introduce the idea of the organisation as an 'open system' from the viewpoint of the individual we are reminded that most conventional organisation theory typically treats employees as the only relevant participants within public sector organisations. Yet much of the work of those organisations involves influencing the lives of the public – as 'customers', 'clients', subjects of regulation and so on. The Weberian model is, as has been shown, pessimistic about control over bureaucracy by politicians, but is not the more important issue control over bureaucracy by the public upon whom it impacts. At least market organisations recognise the need to retain the interest of the customer as the central problem to be addressed in organisational life. Hence the persuasive strength of arguments for 'markets' as against 'hierarchy'. Hirschman (1970) has captured the importance of this issue in his distinction between 'exit' and 'voice' as the two alternatives to continuing 'loyalty' to an organisation. Traditional democratic theory offers 'voice' as the technique for influence over bureaucracy, either through representative government or through more participative devices for citizens to influence policy or ventilate personal grievances. If market models of public service can be developed they provide the alternative 'exit' option.

Conclusions

This chapter started with an outline of the way in which Max Weber developed a model of bureaucratic organisation as part of his analysis of the role of bureaucracy in modern society. The development of the study of organisation theory in the twentieth century can be seen as a growth outward from that. The initial reaction of American sociology to Weber involved a strong emphasis on the nature of the formal organisation and on the processes going on within it. This fitted well with a concern in management theory and the social psychology of organisations about the problems of compliance of employees with managerial goals. Later sociologists returned to Weber's wider concerns, about power and the place of formal organisations in society. Radical organisation theory has paid particular attention to this theme, bringing together the perspectives of Marx and Weber. The radical Right, by contrast (in this case particularly through the work of Williamson) has raised issues about the application of market concepts to the study of organisations. Work with its roots in 'ethnomethodology' has made us look at relationships between organisations and individuals in new ways, which complement some of the questions being raised about power structures by drawing attention to dominant 'discourses'. The last part of the chapter shifted to the rather sharply contrasting emphasis upon human behaviour within organisations provided by the more psychologically oriented studies of the subject.

Some of the points addressed in general terms here are picked up in relation to some specific issues about individual participation and individual action in organisations in the next two chapters, and then we return to some of the overarching themes in the final chapter.

CHAPTER 8

BUREAUCRATS IN THE POLICY PROCESS

Introduction

There has been an extensive debate, particularly in Britain, about the part top officials play alongside politicians in the policy process. This has been linked to arguments about the nature of the power structure, with questions being raised about the class position of civil servants. Some references were made to these issues in Chapters 2 and 3. This chapter looks at rather different issues, the roles of lower level officials in the implementation process. The bureaucrats in the title refer generically to public officials, including many who prefer to be seen as professionals rather than bureaucrats.

Chapter 6 set out the view that a great deal of policy is in fact made, or modified, in the implementation process. It follows that concern about the impact of officials must extend to a larger group than merely the top echelons. Three issues emerge from the literature on this theme: (a) the extent to which 'bureaucratic personalities' give public sector activities a negative and perhaps conservative aspect, (b) a development of that theme, the nature of the pressures upon what have been called 'street-level bureaucrats' and the significance of these for interactions with the public and (c) the impact of the involvement of professionals in much policy delivery inasmuch as they play separate and distinctive roles. Each of these issues will be considered in turn.

Bureaucratic behaviour and the bureaucratic personality

The administrative organisation has typically a complex structure of a kind which many writers have described as bureaucratic. But, for a number of commentators, bureaucracy implies something more than a complex organisation. For them, bureaucracies are characterised as rigid and slow, with effective action hampered by red tape. Although the main arguments on this topic are concerned with the inherent limitations of elaborate formal procedures, several writers have sought to show that bureaucratic rigidity is in some respects a consequence either of the impact of working in a rule-bound context upon the personalities of individuals, or of a tendency for bureaucracies to recruit people with inflexible personalities.

The impact of the demands of complex organisations upon individuals has been a theme developed in several popular American sociological tracts (see, for example, Whyte, 1956). The picture of the independent frontiersman trapped in the bureaucratic organisation is an American equivalent of the happy peasant forced to work in the dark satanic mills as portrayed in some views of the Industrial Revolution in Britain. It involves a nostalgia for an idealised past which contains enough of a germ of truth to appear plausible while, at the same time, it distorts analysis of present realities by oversimplifying them.

In the study of public bureaucracy, the organisation personality theory links up with another theme which has had a place in popular mythology for many centuries, a theme which several European novelists have developed most effectively, the portrayal of the clerk in public service as an individual whose life becomes dominated by the complex rules which have to be followed in dealings with the public (see, for example, Balzac, 1836; Galdos, 1963).

Reference was made in the last chapter to a pioneering essay on organisational sociology by Merton (1957) which takes up this theme and attempts to explain the conditions under which bureaucratic personalities are likely to be found. Merton's essay is therefore the starting point for this discussion.

The position of those in authority is markedly simplified if subordinates are submissive individuals conditioned to following their superiors uncritically, and much of the literature on authority suggests that many subordinates will be of this kind. Moreover, the implication of much managerial training is that the successful operation of a system of authority will depend upon creating bureaucratic personalities. On the other hand, some of the more sophisticated writers in this field have recognised that there are severe dangers in creating over-submissive subordinates, and that there are advantages to be gained from having bureaucrats who are unwilling to be excessively bound by formal rules. Moreover, subordinates will resist over-formalisation, and so it may be said that they will try to avoid becoming bureaucratic personalities.

In his essay, Merton takes issue with Weber because, in his analysis, 'the positive attainments and functions of bureaucratic organisation are emphasised and the internal stresses and strains of such structures are almost wholly neglected' (1957, p. 197). He contrasts this with the popular emphasis upon the imperfections of bureaucracy. Merton argues that bureaucrats are likely to show particular attachment to rules that protect the internal system of social relationships, enhance their status by enabling them to take on the status of the organisation and protect them from conflict with clients by emphasising impersonality. Because of their function in providing security, rules of this kind are particularly likely to be transformed into absolutes. In this sense policy goals are distorted as means are treated as ends.

Merton's essay is applied to bureaucratic organisations in general, but there are reasons why it may be particularly applicable to public administration. First, public officials are placed in a particularly difficult position *vis-à-vis* their clients. They may be putting into practice political decisions with which they disagree; they are facing a public who cannot normally go elsewhere if their demands are unsatisfied, as they often can with private enterprise; and the justice of their acts is open to public scrutiny, by politicians and sometimes by courts of law. They are thus under particular pressure to ensure that their acts are in conformity with rules. Rules are bound to play a major part in their working lives.

Second, the careers of public officials are normally organised very much along the lines of Weber's bureaucratic model. Indeed, in this respect at least, state bureaucracies often come very close to Weber's ideal type. The need for fairness in selection and promotion, because of the need for the public service to be able to withstand criticism, leads to the development of highly regularised career structures. It tends to be very difficult to justify dramatic or unconventional promotions, and therefore public service careers are oriented towards what F.M. Marx (1957) has called 'the economics of small chances'. Marx explains this expression in the following way:

> In the first place, the ideology of service itself minimises the unabashed display of consuming ambition. In some respects, indeed, service is its own reward. Moreover, the mass conditions to which personnel policy and procedure must be addressed in large-scale organisations cry out for recognition of the normal rather than the exceptional. Meteoric rise of the outstandingly able individual is therefore discouraged quite in the same way as favouritism and disregard of rules are discouraged. Advancement, if it is not to attract suspicious or unfriendly eyes, must generally stay in line with the 'normal'. Exceptions call for too much explaining. All this tends to make reward for accomplishment something that comes in small packages at fairly long intervals. (p. 97)

Such a career structure obviously puts an onus upon conformity, and will tend to create a situation in which if a public official becomes conspicuous for disregarding rules it will be more likely to hamper than enhance his or her career.

Marx's book is interesting in developing the picture of the public official as a bureaucratic personality as a result of the factors discussed above. He therefore characterises the public service as 'the settled life' in which security is valued above high rewards (p. 102). He says 'the merit bureaucracy is not the place for those who want to make money, to rise fast, to venture far, or to stand on their own.' Marx concedes that senior public officials are usually required to be of a reasonably high calibre, but suggests that those who compete for entry will be mostly the 'solid – as contrasted with the brilliant but restive, for instance' (p. 102).

Marx goes on to suggest that the career structure he describes in this way reinforces the pressure for uniformity within a government bureaucracy which arises from the political need for equity and consistency. Thus he claims, 'When the common rule and the common mind combine, the natural consequence is a narrowness of perspective – a weakness more aggravating than mediocrity in administrative performance' (p. 103).

Marx suggests, then, that the bureaucratic personality will be both a product of the fact that only certain types of people choose to join the public service, or indeed the fact that selection procedures may pick out certain types of people, and a product of the bureaucratic environment. The two influences upon personality operate to reinforce each other. In the same way, Merton (1957) recognises this interaction as a key problem for research. He asks:

> To what extent are particular personality types selected and modified by the various bureaucracies (private enterprise, public service, the quasi-legal political machine, religious orders)? Inasmuch as ascendancy and submission are held to be traits of personality, despite their variability in different stimulus situations, do bureaucracies select personalities of particularly submissive or ascendant tendencies? And since various studies have shown that these traits can be modified, does participation in bureaucratic office tend to increase ascendant tendencies? Do various systems of recruitment (e.g. patronage, open competition involving specialised knowledge or general mental capacity, practical experience) select different personality types? (p. 205)

There are, therefore, a number of related issues to consider here:

1. To what extent certain types of people choose to embark on bureaucratic careers.
2. The impact of selection processes in selecting certain types from among those who seek to enter bureaucratic careers.
3. The extent to which personalities who do not fit the organisational environment drop out in the course of their careers.
4. The extent to which success or failure in climbing a career ladder is associated with personality characteristics.

Merton and Marx are, of course, attempting to analyse systematically the widely accepted stereotype of the bureaucratic official. But because it deals with a stereotype the bureaucratic personality theory runs into difficulties. On the most superficial level the public official's role is difficult to distinguish from the role played by a very high proportion of the employed persons in a modern complex society. At this level we are all bureaucratic personalities, in which case there is nothing very special about the role of the public official. On the other hand, if an attempt is made to analyse roles more deeply it will be found that distinctions can be made both between the many different roles in a public bureaucracy, and also between alternative adjustments to formally similar roles. The bureaucratic personality theory is both too specific, in trying to single out certain kinds of organisational roles in a context in which most people are organisational employees, and too general, in implying the existence of uniformity of roles in organisations where such uniformity does not exist.

There is a secondary criticism of the theory which can be made that suggests that there is a tendency to assume the existence of bureaucratic personality, when in practice such behaviour may be a means of protecting the individual from total involvement in the work situation. On this theme a more recent vein of writing is more relevant. It focuses on the pressures upon bureaucrats, and helps to explore, more effectively than the bureaucratic personality theory, how policies become reshaped as public officials seek to bring some order into their own lives. This is the work on street-level bureaucracy by Michael Lipsky (1980) and his associates. For these writers the issue is not the apparent total rule conformity suggested by Merton but rather the way in which officials make choices to enforce some rules, particularly those which protect them, while disregarding others.

Street-level bureaucracy

The theory of street-level bureaucracy is set out in Lipsky's book with that title. It is further developed in work by two of his former research students, Weatherley (1979) and Prottas (1979). Lipsky says of his book: 'I argue that the decisions of street-level bureaucrats, the routines they establish, and the devices they invent to cope with uncertainties and work pressures, effectively become the public policies they carry out' (1980, p. xii).

He argues that this process of street-level policy-making does not involve, as might be hoped, the advancement of the ideals many bring to personal service work but rather the development of practices which enable officials to cope with the pressures they face. He says:

> people often enter public employment with at least some commitment to service. Yet the very nature of this work prevents them from coming close to the ideal conception of their jobs. Large classes or huge caseloads and inadequate resources combine with the uncertainties of method and the unpredictability of clients to defeat their aspirations as service workers. (*ibid.*)

Lipsky argues that street-level bureaucrats develop methods of processing people in a relatively routine and stereotyped way. They adjust their work habits to reflect lower expectations of themselves and their clients. They

> often spend their work lives in a corrupted world of service. They believe themselves to be doing the best they can under adverse circumstances and they develop techniques to salvage service and decision-making values within the limits imposed upon them by the structure of work. They develop conceptions of their work and of their clients that narrow the gap between their personal and work limitations and the service ideal. (p. xii)

Thus Lipsky handles one of the paradoxes of street-level work. Such workers see themselves as cogs in a system, as oppressed by the bureaucracy within which they work. Yet they often seem to the researcher, and perhaps to their clients, to have a great deal of discretionary freedom and autonomy. This is particularly true of the many publicly employed semi-professionals – people like teachers and social workers who secure a degree of that autonomy allowed to professional workers. These are the people whose roles Lipsky and his colleagues are particularly interested in.

Lipsky analyses the paradox, suggested above, in the following way. He outlines the many ways in which street-level bureaucrats are able to manipulate their clients. He stresses the non-voluntary status of clients, suggesting that they only have limited resources inasmuch as the street-level bureaucrat needs their compliance for effective action (p. 57). This is a view supported by two other American writers, Hasenfeld and Steinmetz (1981), who argue that it is appropriate to see bureaucrat–client relationships as exchanges, but that in social services agencies serving low-status clients the latter have little to offer except deference . They point out, as does Lipsky, that ' clients have a very high need for services while the availability of alternatives is exceedingly limited' (Hasenfeld and Steinmetz, 1981, pp. 84–5). Accordingly, 'the power advantage social-services agencies have enables them to exercise considerable control over the lives of the recipients of their services' (p. 85). Clients have to wait for help, experience 'status degradation', have problems in securing access to information, and are taught ways to behave (pp. 89–92). They possess a generally weaker range of tactics with which to respond.

Lipsky also stresses that the street-level bureaucrat cannot readily be brought under the control of a superior. He argues:

> The essence of street-level bureaucracies is that they require people to make decisions about other people.
>
> Street-level bureaucrats have discretion because the nature of service provision calls for human judgement that cannot be programmed and for which machines cannot substitute. (1980, p. 161)

In this sense Lipsky portrays the street-level bureaucrat as making policy, carrying out a political role determining 'the allocation of particular goods and services in the society' (p. 84). Weatherley (1980) summarises this view, as follows:

> a view of policy as determining frontline behaviour is insufficient for explaining what workers actually do and why, and how their activities affect clients. Of course, teachers do teach, caseworkers dispense public assistance, public defenders defend indigent clients, and doctors treat patients, and their work activities are certainly responsive to public policy. But their activities are also responsive to a number of other influences over which the policy maker and administrator may only have limited or no control. The pyramid-shaped organisation chart depicting at the bottom the front-line worker as passively receiving and carrying out policies and procedures dispensed from above is a gross oversimplification. A more realistic model would place the front-line worker in the center of an irregularly shaped sphere with vectors of differing size directed inward. (p. 9)

Elsewhere in Lipsky's book the street-level bureaucrat's role is portrayed very differently. He speaks of it as an 'alienated role' (1980, p. 76), stressing such classic features of alienation as that work is only on 'segments of the product', that there is no control over outcomes, or over 'raw materials' (clients' circumstances), and that there is no control over the pace of work. Lipsky also emphasises the 'problem of resources': street-level bureaucrats face uncertainty about just what personal resources are necessary for their jobs, they find that work situations and outcomes are unpredictable, and they face great pressures of inadequate time in relation to limitless needs.

Is there in Lipsky's work, therefore, an element of inconsistency, or can the contradictions in his analysis be explained? Perhaps he is providing a new variant on the Marxist dictum, 'Man makes his own history, even though he does not do so under conditions of his

own choosing.' This is certainly partly the case. Street-level bureaucrats make choices about the use of scarce resources under
pressure; contemporary fiscal pressure upon human services
makes it much easier for officials to emphasise control than to try
to put into practice service ideals.

But Lipsky does not really try to link his analysis to a macro-
sociological perspective which would enable him to claim that the
illusory freedom of street-level bureaucrats only operates as an
instrument of class oppression and manipulation, and not in any
other direction. His analysis, perhaps even more pessimistically,
tends to show that the street-level bureaucrat's *freedom* to make
policy is largely used to provide a more manageable task and
environment. He talks of 'defenses against discretion', emphasising, as Smith (1981) and Zimmerman (1971) have, the extent to
which street-level bureaucrats develop rigid practices which may
be described by the observer as involving rule conformity even
though the rules are imposed upon themselves. He stresses patterns of practice as 'survival mechanisms', a perspective which is
echoed in a British study of social workers which, using older
American theoretical work on organisational roles by Everett
Hughes (1958), has a great deal in common with Lipsky's work.
This is Satyamurti's (1981) study of English urban social work
teams, in the years immediately after their reorganisation in 1971.
There she speaks of the use of 'strategies of survival' by social
workers under pressure which nearly always led people with the
'best of intentions' to do 'less for clients than they might have' and
often behave in 'ways that were positively damaging' (p. 82). Difficult work environments lead to the abandonment of ideals and to
the adoption of techniques which enable clients to be 'managed', is
the conclusion of this literature.

Let us explore a little further what Lipsky argues about the way
street-level bureaucrats actually behave. A problem about match-
ing limited resources to apparently much greater needs is recognised by all sensitive members of social services agencies.
Accordingly, therefore, considerable efforts are made to prioritise
need and to develop rational ways to allocate resources. The problem is that 'theoretically there is no limit to the demand for free
public goods' (Lipsky, 1980, p. 81). Therefore it is important to
accept that welfare agencies will always feel under pressure.
Lipsky says that the resource problem for street-level bureaucrats

is often irresolvable 'either because the number of people treated
... is only a fraction of the number that could be treated, or
because their theoretical obligations call for higher quality treatment than it is possible to provide to individual clients' (p. 37).
Adjustments to caseloads further the quality of work but leave the
worry about quantity and vice versa. It is always possible to make
out cases for new resources. Marginal changes in those resources
will not necessarily result in visible changes in stress for individual
workers.

This equally seems to provide support for the cynical cutting of
caseloads. Certainly Lipsky suggests that this is how it is sometimes seen. An agency which has great difficulty in measuring
success or providing data on quantity of 'output' is inevitably vul-
nerable to cutting. Yet Lipsky cogently shows how this response
heightens the feeling of stress for individual workers and thus
intensifies the recourse to the manipulation of clients. Retrenchment and redundancy are particularly threatening to the remaining
vestiges of altruism in the human services. In this sense it may be
suggested that incremental growth does little to relieve stress, but
incremental decline intensifies it considerably.

A substantial section of Lipsky's analysis is concerned with the
way in which street-level bureaucrats categorise their clients and
respond in stereotyped ways to their needs. There is a large body
of American research on which he is able to draw. In particular
there have been many studies of the police which have shown how
distinctions are made between different kinds of citizens, which
enable officers to develop certain responses in uncertain situations.
It has been argued that it is misleading to attribute police racism
simply to either the predisposition of recruits or to pressures from
peers. Rather, stereotyping offers short cuts to decision-making on
how to approach people, how to determine whether to act on
suspicion and so on (see Brown, 1981). Lipsky argues that such is
the need for street-level bureaucrats to differentiate clients 'that it
seems as useful to assume bias (however modest) and ask why it
sometimes does not occur, than to assume equality of treatment
and ask why it is regularly abridged' (1980, p. 111). Giller and
Morris (1981) offer evidence of similar stereotyping in British social work in their essay 'What Type of Case is This?'

An issue that is related to simplifying assumptions in categor-
ising different kinds of clients is the adoption of stereotyped

responses to clients in general. Lipsky speaks of these as 'psychological coping mechanisms' and elaborates the importance of simplified views of the client, his or her situation and responsibility for his or her plight to facilitate this (1980, Ch. 10).

Lipsky has already been quoted as asserting that street-level bureaucrats make policy. What does this imply for the implementation of new policy initiatives? A key preoccupation of all those concerned about the need for change in social policy must be with the extent to which it is possible to make things happen at the street level. Lipsky offers a pessimistic view of the feasibility of top-down policy change.

Richard Weatherley (1979) has specifically applied the street-level bureaucracy perspective to the study of the implementation of special education reform in the State of Massachusetts. A new law, enacted in 1974, required schools to operate much more sophisticated procedures for assessing needs for special education and to develop individualised programmes for children. The problem for staff was that they were required to do this without significantly more resources. 'Administrators were caught between the requirements to comply with the law, which they took quite seriously . . . and the certainty that their school committees would rebel against expenditures that led to increased taxes' (Weatherley and Lipsky, 1977, p. 193). Accordingly, a response to the reform was developed which accommodated to the new requirements without substantially disrupting established ways of working. Implementation involved the adjustment of the law to local needs and requirements (see also Hudson, 1989, for a discussion of Lipsky's work to a similar policy context in Britain).

In his last chapter Lipsky connects his concerns about street-level bureaucracy with some of the discussion of professionalism in bureaucracy. Are professionals different, and can the enhancement of professionalism provide a corrective to forms of bureaucratic behaviour outlined in Lipsky's analysis? Our view is that the presence of professionals in bureaucracy does make some difference to the ways in which policy is implemented, but this does not imply that our answer to the normative question posed by Lipsky is a clear 'yes'. Professional power is in our view a subcategory of bureaucratic power in this context, with some distinctive characteristics of its own which raise equally important value questions.

Professionals in the bureaucracy

Sociologists have made many attempts to define professions. Their findings are summarised by Greenwood (1957) in the following terms 'all professions seem to possess: (1) systematic theory, (2) authority, (3) community sanction, (4) ethical codes, and (5) a culture' (p. 45).

However, this list of attributes of a profession mixes occupational characteristics with societal treatment of that occupation. Systematic theory, ethical codes and culture fall into the former category, and authority and community sanction in the latter. An analysis of professions needs at the very least to separate the occupational characteristics which give some groups high prestige, and corresponding power if they possess scarce and needed skills, from the way in which the state and society treats them. In practice there is a very complex interaction between these two groups of factors. This can be explained better by the examination of a concrete case, that of the medical profession.

Of course it is true that doctors possess expertise, and that the public, in its quest for good health, values that expertise. But much medical knowledge is accessible to all. What is also important about the position of the medical profession today is that the state has given that profession a monopoly over many forms of care, allowed it to control its own education and socialisation process, and created, in Britain, a health service in which it plays a dominant part (Eckstein, 1960; Ham, 1985; Klein, 1989; Harrison, Hunter and Pollitt, 1990).

There is a vein of writing on professions within organisations which sees professional power and autonomy as threatened by bureaucratic employment (see Wilensky, 1964). This is misleading since professionals may secure dominant roles within organisations. However, to explore that argument fully would be to depart from the main object here, that is, to emphasise ways in which professionalism is a source of power *within* organisations. The core of that argument is contained in the example of the doctors quoted above. They have succeeded in persuading politicians and administrators that the public will receive the best service if their discretionary freedom is maximised, and if they are given powerful positions in the organisations which run the health services. This expertise, linked with the emotive nature of our concerns about health and the social status which the profession acquired before medical services were provided on any large scale by the state, has reinforced that claim. Other, later established professions, with a weaker base either in expertise or social status, have claimed similar privileges – teachers and social workers, for example.

Ironically, the argument about the role professions may play in bureaucracy has been fuelled by the contrast popularly drawn between the concepts of bureaucracy and professionalism. As Friedson (1970) has argued:

> In contrast to the negative word 'bureaucracy' we have the word 'profession'. This word is almost always positive in its connotation, and is frequently used to represent a superior alternative to bureaucracy. Unlike 'bureaucracy' which is disclaimed by every organisation concerned with its public relations, 'professions' is claimed by virtually every occupation seeking to improve its public image. When the two terms are brought together, the discussion is almost always at the expense of bureaucracy and to the advantage of profession. (pp. 129–30)

Hence professionals stress their altruism, arguing that they are motivated by an ethic of service which would be undermined if their activities were rigidly controlled. In some respects this is a question-begging argument. If public servants are given a high degree of autonomy their actions need to be motivated by ideals of service. The maintenance of ethical standards is important if a group of people have extensive influence on the welfare of individuals. However, the ethical codes of the major professions are often more concerned with protecting members of the group from unfair competition from their colleagues than with service to the public. Moreover, even the public concept of 'good health' is to a considerable extent defined for us by the medical profession; in particular the measures necessary to sustain it, or restore it when it is absent, are largely set out in terms of the activities of the medical profession when in practice many other aspects of our lifestyles and forms of social organisation are also important (Kennedy, 1981; Illich, 1977).

There is, of course, more to medical prestige than expertise, hence Greenwood's fourth and fifth attributes: 'ethical codes' and 'a culture'. We trust and respect doctors, and ask them to take responsibilities far beyond those justifiable in terms of expertise. They are allowed to take decisions on when the life support systems for handicapped babies may be withdrawn, to ration kidney machines and abortions, to advise on where the limits of criminal responsibility may lie and so on. Such powers have emerged gradually as a complex relationship has developed between the state, society and the profession – the last of which has become legitimate partly as a result of the evolution of its ethics and culture and partly because those with power in our society have been willing to devolve authority (see Johnson, 1972). The two phenomena, moreover, have been closely interrelated – internal professional control has made feasible the delegation of responsibility, but equally the latter has made the former more necessary to protect professional autonomy.

The point of this digression on the medical profession is thus to emphasise that occupations are not simply accorded the status of professions by virtue of their own characteristics. Professional status cannot simply be won, as some of the aspirant occupations seem to assume, by becoming more expert and devising an ethical code. It depends upon the delegation of power, and on the legitimisation process in society. In the case of the doctors that legitimisation process may well owe a great deal to our fears about ill health and their special expertise, nevertheless some theorists have argued that it must also be explained in class terms. Johnson (1972) and Parry and Parry (1976) have analysed the way in which medical power was established during the nineteenth century, through a developing relationship with other powerful groups in society. It is clearly relevant, therefore, to raise questions about the comparable autonomy enjoyed by other established professions whose expertise is much more accessible (lawyers, for example). Dunleavy (1981a) has provided an interesting analysis of the influence on public policy and implementation of one such group, the architects, tracing the close connections between conventional professional wisdom and economic interests within the building industry.

The argument for high autonomy within organisations is also based upon Burns and Stalker's evidence on the link between this and adaptability and flexibility (see Chapter 7). Where it is hoped that public officials will play an active role in developing new approaches to their tasks and more sophisticated service to the public, there may be a strong case for granting them a high degree of autonomy. In individual services there is a need to make a choice between the case for a reliable service which can only be changed by initiative from the top, and a less predictable service which may nevertheless be flexible in practice. A further issue here is the extent to which professional tasks are carried out in contexts, such as interactions with individual clients, in which supervision is inherently difficult. The organisation which makes extensive use of professionals is one in which there is high expertise in the lower ranks, a complex task to perform, difficulties in developing effective patterns of supervision and a need for flexibility and openness to change. A strong group of arguments for autonomy come together. In this sense professionals are street-level bureaucrats who have been able to develop special claims to autonomy. But they claim to differ from other public officials in that their relationship with their clients is governed by ethical codes and by altruistic values which others lack.

Various writers have questioned whether these special claims are justified. Lipsky's analysis of this issue comes to the conclusion that high standards of performance and behaviour are eroded by 'peer pressures which leave self interest dominant' (1980, p. 201 *et seq.*). He argues for a new approach to professional accountability in which there is more emphasis upon client-based evaluation of their work. Similarly, Wilding (1982) writes of the need to realise 'a new relationship between professions, clients and society' (p. 149), precisely because others have so little control over them.

We see, therefore, in contemporary writing on professionalism two related, but separate, observations on that phenomenon. Professionals are seen as members of groups able to secure and protect autonomy in their own interest. But they are also, as argued above, identified as able to do this because of their relationship to other elites or dominant class elements in society. There is an important area of debate about the relative importance of these two propositions. Are professions separate power elites, or part of a wider ruling class? Where they are employed by the state, are they able to coopt state power in their own interests, or are they, like most street-level bureaucrats, only able to secure limited power *vis-à-vis* their clients in a context in which influence on the major decisions is beyond their reach?

Concern about professional power has become a shared concern of critics of public bureaucracies on both Left and Right. It has fuelled movements to increase control over or to break up organisations. New devices, made feasible by new technologies, have offered approaches to increasing accountability of street-level workers. Yet these run risks of enhancing some of the problems identified by Lipsky, of stereotyped behaviour and low morale. Furthermore, they may enhance, at the expense of professional service staff, the power of those who monitor their work, creating new kinds of 'professional dominance' from accountants, lawyers and managers (see Alford, 1975a, and Ham, 1985, on 'corporate rationalizers', and developments of this theme in Harrison *et al.*, 1990 and in Flynn, 1991).

Conclusion

The use of the term 'bureaucracy' has often been taken to imply a rigid red tape-bound organisation. In both Chapter 3 and in the last chapter the term was generally used in the way employed originally by Max Weber to connote a complex, regulated organisation. This chapter, by focusing upon bureaucrats rather than bureaucracy, has explored some of the generalisations about organisational behaviour. It showed how theorists like Merton and F.M. Marx seek to explain how rigid behaviour develops in complex organisations. It then outlined how Lipsky's approach to the study of public officials has extended the understanding of this issue by explaining behaviour in terms of the pressures upon street-level bureaucrats. This theory pays considerable attention to officials who are to some degree professionalised, and it poses questions about the way in which professionalism has an impact upon the problem of bureaucracy. Accordingly, the chapter went on to look at professionalism in more detail, arguing that it may provide a different face to public organisations. Professional power may have a significant influence upon the way organisations are run, but that does not necessarily mean that it will protect the public from the dysfunctions of bureaucracy. It may well be used principally to protect the interests of the professionals, and to link those interests to those of other elites.

Both the street-level bureaucracy work and the arguments about professional power have as a central concern the inevitability of high discretion in a great deal of public policy implementation particularly where, as the title of Prottas' contribution to this thesis suggests, 'people processing' is involved. This is a theme which is carried further in the next chapter, when the phenomenon of discretion in the policy-implementation process is explored further.

CHAPTER 9

DISCRETION IN THE POLICY PROCESS

Introduction

Discretion is a concept used in the discussion of public policy implementation in several, partly distinct, ways. In organisational and industrial sociology many writers have drawn attention to it as a ubiquitous phenomenon, linked to the inherent and logical limits to control. In the study of social policy a concern has developed to use and elaborate on the distinction between rules and discretion, linking it to the issues of welfare rights and of arbitrary decision-making by officials, particular staff responsible for the provision of cash benefits. In discussions of administrative law, discretion figures as an issue of some importance in relation to the question of the feasibility of citizen control over administrative acts through the judicial process. Administrative lawyers have long warned against statutes which give government departments unfettered discretionary powers. Studies of law enforcement have drawn attention to the role of discretion in the behaviour both of the police and of the courts, and of other law-enforcement bodies, relating it to the analysis of bias and discrimination.

Hence, ideas about discretion come from a number of different academic sources, where they have been developed, often on the basis of different normative concerns, and sometimes using rather different concepts. The theory available is vague and general. Some contributors to the debates about discretion within a series of sponsored workshops on discretion in social policy held in Britain in 1979–80 expressed scepticism about the value of a priori definitions of discretion. For example, Gilbert Smith (1981) argues:

> the merits of specifically 'discretionary decisions' as a weapon in the research worker's conceptual armoury are dubious. It seems likely to backfire and give rise to a great deal of definitional debate which confuses as much as it clarifies. The *a priori* definitions of discretion tend to be either arbitrary or prejudiced. (p. 67)

While that is a valuable warning on the difficult nature of this concept it does seem to us that its widespread usage in discussions of policy implementation justifies some further explanation.

Definitions of discretion

Some writers who have used the concept of discretion define it very loosely so that it embraces a wide range of phenomena. For example, Davis (1969), in what has been perhaps the most influential book on the subject, says, 'A public officer has discretion wherever the effective limits on his power leave him free to make a choice among possible courses of action and inaction' (p. 4). By contrast others have used quite restrictive definitions, reserving the concept for only some of the phenomena embraced by Davis's definition. For example, Bull (1980) and Donnison (1977), in their separate discussions of social security discretion, draw a distinction between judgement, where the simple interpretation of rules is required, and discretion where the rules give specific functionaries in particular situations the responsibility to make such decisions as they think fit.

It is acknowledged that the use of a wide definition like Davis's implies a concern with almost all decision-making situations since, as Jacques (1967) points out, almost all delegated tasks involve some degree of discretion. A study of discretion must involve, by implication, a study of rules, and may alternatively be defined in that way as being concerned with the extent to which actions are determined by rules. This also means that students of discretion must be concerned with rule-breaking since in real-life situations the interpretation of the extent to which rule following allows discretion merges imperceptibly into the witting or unwitting disregard of rules. The approach here is to use the concept of discretion in the wide sense embodied in Davis's definition. This is partly influenced by a belief that social scientists should try to avoid imposing their own restrictive definitions of concepts used in everyday speech. But it is also justified by the fact that this discussion is concerned to see to what extent discretion is a useful concept with which to explore delegated decision-making processes.

Discretion in organisational sociology

All work, however closely controlled and supervised, involves some degree of discretion. Wherever work is delegated, the person who delegates loses some amount of control. To approach the concept in this way is, of course, to examine it from the perspective of superordinate authority. Viewed the other way round the equivalent phenomenon is rules which apparently guarantee benefits or services but nevertheless have to be interpreted by intermediaries. It is not accidental that the most common academic usage of the concept of discretion has occurred in industrial sociology and the study of organisations. It is in the twin contexts of task complexity and the delegation of responsibility that the phenomenon of discretion becomes of salient importance. In complex organisational situations gaps readily emerge between intentions and outcomes. Logically, people running one-person businesses have discretion but the concern here is with it as a relational phenomenon. The *problems* about discretion are perceived, not surprisingly, as arising when one person's discretionary freedom subverts the intentions of another and so on.

Running through much organisation theory, and in particular through the work of those writers who are seeking to help those they see as in control of organisations to determine the right way to approach the delegation of tasks, is therefore a concern about the balance between rules and discretion, even when different words are used.

Hence Simon in his classic work *Administrative Behaviour* (1945) emphasises the importance of the various premises upon which decisions are based. Rule-making and control within organisations is concerned with the specification of premises for subordinates. Simon argues:

> The behaviour of a rational person can be controlled, therefore, if the value and factual premises upon which he bases his decisions are

specified for him. This control can be complete or partial – all premises can be specified, or some can be left to his discretion. Influence, then, is exercised through control over the premises of decision. (p. 223)

One reservation must be made about this statement, namely that, as suggested above, the notion of total control in an organisational context is unrealistic. Otherwise this is a valuable statement of the place of discretion in a hierarchical relationship. Simon goes on to suggest that what occurs within an organisational system is that a series of areas of discretion are created in which individuals have freedom to interpret their tasks within general frameworks provided by their superiors. He quotes a military example relevant to the 'modern battlefield':

> how does the authority of the commander extend to the soldiers in the ranks? How does he limit and guide their behaviour? He does this by specifying the general mission and objective of each unit on the next level below, and by determining such elements of time and place as will assure a proper coordination among units. The colonel assigns to each battalion in his regiment its task; the major, to each company in his battalion; the captain, to each platoon in his company. Beyond this, the officer does not ordinarily go. The internal arrangements of Army Field Services Regulations specify that 'an order should not trespass upon the province of a subordinate. It should contain everything beyond the independent authority of the subordinate, but nothing more. (p. 224)

Thus Simon recognises the importance of discretion even in the most hierarchical and authoritarian organisation. Dunsire (1978a) has seized upon the interesting reference to the 'province' of the subordinate in this context. He portrays organisational activities as involving 'programmes within programmes'. In a hierarchy subordinate programmes are dependent upon superior ones but they may involve very different kinds of activities. He elaborates an example of a railway closure to show that while activities such as the rerouting of trains, the selling of railway property and, at the very end of the chain, the removal of ballast from abandoned tracks are necessarily dependent upon superior decisions about the closure, the way they are carried out is not predetermined by the decisions taken at the top of the hierarchy. He argues that decisions at the higher level are of high generality, those at the bottom of high specificity. This does not mean, however, 'that a worker at a high specificity level necessarily has a smaller amount of discretion (in any of its senses) than a worker at a high generality level' (p. 221). This approach helps us to make sense of the use of the concept of discretion in relation to professional hierarchies, such as education or medicine. The organisational or planning activities at the top of such hierarchies set contexts for, but do not necessarily predetermine, decision-making at field levels, where very different tasks are performed and very different problems have to be solved.

All the writers who have been concerned about the complexity of organisations have acknowledged that there are related problems of control, coordination and communication between these different provinces and linking these programmes within programmes (see Dunsire, 1978b). Attention has been drawn to the interdependence involved, and therefore to the fact that in a hierarchical situation superiors may be dependent upon subordinates. This is taken further by Gouldner (1954) who shows that the top-down presentation of hierarchical relationships with superiors promulgating rules to restrict the discretion of the subordinates may sometimes be turned on its head. He draws attention to the development of rules which limit the discretionary freedom of superiors in the interests of their subordinates. The classical discussion of this occurs in Gouldner's *Patterns of Industrial Bureaucracy* in which he shows the part that workers may play in securing rules to protect their interests. Overall his emphasis is upon the appeal to rules, by either party, in a situation in which a previously obtaining relationship breaks down: 'Efforts are made to install new bureaucratic rules, or enforce old ones, when people in a given social position (i.e. management or workers) perceive those in a reciprocal position (i.e. workers or management) as failing to perform their role obligations' (p. 232).

Gouldner is concerned about the many functions of rules in situations of social conflict. He draws our attention, therefore, to the extent to which rules and discretion must be studied in the context of relationships in which the parties on either side seek to influence the freedom of movement of the other.

It is important to move away from the older emphasis in organisation theory which saw the rules/discretion relationship from the perspective of superiors concerned to limit discretion, as far as acceptable, in the interests of rational management. Instead, attention should be directed towards the extent to which both rules and discretion are manipulated and bargained over within hierarchies. Fox (1974), coming to the examination of this issue from a concern with industrial relations, has interestingly related rule imposition to low-trust relationships. He picks up the top-down concern with detailed prescription and shows how this creates or reinforces low-trust relations:

> The role occupant perceives superordinates as behaving as if they believe he cannot be trusted, of his own volition, to deliver a work performance which fully accords with the goals they wish to see pursued or the values they wish to see observed. (p. 26)

A vicious circle may be expected to ensue. The subordinate, who perceives he or she is not trusted, feels little commitment to the effective performance of work. This particularly affects the way the remaining discretionary parts of the work are carried out. The superior's response is to try to tighten control, and further reduce the discretionary elements. The irreducible minimum of discretion left leaves the subordinate with some weapons against the superior; the prescribed task is performed in a rigid, unimaginative and slow way.

Hence, some rather similar phenomena may emerge by different routes. One may be defined as discretion, the other as rule breaking. The former emerges from a recognition of the power and status of implementers (this word is used deliberately instead of subordinates). This is the high-trust situation described by Fox, and applies to much professional discretion within public administration. The latter is seized by low-level staff regarded as subordinates rather than implementers who, in practice, superiors fail to control. One is legitimised, the other regarded – by the dominant elements in the hierarchy – as illegitimate. To the member of the public on the receiving end they may be indistinguishable.

Discretion and rule-breaking cannot be simply contrasted. Actors may be faced with situations in which rules conflict, in which rules are ambiguous, or in which so many rules are imposed that effective action becomes impossible. In these situations choices are made between rules, or about the spirit in which they are to be respected. Hence occasions arise in which subordinates can paralyse the organisation by working to rule, obsessively following rules which under normal operating conditions everyone tacitly recognises as only to be applied in unusual situations. The overconforming bureaucrats described by Merton (see the discussion in the last chapter) create problems because they apply the letter and not the spirit of the law. Michael Hill has elsewhere discussed the way in which social security officials may operate when they suspect fraud. They are able to operate rules and procedures in a heavy-handed way to ensure claims are fully investigated and claimants are made fully aware of the consequences of detection. If, however, they operate like this in more normal situations they will severely slow down the processing of claims and deter genuine applicants (Hill, 1969).

While Merton emphasises over-conformity within bureaucracy, one of his students, Blau (1955), stresses very different aspects of subordinate behaviour. He shows how front-line bureaucrats disregard rules to enable them to relate more effectively to their peers and to the members of the public with whom they deal. He also demonstrates how performance indicators used in the evaluation of work may distort bureaucratic behaviour. The latter is an issue very relevant to the consideration of the use of rational devices in the control of administrative behaviour, for example management by objectives and quantitative staff assessment. Individuals not only set out to cook their own performance statistics but choose to emphasise those activities which will maximise the score achieved by themselves and their agency. Quantitative rather than qualitative performance becomes emphasised. Nevertheless, it is through the use of output measures, whose collection and analysis is facilitated by computer technologies, that much retrospective control over discretion is sought. This is one of the ingredients in the reversion to Taylorism identified by Pollitt in the public sector (Pollitt, 1990).

The decision-making freedom enjoyed by professionals may be seen as a form of discretion, rooted in – as was suggested – the difficulties to be faced in effectively controlling the work of staff who have to apply their expertise in a wide range of situations. But professionalism is also seen as legitimising the exercise of discretion, so much so that many individuals resist the application of the latter term to this kind of decision-making.

This brief excursion into the treatment of discretion in organisation theory suggests, therefore, that there are a number of reasons why discretion is likely to be an important phenomenon in bureaucracies. At times confusion emerges between notions of

organisation flexibility in which discretion, particularly professional discretion, is accepted as an inherent feature, and notions of
conflict between formal requirements and informal behaviour (or
more explicitly between rule-making or enforcement and rule-
breaking). This confusion may be a reflection of the fact that in
reality these phenomena are confused. Organisations are not
simply fixed entities within which informal behaviour may develop. They are in a permanent state of change with both new rules
and new forms of rule-breaking occurring as conflicting interests
interact. The granting of discretion may be a conscious ingredient
of the formal design, at one extreme, or a reluctant concession to
organisational realities at the other. Conversely, new limitations
upon discretion may stem from attempts by superiors to assert
their hierarchical rights, or from aspirations of subordinates to
introduce greater certainty for their activities. In the last sense,
therefore, there is no simple equation between rule-making and
hierarchical control or between the preservation of discretion and
subordinate freedom.

The application of the concept of discretion to relationships
within bureaucracies has been extended in some writing about
organisations to relationships between bureaucracies (Page and
Goldsmith, 1987; Lidstrom, 1991). The first edition of this book
had a section analysing central–local relations in these terms.
There are, however, difficulties in doing this which arise because
the arguments about rules and discretion belong to situations in
which there is ambiguity or a dispute about autonomy. One party
claims a superordinate position, whilst the other asserts that it has
a measure of independence. This is something particularly likely to
occur in inter-organisational relationships. We prefer to explore
these issues in the terms discussed in Chapter 7, of environmental
constraints and power.

The treatment of discretion in the study of social policy

The dominant perspective in the study of social policy in Britain
has approached the issue of discretion by emphasising it as a problem, as something that gets in the way of social rights.

But more recently it has become recognised that it is important not merely to complain about the problem of discretion, but to analyse its nature. Michael Hill (1969; see also 1972) made one of the earliest attempts to do this in an analysis of the relationship between government policy, internal rules (codes and circulars) and individual officer discretion, based on his own experience as an executive officer in the National Assistance Board from 1960–3. It was stressed that the National Assistance Board was required by the government to maintain people at a low subsistence level and at that level people differ markedly from each other in their basic needs; this situation meant that the Board needed to grant its executive officers considerable discretion in the assessment of client need. These decisions were guided by the rules contained in the various codes and circulars which attempted to specify those cases that required a reduction in the rent allowance or the basic scale rates and those cases that required an addition for exceptional needs or circumstances. However, such decisions were not only inherently hard to define by such guidelines but the guidelines were in any case ambiguous protecting the public purse. The net result was that 'it was inevitable that individual attitudes would lead to wide variations in the treatment of the public' (p. 2) This situation was likely to produce inconsistency in decision-making, a process furthered by two other factors. First, the persistent claimant who questioned the level of benefit could be appeased by the executive officer because of the ambiguity in the rules. Second, supervisors could use the discretionary powers in the rules to overrule their executive officers in cases where complaints had been received from politicians and others.

The welfare rights 'movement' which developed in Britain in the 1960s focused on these discretionary powers. Campaigners argued that basic benefit scale rates were too low for most clients and that consequently they should be encouraged to apply for additional payments, either lump-sum emergency-needs payments or as weekly exceptional circumstances additions. Refusal of such requests should be followed by appeal from which it was hoped to encourage the government to amend the internal rules so that such additions became accepted as the norm.

These tactics have not received unqualified support. Titmuss (1971) attacks this 'pathology of legalism' (p. 124) and argues 'that the real need is to achieve the correct balance between legal rule and administrative discretion' (p. 113). In particular, he is concerned that such tactics pressurise the system towards an excessive itemisation of entitlement in terms of individual articles of clothing.

Bull (1980) has rebutted Titmuss's attack, arguing that there has never been a movement against discretion in Britain but rather a range of unrelated groups and advisers who have been concerned about various aspects of the relief system. He also argues that there has been great confusion from authors such as Titmuss on what poverty campaigners meant by discretion. There are various types of discretion and only some of these are a major cause for concern. Bull distinguishes between discretion exercised by an individual officer (officer discretion) and that exercised when an organisation provides interpretation of the law (agency discretion). He then argues that officer discretion can be divided into:

1. Interpreting rigid rules.
2. Taking decisions in areas where it is deemed inappropriate to have such rules.
3. Using their freedom to depart, in exceptional circumstances, from these rules.

Bull suggests that the first two of these are most appropriately referred to as 'judgement' and only the third as 'discretion'. Bull's concern is that:

> a failure to distinguish these different levels and types of activity can contribute to a confusion of two issues: the extent to which law makers should leave scope for agencies and/or officials to exercise discretion in exceptional circumstances, and whether and how checks can be imposed on the inevitable power of officers, at the point of delivery of a service, to make judgements about claims by their fellow human beings for that service. (p. 68)

Such a confusion has occurred, he contends, in the discussion of social security implementation in Britain.

This strand of writing on discretion has been described because it has had a great influence upon the present state of theoretical thinking about this concept. At first, reference to discretion in Britain was a loosely defined term of abuse used in pressure-group activity against the residual cash benefit system. Arguments over tactics led to attempts to clarify the nature of those practices, referred to as discretion, which needed to be challenged. This search for clarification led several writers to study the literature on legal techniques for controlling the growth of executive power.

The interest in discretion in social policy in Britain therefore has begun to widen out in new directions. Attention has extended beyond the narrow normative concern, towards an interest in how and why discretionary powers emerge. At the same time a need has been recognised to make connections between the use of the concept of discretion in this context and its use in administrative law (see particularly Adler and Asquith, 1981). The latter topic is taken up in the next section.

Discretion in administrative law

Traditionally British administrative law text books give attention to administrative discretion as a 'taken for granted' phenomenon within the political system. They point out that the concern of the courts has been with (a) whether or not discretionary powers which are exercised have been clearly delegated by statute; (b) whether the exercise of those powers is within the boundaries of natural justice (are they exercised reasonably and with regard to due process?); and (c) the principle that if a statute grants discretionary powers then the officials using them should not devise rules which in practice fetter that discretion.

The role of the courts in relation to administrative discretion is an interesting phenomenon in its own right. The textbooks provide a portrait of the law as trying to keep administrative discretion under control. The law is presented as the defender of the citizen against the arbitrary exercise of power. Wade (1967), for example, perceives administrative law as an attempt to ensure that the 'whole new empires of executive power' conform to the principles of liberty and fair dealing. This perspective leads Wade to argue that the key issue is ensuring that the law can control 'the exercise of the innumerable discretionary powers which Parliament has conferred on the various authorities' (p. 4). His emphasis is on ensuring that such authorities do not act *ultra vires* by exceeding their statutory power or following the wrong procedures. Authorities cannot escape such control by being offered statutes that give them unlimited power since 'in practice all statutory powers have statutory limits, and where the expressed limits are indefinite, the courts are all the more inclined to find that limits are implied. The notion of unlimited power has no place in the system' (p. 50).

In this way, the courts can protect the citizen from arbitrary power by blocking activities and individual decisions that no reasonable public body would have come to. At the same time, the courts can rarely do anything to protect the citizen from incompetent rather than illegal decision-making since 'it is of the essence of discretion that it involves the power to make mistakes' (p. 45), although the court may be tempted to interfere on the grounds that 'there is some implied statutory restriction which gives the offending act an aspect of irregularity' (p. 64).

An alternative perspective is to raise questions about the circumstances under which the courts do, and the circumstances under which they do not, intervene to curb discretionary power. This viewpoint sees the judges as just as much exercisers of discretion as the officials whose actions they may scrutinise. This is a perspective being given increasing recognition in Britain, a country which has hitherto treated its Law Lords with rather excessive reverence. In the United States the political role of the Supreme Court has been more clearly identifiable for some time, together with the recognition that, at least in the short run, the evolution of the law depends upon the dispositions of sometimes fairly eccentric elderly people (see Bickel, 1970; Scheingold, 1974, among others).

A British analysis of the politics of the judiciary concludes:

> Judges are concerned to preserve and to protect the existing order. This does not mean that no judges are capable of moving with the times, of adjusting to changed circumstances. But their function in our society is to do so belatedly. Law and order, the established distribution of power both public and private, the conventional and agreed view amongst those who exercise political and economic power, the fears and prejudices of the middle and upper classes, these are the forces which the judges are expected to uphold and do uphold. (Griffith, 1977, p. 214)

Thus, an approach to the study of discretion in administrative law which seeks to counteract the discretionary behaviour of officials with the rule of law merely comes up against a further set of discretionary actors, the judges. But another group of academic students of administrative law have directed their attention to what goes on within administration, seeing this as a law-creating process in its own right which may be checked by courts but where equally the problem identified by the other academics discussed so far in this chapter, of the relationship between rules and discretion, is deserving of attention. Thus in the United States, Davis (1969) argues that:

> we have to open our eyes to the reality that justice to individual parties is administered more outside courts than in them, and we have to penetrate the unpleasant areas of discretionary determinations by police and prosecutors and other administrators, where huge concentrations of injustice invite drastic reforms. (p. 215)

Citizens have a right to procedural justice when being dealt with by state officials and Davis argues that this can best be achieved through earlier and more elaborate administrative rule-making and in better structuring and checking of discretionary power (p. 219). Davis is thus concerned with the need for the organisation to control the discretionary power of the individual public officer and he feels this should be primarily attempted through rules which are open to public inspection.

In Britain, Jeffrey Jowell has played a major part in carrying forward the kind of concern about discretion shown by Davis in the United States. Jowell's definition of discretion is like Davis's. He defines it as 'the room for decisional manoeuvre possessed by a decision maker' (Jowell, 1973, p. 179), and argues that the key need is to ensure that decision-makers cannot make arbitrary decisions. However, Jowell lays a far greater stress than Davis upon the limitations of rules and tribunals in reducing administrative discretion. In particular he shows how many of the considerations with which decisions must be concerned are inherently difficult to specify in rules. Legislators are concerned to prevent *dangerous* driving, to ensure that food is *pure*, and that factories are *safe*. The provision of clear-cut rules to define what is safe or dangerous, pure or polluted, is often difficult. It may be that legislators need the help of the experts who are to enforce the law to provide some specific rules. In this sense discretion may be limited at a later date when experience of enforcement enables explicit rules to be devised. It may be that conflict over the legislation has led to the blurring of the issues, and that legislators have evaded their responsibility to make more explicit rules. But it may be the case that the translation of standards into explicit rules is so difficult as to be practically impossible.

Jeffrey Jowell provides a valuable discussion of the problems of fettering discretion where concern is with the enforcement of standards. He argues that standards may be rendered more precise by criteria, facts that are to be taken into account. However, he argues that 'the feature of standards that distinguishes them from rules is their flexibility and susceptibility to change over time' (p. 204). Very often, too, standards involve questions of individual taste or values. Jowell quotes with reference to this point an appeal-court case in which the judge was unable 'to enforce a covenant restricting the erection of "any building of unseemly description" ' (*ibid.*). Jowell similarly suggests that situations in which unlike things have to be compared, or which are unique and non-recurring, cannot be regulated by reference to a clearly specified standard. He argues,

> It is not difficult to appreciate that it would be asking too much of the English football selectors to decide after a public hearing and with due representation, to state reasons why the national interest would be served by having X rather than Y or Z to play centre forward in the coming match. (p. 206)

This issue about standards has been taken up in other legal writing on discretion. Dworkin (1977) distinguishes strong discretion where the decision-maker creates the standards from weak discretion where standards set by a prior authority have to be interpreted. This is rather like Bull's distinction between discretion and judgement. Galligan (1986) is similarly concerned to analyse discretion in this way, identifying that decision-makers have to apply standards to the interpretation of facts. These distinctions may seem very academic; they are, however, important in administrative law for distinctions between decisions which are within an official's powers and ones which are not, and therefore for determining whether intervention by an appeal body is appropriate.

Issues about conflicting facts arise where evidence is ambiguous, or where individuals present different versions of the same events. One of the surprising aspects of some of the less sophisticated attacks on discretionary administration by lawyers is that, in practising their own profession, while they talk of facts and law and of proof and disproof, they very often require judges and juries to decide between conflicting evidence. The proper distinction to make is not between the precision of judicial decision-making and the imprecision of much administration, but between the extent to which procedural safeguards for the individual, or due process, exist in each situation. Here again, Jowell's work is helpful since he distinguishes between two approaches to the control of discretion: 'legalisation', the 'process of subjecting official decisions to pre-determined rules' and thus, of course, the elimination of discretion; and 'judicialisation', involving 'submitting official decision to adjudicative procedures' (1973).

Jowell does not accept a simple dichotomy between rules and discretion as suggested by Davis but rather argues that discretion 'is a matter of degree, and ranges along a continuum between high and low' ((1973) p. 179). At first glance, rules may appear to abolish such discretion 'but since rules are purposively devised . . . and because language is largely uncertain in its application to situations that cannot be foreseen, the applier of a rule will frequently be possessed of some degree of discretion to interpret its scope' ((1973) p. 201). This last comment suggests that any study of discretionary decision-making requires a consideration of social processes internal to the organisation and a study of the attitudes and beliefs of those who have to interpret the rules.

Jowell's work also stresses the need to see discretion in a political context. He has examined the role of bargaining, logically an important form of discretionary behaviour, in planning policy implementation (Jowell, 1977). British local authorities are often able to bargain with developers to try to secure planning gains, such as infrastructure improvements, for the community. While the law appears to suggest that the authorities have merely a quasi-judicial function, in practice they may seek to pursue wider political goals. Jowell recognises that community gains may be being achieved at the expense of over-powerful citizens but is fearful, as a lawyer concerned about rights, about the private governmental processes involved. He identifies the phenomena with which his study was concerned as paralleled by other bargaining behaviour by governments, in attempting to impose informal pay norms or secure beneficial trading agreements (Jowell, unpublished paper), which other writers identify as manifestations of the 'corporate state' (Winkler, 1976).

Hence the work of Davis and of Jowell is starting to initiate an approach to the examination of the role of law in public policy implementation in which discretion is recognised as a fundamentally important phenomenon, and not as an undesirable manifestation of the collectivist state which ought to be eliminated, as earlier legalistic analyses such as those by Dicey (1905) and Hewart

(1929) had suggested. At the same time they keep alive the older concern about the threat posed by discretion to the rule of law. Not surprisingly there are significant cultural differences between societies in the extent to which the issues about discretion are regarded as susceptible to judicial control, with a strong emphasis on this theme coming from the United States.

Discretion in law enforcement

The traditional defenders of the rule of law in public administration do not seem to have had the same concern about its place in the prevention of crime. It is a modern group of criminologists and radical students of law who have drawn attention to the all-pervasive presence of discretion in the criminal law.

The areas in which discretion occurs in criminal law enforcement are extensive. They can be listed from the beginning to the end of the process as follows:

- Police decisions about the deployment of manpower.
- Police decisions on the extent to which reported breaches of the law should be investigated.
- Police and/or Crown Prosecution Service's decisions on whether to prosecute.
- Decisions on bail.
- Plea bargaining, in which lawyers try to negotiate lower sentences in return for pleas of guilty.
- Assessment of evidence by judges, magistrates and juries.
- Sentencing decisions.
- Parole decisions.

Some cannot be denied, but are vested in an aura of rationality which recent research studies have questioned (Bottomley, 1973). This applies, for example, to sentencing. Others are relatively unacknowledged, at least in Britain, and efforts to research them have met with resistance. This is particularly the case with plea bargaining (Baldwin and McConville, 1977).

The phenomenon of police discretion has been relatively thoroughly studied (see *inter alia* Cain, 1973; Brown, 1981; Lambert, 1967; Wilson, 1970), and is worth further comment because of its parallels with discretion exercised by administrative officials. The fundamental reason for police discretion is that were policemen to arrest all who break the law a gigantic police force would be necessary, the courts would be hopelessly over-strained and the prisons filled many times over. The police need, therefore, to choose where they operate, where they concentrate their attention, and where efficiency – and to some extent justice – is enhanced by turning a blind eye. Choice is particularly necessary in respect of what are often called crimes without victims – drug and alcohol offences, gambling, and of course traffic offences not involving accidents – where the police cannot depend upon reports of crimes and yet still require public cooperation in law enforcement.

Tax officials, public-health inspectors, and factory inspectors, as law-enforcement agents, have to operate in a similar way. Paulus (1974) has shown how the enforcement of the laws against the adulteration of food developed from a battle between public-health authorities and the powerful food manufacturers and grocers in which convictions were hard to obtain, to a more voluntaristic but effective system in which the inspectors use extensive discretion to maintain standards with a minimal use of the prosecution weapon. The case for discretion in these examples rests not so much upon an argument that it is impractical to regulate the behaviour of law-enforcement officials, as upon a view that the ends of the system would not be effectively achieved by undue rigidity.

Hawkins (1984) and Richardson (in Downing and Hanf, 1983) have shown how law enforcement in an area like pollution often entails processes of negotiation in which considerations about the overall pattern of behaviour are taken into account. Such procedures have fuelled an argument between those who see this as a necessary feature of effective law enforcement and those who see it as regulator cooptation by powerful interests (see discussion of British air pollution control policy in Ashby and Anderson, 1981, ch. 11; and in Hill's essay in Downing and Hanf, 1983).

Davis (1969), in *Discretionary Justice*, rightly points out that some of the problems of differential enforcement, particularly in the United States, arise from the over-eagerness of legislators to try to regulate behaviour. The classic example of this was Prohibition. Similarly many States have on their statute books laws which proscribe all forms of gambling from the large-scale rackets to church-hall bingo. Naturally, police attention is focused upon the major violations of such laws and the minor cases are often ignored. Davis rightly argues that many forms of discretion can therefore be confined if the laws are more realistic.

The particularly important contribution of studies of law enforcement to our understanding of discretion has been their emphasis upon the way in which bias operates. From an initial concern simply to demonstrate that social class, gender and race affect discretionary decision-making, studies have gone on to explicate the ways in which these effects occur. They do not arise merely from prejudice but also from situational characteristics of the enforcement official's task. Such phenomena as the relationship between the official and the community being 'policed', the way the official's day-to-day work is organised, the particular sources of stresses and conflicts in the task and the way the official is encouraged to define law-enforcement problems have been shown, particularly by the police discretion studies, to influence the pattern of formal enforcement action.

The role of normative considerations in the study of discretion

In each of the sections of this discussion some references have been made to normative concerns. It is appropriate to examine these a little more closely.

There is an overriding difference of perspective between those who come to the study of discretion because of a concern about its place in some area of public policy, and those who primarily want to use it as a concept for the analysis of official behaviour. There is also a division between those who see law as a product of the social system and discretion as a manifestation of this relationship, but are not particularly interested in its detailed character in specific policy areas, and those who are much more interested in the latter than the former. Differences of point of view between those who, to put it crudely, see discretion as a 'good' thing and those who see it as a 'bad' thing are likely to derive as much from the concrete issues in which people are interested as from any more fundamental stance on discretion.

As Adler and Asquith (1980) put it:

> Whether or not discretion is a 'bad thing' is in part a question of fact and in part a value judgement. It is a question of fact in as much as it

depends on the ways in which discretion is exercised and on the outcome of the discretionary decision making – it is a value judgement in as much as these outcomes are regarded positively or negatively.

Furthermore, one person's discretion is likely to be another person's constraint.

What then are the particular normative preoccupations of students of discretion? In the study of organisations it has been the problem of top-down control, but later writers such as Fox have replaced this by a concern about the autonomy of subordinates in low-trust situations. In social policy the welfare-rights movement has been concerned about the tyranny of the low-level official. Against this has been counterposed arguments against the rigidity of rules, and in favour of the benign impact of some social policy practitioners (Titmuss, 1971). In administrative law the absence of public accountability has been given attention, but political flexibility has been suggested as preferable to legal rigidity. In criminal law the major concern has been with bias, but again it has been questioned whether police without a capacity to turn a blind eye and magistrates required to use fixed tariffs would be desirable even if they were a practical possibility.

Hence value questions are continually mixed up with attempts to analyse discretion. But perhaps the most important way in which such issues confuse the study of discretion is that they are essentially bound up with what may be called ameliorative concerns. The arguments cited in the last paragraph are about the balance of power within the existing political and administrative system. As such they relate to the micro-sociology rather than the macro-sociology of that system. The arguments all regard discretion *per se* as mattering, not as taking forms which are merely epiphenomenal manifestations of much broader social, economic and political forces.

The alternative view is to regard the issues discussed as of interest, not as *problems* to be solved within the system, but as products of broader social forces (see, for example, Offe, 1984). A literature which has been so problem-focused has perhaps played down these wider issues. Phenomena which are attributable to social forces have sometimes been dismissed as products of incomplete anticipation by legislators, or difficulties in laying down rules, rather than satisfactorily explained.

In his discussion of administrative discretion, Davis stresses that it is unrealistic to expect legislative bodies to settle all policy questions. Primarily, this is a matter of being unable to identify specific cases to which a general principle will be applied. Here, as Davis argues, it may be possible to pass further legislation at a later date, to close the gaps initially filled by discretionary powers. It seems realistic to expect therefore that new policy problems will be tackled by loosely framed laws, and that those laws will then evolve from the general to the specific.

Yet such evolution does not always take place, and there seem to be examples where legislators could easily make their requirements much more specific. Davis suggests a political explanation for their failure to do this:

> Even questions suitable for legislative determination are often delegated for some such reason as failure of legislators to agree, preference of legislators to compromise disagreements by tossing the problem to administrators, draftsmanship which is intentionally or unintentionally vague or contradictory, or some combination of such factors. (1969, pp. 38–9)

Studies of legislation, to deal with such problems as pollution, unsafe factories and impure food, suggest that such fudging of the issues particularly occurs when powerful economic interests are involved (see Knoepfel and Weidner, 1982; Gunningham, 1974).

Davis's argument here is very similar to one advanced by one of the authors in an earlier article on the National Assistance Board, explaining many of the discretionary powers found there in terms of unresolved value-issues:

> in many ways the framers of the National Assistance Act failed to follow Simon's advice to politicians to deal with the main value problems at the policy making stage. The traditional attitude to the poor had been to regard them, in the absence of unambiguous evidence to the contrary, as undeserving individuals on whom public-money should be spent most sparingly. The National Assistance Act seemed to turn its back on the doctrine, yet it failed to jettison the view entirely and it failed to provide financial resources sufficient to enable the Board to avoid having to distinguish between the claims made by applicants, particularly as regards their more unusual needs. Consequently the onus of distinguishing between the 'deserving' and the 'undeserving' poor tended to fall upon the officer dealing with the applicant in the field, just as it had fallen upon the relieving officer in the past. While the politicians and administrators

who framed the Act would not have wished to have espoused the notion of the 'undeserving poor' they felt unwilling to risk the public criticism that would have resulted from an approach to poverty that involved ignoring the potential waste on the 'work-shy' and the fraudulent applicant in order adequately to meet the needs of the majority of applicants. Extravagance in meeting the needs of the poor produces public criticism of the government more readily than any other form of extravagance. (Hill, 1969, pp. 85-6)

This theme has been effectively developed in a later analysis of discretion in social security by Prosser (1981). Where such political ambivalence exists it may be particularly unrealistic to call for legislation to eliminate discretion. But it is precisely in circumstances like these that discretion will arouse controversy. The unresolved value-issues will trouble those who implement policy, and those whose welfare is affected by its implementation, just as much as it troubled the politicians.

This discussion of normative considerations in the study of discretion contains echoes of the distinction between analysis of and analysis for policy outlined in our introductory chapter, and of the discussion of decision theory and of implementation theory. Discretion can be analysed at two levels, one of which is relatively value-free. At this level the study of discretion is concerned to try to identify the factors which influence the way in which an amalgam of rules and discretion has been developed and is implemented, bearing in mind both specific characteristics of the issues at stake and wider social, political and economic forces. The other level involves a concern with who gains what out of a particular configuration of rules and discretion, and what concrete changes might be made to alter that. At that level ameliorative concerns about the interests of gainers and losers are inevitably brought into play.

Conclusion

In examining discretion several issues need to be given attention. First, policy must be seen in a wider social and political context, which is likely to affect the way discretion manifests itself and the attempts that are made to control it. We should note Prosser's (1981) dissatisfaction 'with the "black box" model of discretion . . . in which the determined legislative purpose is "shone into" an administrative agency, but then "refracted" by the various influences affecting the exercise of discretion' (p. 149). Discretion may arise from ambiguity, sometimes deliberate, in public policy.

Second, while there are political sources of discretion we have not disregarded the extent to which this phenomenon arises as a consequence of inherent limits to control. Hence attention has been given to the issue of standards, raised by Jowell, and to some of the supervision problems which must face those who seek to control discretion. As Prottas (1978) argues, echoing the general point made in many references to discretion within organisations:

> A general rule in the analysis of power is that an actor with low 'compliance observability' is relatively autonomous. If it is difficult or costly to determine how an actor behaves and the actor knows this, then he is under less compulsion to comply. The compliance observability of street-level bureaucrat slotting is typically low. (p. 298)

Third, as this last observation reminds us, there is a need to analyze discretion as a facet of organisational life, in a complex relationship to rule-breaking. It is important to relate discretion to issues about organisational complexity, reward systems, motivation and morale.

Fourth, we should not disregard the extent to which the concern about discretion is a normative one. Under what circumstances may discretion be said to be a problem, and for whom? To what extent does the balance established between discretion and rules distribute differential advantages and disadvantages to the parties involved, and particularly to the members of the public affected by the policy?

Finally, in noting that discretion has been regarded as a problem, we should recognise that a variety of strategies of organisation control have developed to try to deal with it. The traditional approach has been to try to control it through tighter rules and procedures (as discussed in Chapter 7). More recently, identification of the ubiquitous nature of the phenomenon has led rather to attempts to structure it, through budgetary controls and through systems which have been described as 'loose-tight' (Elcock, 1991, p. 41) to imply a combination of rigid procedures with the deliberate delegation of areas of discretion. The 1986 changes to the British system of means-tested social security benefits offers a good example of this (Hill, 1990, Ch. 7). A more radical variant on this theme is offered (see also Chapter 7) by models which aim to create market or quasi-market systems leaving the problems of discretion to be tacked by consumer control through the use of the capacity to 'exit' (Hirschman, 1970). This approach is certainly not applicable to policy areas like social security and regulation, the extent of their applicability to consumer services like health, social care and education remains an area of controversy (see Ham, Robinson and Benzeval, 1990; Glennerster, Power and Travers, 1991).

CHAPTER 10

CONCLUSION: LINKING LEVELS OF ANALYSIS

We began this book by arguing that the term policy analysis encompasses a wide range of activities all concerned in one way or another with examining the causes and consequences of government action. In discussing the various attempts to define and describe policy analysis, we drew particular attention to Wildavsky's view (1979) that policy analysis takes as its subject matter the problems facing policy-makers and aims to ameliorate those problems through a process of creativity, imagination and craftsmanship. At the same time we argued that policy analysis should give due consideration to the social, political and economic contexts within which problems are tackled. On this basis we suggested that the student of the policy process should stand back from the world of everyday politics in order to ask some of the bigger questions about the role of the state in contemporary society and the distribution of power between social groups. We indicated that it was necessary to focus on different levels of analysis: to look at decision-making within organisations, policy formulation and the relationship between state and society. We pointed out that it is the interaction between these three which is particularly significant and problematic.

In subsequent chapters we sought to demonstrate the utility of this kind of approach to policy analysis. Chapter 2 reviewed different theories of the state and questioned the validity of the pluralist assumptions which inform much policy analysis work. Chapter 3 concentrated on the role of bureaucracies and assessed the ability of macro theories to explain adequately the part played by bureaucracies in advanced societies. Chapter 4 examined the literature on power and decision-making, again exposing the weaknesses of pluralist analyses of the power structure and favouring the more radical approach set out by writers such as Bachrach and Baratz (1970) and Lukes (1974). Chapter 5 focused on the relationship between rationality and decision-making, tracing the debate between comprehensively rational and incremental models of decision-making, and examining the relationship between the incrementalist thesis and pluralist theories of power. Chapter 6 analysed approaches to the study of public policy implementation, questioning the value of the top-down model of implementation which lies behind many implementation studies, drawing attention to the normative assumptions often to be found in the model, and noting that policy is frequently made during what is conventionally described as the implementation stage of the policy process. Chapter 7 concentrated on the relevance of organisation theory to the study of public policy, making connections between issues about internal organisational power and the external context. Chapter 8 examined the role of bureaucrats in the implementation process, paying particular attention to theories concerned with bureaucratic personalities, professionals and street-level bureaucrats. Chapter 9 concentrated on the analysis of discretion in the implementation process, noting the various ways in which discretion has been treated in different policy contexts.

In this final chapter we want to bring the various strands of our argument together and analyse in a more focused way how the agenda identified at the beginning of the book, that of linking different levels of analysis, may be taken forward. The concept of levels is, in the context of the concerns of this book open to interpretation in terms of different parts of the system and in terms of the policy-making/implementation distinction (which we have portrayed as difficult and frequently overemphasised). These distinctions are dwarfed in analytical importance by the issue of the relationship between action and the structure in which it occurs, or is constrained, touched on briefly at the end of Chapter 4, which is relevant for the whole of the policy process. It is this which is our concern here.

We propose to draw on a body of literature referred to in Chapter 7 as radical organisation theory. The central concern of much of this literature – represented by writers such as Benson, Clegg,

Dunkerley, Salaman, and Burrell and Morgan – is to suggest ways in which organisations are shaped and influenced by the societies in which they operate. Since our emphasis is upon the need to ensure that the analysis of the state is based upon an understanding of its relationship to society, and state activity in modern society is essentially organisational activity, the insights of these writers clearly contribute to the exploration of our subject. This chapter will therefore review the perspective adopted by the radical organisation theorists and will outline a framework of analysis which may serve as a guide to future research.

Benson: the rules of structure formation

Benson is one of the theorists of organisations who has stressed the importance of linking different levels of analysis (Benson, 1983). In his work on inter-organisational relationships, Benson has criticised writers who concentrate on the problems of securing the coordination of public services and neglect the broader influences which affect coordination. Benson maintains that inter-organisational analysis is at one level concerned with examining the dependency of organisations on each other for resources such as money and authority, but at another level it must focus on the interests built into the structure of a particular policy sector. Benson defines a policy sector as 'a cluster or complex of organisations connected to each other by resource dependencies and distinguished from other clusters or complexes by breaks in the structure of resource dependencies' (1983, p. 3). Defined in this way, the concept of policy sectors is similar to Richardson and Jordan's idea of policy communities discussed in Chapter 2. As well as examining the interests built into a policy sector, Benson suggests that it is necessary to examine the system of rules which govern relationships between these interests. In essence, then, there is a need to explicate the interaction between the surface level and the 'deep structure which determines within limits the range of variation of the surface levels' (1983, p. 5). As Benson notes, the concept of a deep structure parallels the idea of the mobilisation of bias as set out by Bachrach and Baratz in their discussion of nondecision-making (see Chapter 4).

Thus, according to Benson, a complete analysis of inter-organisational relationships needs to explore three levels in the structure of policy sectors (1983, p. 6): first, there is the administrative structure, that is, the surface level of linkages and networks between agencies held together by resource dependencies. Second, there is the interest structure, that is, the set of groups whose interests are built into the sector either positively or negatively. These groups comprise demand groups, support groups, administrative groups, provider groups and coordinating groups. The interest structure is important in that it provides the context for the administrative structure which cannot be adequately understood except in terms of the underlying power relations manifested within the interest structure. In turn, the interest structure has to be located within the third level, that is, *the rules of structure formation*. In advanced societies, these rules are principally those which relate to the maintenance of capital accumulation. Drawing on the work of neo-Marxists such as Offe, Benson points to the role of state agencies in advanced capitalist societies in assisting the process of capital accumulation and performing the function of legitimation. As we noted in Chapter 4, Offe (1974) argues that within capitalist societies various exclusion rules operate to select some issues for attention and not others. The operation of these rules, which are built into the institutions and structures of capitalism, help to maintain political stability by filtering out demands which threaten the basis of capitalist societies. Exclusion or selection rules are both negative and positive. Negative rules function at a general level to exclude challenges, for example to the right to private property, which are inimical to the intrinsic features of the capitalist state. They also operate within specific policy sectors, and are manifested both in nondecision-making procedures which keep certain issues off the agenda for discussion and in ideological mechanisms which define issues and problems in a particular way. The same point is made in a slightly different way by Lindblom (1977, 1979) who notes the power of business corporations to exercise agenda control through the heavy indoctrination of opinion. The overall impact of negative selection rules and indoctrination is to place limits or boundaries on what is possible.

Positive selection rules refer to those rules that require action consistent with the maintenance and development of the dominant forms of economic organisation. Examples would be rules which lead the state to intervene through specific policies to further the process of accumulation, such as providing support to industry and infrastructure for industrial development. One point to note is that the rules of structure formation are not always consistent, as, for example, in the conflicts which may emerge between the requirements of accumulation and the demands of legitimation. We discuss this further below.

Benson summarises his argument in the following terms:

> For each policy sector, then, it would be necessary to explore the impact of deep rules of structure formation. These would not determine the structure of the sector in every detail. It is reasonable to assume some measure of autonomy for the other levels – administrative organisation and structural interests. In broad terms, however, the events at those levels are to be explained at the level of rules of structure formation. The rules limit and enable action at other levels. Social science accounts which do not consider these deeper rules are to varying degrees incomplete. (1983, p. 31)

One of the issues this raises is: what precisely is the relationship between levels? While the main thrust of Benson's argument is that action at the surface level cannot be understood without reference to the interest structure and the rules of structure formation, he is careful not to suggest that the relationship between levels is simply deterministic. Indeed, in discussing how changes might occur within sectors, he notes the possibility that the administrative structure might become independent of the structural underpinnings and that bureaucracies might develop a life and logic of their own. There are echoes here of Weberian analyses of bureaucracies and the growth of corporatism, with the suggestion that state agencies in capitalist societies may be able to shake themselves free of class control and act in their own interests. What is not clear from Benson's analysis is how far and in what circumstances bureaucratic action is determined by deep structures or is independent of these structures.

Clegg and Dunkerley: the structure of domination

A parallel but slightly different approach to these issues can be found in the work of Clegg (1975). Like Benson, Clegg maintains that studies which focus on the surface level of power, such as pluralist analyses of community power, are incomplete. In their place, he proposes that students of power should seek to identify

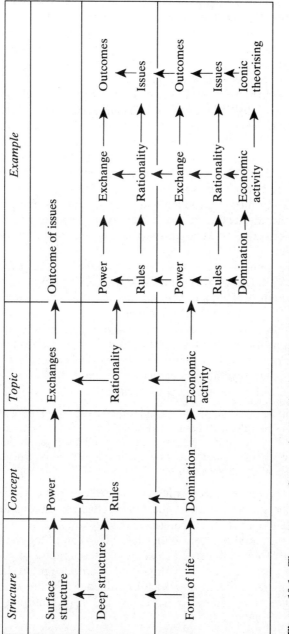

Figure 10.1 The structure of power in organisations (Source: Clegg, 1975)

the structure of domination within which power is exercised, and should analyse the rules which link power and domination. It is these three concepts – power, rule and domination – which in Clegg's work hold the key to understanding relationships within organisations. Clegg represents the structure of power within organisations in the form shown in Figure 10.1.

These points are illustrated by Clegg in a study of relationships between workers and managers on a construction site. Underlying these relationships is the capitalist mode of production within which the profitability of productive organisations is of paramount importance. The capitalist mode of production is an 'iconic' (Clegg, 1975, p. 77) system of domination because it constitutes the form of life of capitalist societies. It is this form of life which gives rationality to the construction company and guides its operation. Hence, the production of profit acts as the organisational ideal, and actions by workers and managers are oriented towards profitability.

These arguments are reiterated and developed by Clegg and Dunkerley (1980). Drawing on the work of writers who have emphasised the importance of nondecision-making and political routines (see Chapter 4), Clegg and Dunkerley maintain that the power of capital does not have to be exercised to be present because it is enshrined in the routines of capitalist societies. These routines or rules result from 'an economically conditioned structure of domination' (1980, p. 456). Taken together, the structure of domination and the rules contained within the structure are such that

> The individual is essentially a social being, who, as a bearer of social relations, is ruled and dominated in the last instance by economic power. This economic power is embedded and displayed within the framework of a 'structure of domination' which is articulated through different types of 'rule'. (1980, p. 456)

Thus, studies of power which examine exchanges between individuals or groups without questioning the structure and rules which set the terms of exchange are inadequate.

To a considerable extent both Clegg (1975) and Clegg and Dunkerley (1980) are concerned to analyse the operation of power in private enterprises which are organised to produce profit. In so far as other kinds of organisations are examined, a less direct relationship between economic imperatives and organisational action seems to be suggested:

In spheres other than those concerned with the institutional area of the economy the level of domination is only contingently determined by the mode of production. This allows subjects considerably more choice, theoretically, at the surface level of social practice and action. Nonetheless, this freedom, like all freedom, is conditioned, and one can hypothesise rules which condition the selection of strategies of action. (1980, p. 503)

This seems to indicate that organisations functioning outside economic policy sectors may be able to escape the constraints imposed by the demands of profitability.

What does this imply for state agencies? In broad terms Clegg and Dunkerley argue that the state in capitalist society is subject to the same structure of domination as private corporations. Thus, state-owned enterprises or capitalist state activities (CSA) such as nationalised industries and coal mines are driven by considerations of profit and accumulation in the same way as private enterprises operating in these fields. At a more general level Clegg and Dunkerley maintain that:

The state cannot afford to neglect the profitable accumulation of certain key organisations: to do so is to risk drying up the source of its own power, the surplus production capacity of the economic system, the taxes drawn from this surplus and the labour that produces it. (p. 550)

As well as promoting accumulation, the state must guarantee legitimation through both repressive and ideological mechanisms. It is in relation to legitimation that Clegg and Dunkerley suggest that state agencies may be relatively free of the structure of domination which guides other institutions. In other words, non-capitalist state activities (non-CSA), for example housing, education and health, do not operate in the same mode of rationality as capitalist state activities and private enterprises organised for profit. The economic imperatives which in other organisations place a premium on efficiency and cost-cutting as a way of maximising profit are less evident in agencies concerned with non-capitalist state activities. In these agencies other rules have greater prominence, and may push the agencies to expand their resources in order to improve the quality of the services they provide to consumers. The resulting agency autonomy is, however, incomplete because the underlying structure of domination limits the extent to which legitimation activities can increase at the expense of accumulation. In these circumstances there may develop a crisis if the state spending required to maintain legitimation places pressure on the accumulation process. In Benson's terms, this represents a contradiction in the rules of structure formation. The consequence for the capitalist state is either a legitimation crisis (see also Habermas, 1976; Offe, 1975) as social expenses are cut back, or a fiscal crisis (O'Connor, 1973) as tax revenues place an increasing burden on capital. It is not appropriate to examine this crisis theory here, it is one on which a great deal has been written (see Mishra, 1984), and there is considerable argument about whether it is real or perceived (Hill and Bramley, 1986). In this context it is sufficient that the idea of crisis becomes a basis for action. Clegg and Dunkerley conclude:

> Rather than acting as purposefully rational organisations, state organisations, particularly in the non-CSA sector, are characterised by a reactive avoidance of responsible rational planning in the face of competing and contradictory pressure and conflicts. In the face of crisis, the contradictory role of both successfully maintaining accumulation and simultaneously retaining legitimacy, without producing a crisis of practical reason, appears almost impossible. (1980, p. 555)

Salaman: class and the corporation

A number of the themes discussed by Clegg and Dunkerley are also considered by Salaman (1981) who argues for a Marxist approach to the study of organisations to be combined with elements from Weberian theory. In Salaman's view, this means reaffirming the continued importance of capitalism as an economic system and of class relations under capitalism, while acknowledging the growth of the middle classes, the key place occupied by bureaucracies and the increasingly interventionist role of the state. Applied to the study of business organisations, Salaman's perspective draws attention to the significant influence which the profit motive exercises over the structure of organisations and decision-making. Specifically, the fact that organisations have to make a profit to survive has an important bearing on moves to improve efficiency and make use of technological advances. Yet the relationship between changes in the capitalist economy and organisational responses to these changes is by no means straightforward. As Salaman notes, 'To argue for the continuing relationship between capitalism as a form of economic system based on class conflict and class interest and organisation structure and design of work is not to assert that this relationship will be automatically achieved' (p. 249).

In Benson's terms, what this means is that the administrative structure may be influenced by the rules of structure formation (in Clegg's terms the structure of domination) but it will not be determined by these rules. Much depends on how individuals and groups in the administrative structure and the interest structure perceive the pressures emanating from the rules. These comments apply to state agencies as well as business corporations. Although, as Salaman notes, the major role of the state under capitalism is to support the economy, it is just as plausible to argue that public officials and politicians mediate the pressures to promote accumulation as it is to point to the role of managers and experts in doing so.

There is, here, a somewhat different emphasis to that found in Clegg and Dunkerley's analysis. As we noted above, the latter writers argue, in terms similar to Poulantzas (see Chapter 2), that individuals are 'bearers' of social relations, and therefore have little or no autonomy. In contrast, Salaman, while pointing to the influence of economic factors on individual and organisational action, maintains that individuals do have some scope for interpreting these influences. Benson similarly avoids expressing the relationship between levels of analysis in deterministic terms, and points to the possibility of state agencies liberating themselves from the demands of accumulation. The difference between Clegg and Dunkerley on the one hand, and Salaman and Benson on the other, is in part explained by their dependence on Marxist and Weberian approaches respectively. The influence of these approaches, and in particular their attack on functionalist theories of organisation represented by writers such as Taylor, Fayol and Mayo (see Chapter 7), has been explored by Burrell and Morgan (1979), and we can take the argument a stage further by examining Burrell and Morgan's thesis that a radical organisation theory has developed out of the critique of functionalism.

Burrell and Morgan: the contribution of radical organisation theory

Burrell and Morgan point out that the functionalist approach has been attacked by radical structuralists who have found the approach wanting for, among other reasons, ignoring class analysis, omitting to consider the role of the state and being unaware of the importance of macro-societal factors. The unifying themes which join together radical structuralist writers are:

1 Totality – a concern to look at the whole, at organisations in context.
2. Structure – an emphasis on organisations as structures within wider structures.
3. Contradiction – organisations are the stage where conflicts and cleavages are visible.
4. Crisis – macro-social change results from crises which develop out of contradictions (pp. 358–9).

Burrell and Morgan note that radical organisation theory embraces a diverse range of writers and in many ways is only embryonic. Nevertheless, two broad approaches within the theory may be discerned: the radical Weberian and the Marxian structuralist.

The distinctive feature of the radical Weberian approach is that it examines the role of bureaucracy, the increased role of the state, and is linked to ideas about corporatism. It offers 'a mode of analysis which, in focusing upon the totality of contemporary social formations, allows one to transcend the insights which emerge from an exclusive preoccupation with the middle range level of analysis characteristic of functionalist organisation theory' (p. 388). The distinctive feature of Marxian structuralist approaches is their focus on the economic structure of society and their use of the method of political economy to analyse organisations. Burrell and Morgan argue that the strength of Marxian structuralist approaches in highlighting the importance of economic relationships points up a weakness in radical Weberian approaches which tend to assert the primacy of political relationships. Although the two approaches are 'relatively distinct' (p. 385), Burrell and Morgan suggest that a synthesis might be possible.

It should be possible to incorporate analysis of the economic structure within a radical Weberian approach. In essence this is what a number of the writers whose work was discussed earlier in the chapter have attempted to do. As Burrell and Morgan note, the radical Weberian approach does not ignore the ideas of Marx.

Rather, it 'explores that intellectual terrain in which the interests of Marx and Weber may be thought to coincide' (p. 371).

As we argued in Chapter 2, one of the strengths of Marxist theory is its analysis of the economic context of political activity. By reminding us that the state in Western industrialised societies functions in a capitalist economy in which the goal of capital accumulation is fundamental, Marxists avoid the trap of analysing political behaviour in isolation from factors which have a significant influence on that behaviour. However, a major difficulty with Marxist approaches is their treatment of the relationship between economic power and political power. We noted in Chapter 2 the inadequacy of the concept of relative autonomy in handling this relationship, and we would want to reject the view that political action is structurally determined in the way suggested by much recent Marxist theory. Yet a rejection of structural determinism does not mean focusing solely on the role of political actors in seeking to explain public policy. Rather, as Saunders (1981a) maintains, it is necessary to recognise that actors, in mediating structural influences, behave in ways that are meaningful to themselves. This approach, which acknowledges the importance of Weber's emphasis on the need to understand human action in terms of the perspective of the actor, is very different from arguing that individuals are bearers of social relations.

The kind of analysis favoured here owes two further debts to Weber. First, it attaches significance to the intermediate social groupings who do not fit neatly into either of the social classes which have a central place in Marxist analyses. Weber rejected the Marxist analysis of class in terms of ownership or non-ownership of property in favour of a classificatory system based on a market situation model in which the complexity of the market structure within society is seen as producing a highly differentiated stratification system. The complexity of social divisions within contemporary capitalist societies is testimony to the value of Weber's approach. As we argued in earlier chapters, any theory of policy formulation must take account of the role played by professionals, bureaucrats and other members of the salaried middle class. Not least, the interest of these groupings in the maintenance and growth of the large-scale bureaucracies which have accompanied the development of the welfare state may conflict with the interests of the bourgeoisie in promoting accumulation. This conflict is one of the factors which helps to explain how it is that state agencies may enjoy some autonomy. It is for this reason that we reject explanations expressed in terms of structural determinism.

Our second debt to Weber is connected with the first, and concerns the growing power of bureaucracies. As we have argued throughout the book, state agencies and the officials who work in them are powerful in their own right and are not simply a means of perpetuating the dominance of a particular class. In relation to both issues of production and issues of consumption, these agencies play a key role, typically negotiating production policies with business and trade union elites in a corporatist system, and working out consumption policies with a variety of pressure groups in a system of biased pluralism. In these relationships, state agencies derive power from their command of legal, financial and organisational resources, and are not merely instruments of capital.

In drawing on the ideas of both Marx and Weber, then, our broad stance is similar to that set out by Salaman and discussed earlier in the chapter. There are also parallels between our approach and the work of Alford (1972 and 1975a) and Dunleavy (1981b). In his analysis of health-care planning, Alford maintains that there is a need to look beyond the surface level of pressure-group politics in order to identify the underlying structural interests who gain or lose from the form of organisation of health services. There are three sets of structural interests: dominant, challenging and repressed. This is a formulation we prefer to Benson's analysis of the interest structure in terms of demand groups, support groups, administrative groups, provider groups and coordinating groups. Alford notes that the medical profession is dominant in health services, and the profession's interests are served by the way in which these services are organised. One of the reasons why the medical profession is the dominant structural interest is that the medical model of health and illness is pre-eminent. The medical model, as the dominant value-system in the health field, defines illness as a phenomenon which is suitable for intervention by doctors, thereby legitimising the profession's claim to control. Alford suggests that structural interests are created and sustained by the 'institutional and class structure' (1972, p. 164) which forms a basic part of market societies. Yet in his other writings Alford notes that the way in which the process of accumulation and class conflicts influence structural interests and policy development is

highly complex. As he has argued, 'The translation of class interests (or a cultural consensus) into organisational form and then
into action is problematic and contingent' (1975b, p. 153).

A similar conclusion is reached by Dunleavy in his search for
'mediating frameworks to connect macro-theory with specific policy issues' (1981b, p. 4). According to Dunleavy, it is possible to
identify systems of 'ideological corporatism' (p. 7) in operation in
policy communities. These systems derive from 'the acceptance or
dominance of an effectively unified view of the world across different sectors and institutions' (p. 7). In many cases the unified
view of the world emanates from a profession – the medical model
is a good example – and provides 'ideological cohesion' (p. 7).
Dunleavy goes further to suggest that

> underlying apparent instances of policy shaped by professional in-
> fluences it is possible on occasion to show that structural parameters
> and dynamics shaped by production relations and movements of
> private capital play a key role in shifts of welfare state policy. But I
> doubt if fairly specific policy changes can ever be reduced to explan-
> ation in such terms alone. (p. 15)

We endorse these views which widen the range of *interests* which
may be seen as supporting the *status quo* to include professional
and bureaucratic interest groups. There will be other such interests
relating to sexual, racial, religious and other divisions in society
and the inequalities they engender.

As we noted earlier in the chapter, in the sphere of consumption
of welfare services the relationship between policy formulation
and underlying economic processes is by no means direct and deterministic. The relationship is often clearer in the sphere of production policies, yet even here state agencies and the officials who
work in them play an important mediating role in translating the
pressures deriving from the economy into political action. Alford's
description of the relationship between different levels as 'problematic and contingent' expresses very well the nature of the relationship as we understand it. The framework outlined here has
much in common with the analysis of Alford and Friedland (1985).
In a review of different theories of the state, these authors argue
that pluralist, elitist and Marxist perspectives offer partial explanations of political actions. Alford and Friedland put forward a 'syn-
thetic framework'(*ibid.* p. 3) drawing upon the major contributions
of each perspective. Their thesis is that contemporary political

situations involve factors relevant to different theoretical traditions. As a consequence, analyses which combine elements of each tradition are likely to be more plausible than those which focus on only one perspective.

As a final comment, it is worth returning to the point of departure of our discussion, that is, Benson's critique of analysts who focus only on the surface level of power and control within and between organisations. One of the writers criticised by Benson is Strauss, whose work on organisations as systems of negotiated order has received considerable attention (Strauss, 1978). In reply to Benson's critique, Strauss maintains that it is necessary to examine both the process of negotiation and the social structure within which negotiations take place, and he argues that this has always been recognised by the negotiated order perspective. In this context, Strauss quotes with approval Gerson's statement that

> smaller-scale negotiations are continuously taking place in very large numbers *within* the context of the larger-scale arrangements which are changing more slowly and less visibly to participants. The larger-scale arrangements appear to individuals at particular times and places as 'givens', the 'system', the 'natural order of things', even though a larger-scale (that is, macrosociological and historical) perspective shows them as changing, often 'rapidly'. (Gerson, 1976, p. 276)

In this sense we would not wish to carry the emphasis upon structure to the extent to which it is seen as the essential determinant of action. The study of the policy process is the study of conflicts between interests, as embodied in the pluralist model, the study of individuals and groups securing positions within the autonomous state and then being able to make choices in both the making and the implementation of policy and the study of action constrained by strong, but not unalterable, structural forces.

Studies of the policy process need to link the various kinds of explanations of action and its determinants along the lines explored in this concluding chapter.

BIBLIOGRAPHY

Aberbach, J.D., R.D. Putman and B.A. Rockman, *Bureaucrats and Politicians in Western Democracies* (Harvard University Press, Cambridge Mass., 1981).

Adler, M. and S. Asquith, *Report to SSRC on Workshops on Discretion and Social Policy* (unpublished, 1980).

Adler, M. and S. Asquith (eds), *Discretion and Welfare* (Heinemann, London, 1981).

Albrow, M., *Bureaucracy* (Pall Mall, London, 1970).

Albrow, M., *Max Weber's Construction of Social Theory* (Basingstoke, Macmillan, 1990).

Aldrich, H.E., *Organizations and Environments* (Prentice Hall, Englewood Cliffs N.J., 1979).

Alford, R., 'The Political Economy of Health Care: Dynamics without Change', *Politics and Society* (Winter 1972).

Alford, R., *Health Care Politics* (University of Chicago Press, Chicago, 1975a).

Alford, R., 'Paradigms of Relations between State and Society', in L.N. Lindberg, R. Alford, C. Crouch and C. Offe (eds), *Stress and Contradictions in Modern Capitalism* (Lexington Books, Lexington Mass., 1975b).

Alford, R. and R. Friedland, *Powers of Theory* (Cambridge University Press, Cambridge, 1985).

Allison, G.T., *Essence of Decision* (Little Brown, Boston, 1971).

Argyris, C., 'Individual Actualization in Complex Organisations', *Mental Hygiene* (1960).

Ashby, E. and M. Anderson, *The Politics of Clean Air* (Clarendon Press, Oxford, 1981).

Ashford, D.E., *British Dogmatism and French Pragmatism: Center–Local Relations in the Welfare State* (Allen and Unwin, London, 1982).

Ashford, D.E., *The Emergence of the Welfare States* (Blackwell, Oxford, 1986).

Auster, R.D. and M. Silver, *The State as a Firm: Economic Forces in Political Development* (Martinus Nijhoff, The Hague, 1979).

Bachrach, P., *The Theory of Democratic Elitism* (University of London Press, London, 1969).

Bachrach, P. and M.S. Baratz, 'Two Faces of Power', *American Political Science Review*, 56 (1962).

Bachrach, P. and M.S. Baratz, 'Decisions and Nondecisions: An Analytical Framework', *American Political Science Review*, 57 (1963).

Bachrach, P. and M.S. Baratz, *Power and Poverty* (Oxford University Press, New York, 1970).

Baldwin, P., *The Politics of Social Solidarity* (Cambridge University Press, Cambridge, 1990).

Baldwin, J. and M. McConville, *Negotiated Justice: Pressures on Defendants to Plead Guilty* (Martin Robertson, Oxford, 1977).

Balzac, M., *Les Employées* (Paris, 1836).

Banting, K.C., *Poverty, Politics and Policy* (Macmillan, London, 1979).

Barnard, K., K. Lee, A. Mills and J. Reynolds, 'NHS Planning: An Assessment', *Hospital and Health Services Review* (1980).

Barrett, S. and C. Fudge (eds), *Policy and Action* (Methuen, London, 1981).

Barrett, S. and M.J. Hill, *Report to the SSRC Central–Local Government Relations Panel on the 'Core' or Theoretical Component of the Research on Implementation* (unpublished, 1981).

Beer, S.H., *Modern British Politics* (Faber & Faber, London, 1965; 2nd ed. 1969).

Bendix, R., *Max Weber, an Intellectual Portrait* (Heinemann, London, 1960).

Benson, J.K., 'Organisations: A Dialectical View', *Administrative Science Quarterly*, 18 (1) (1977).

Benson, J.K., 'Interorganizational Networks and Policy Sectors' in D. Rogers and D. Whetten (eds), *Interorganizational Coordination* (Iowa State University Press, Iowa, 1983).

Bickel, A.M., *The Supreme Court and the Idea of Progress* (Harper & Row, New York, 1970).

Blackstone, T. and W. Plowden, *Inside the Think Tank* (London, Heinemann, 1988).

Blau, P.M., *The Dynamics of Bureaucracy* (University of Chicago Press, Chicago, 1955).

Blowers, A., *Something in the Air: Corporate Power and the Environment* (Harper & Row, London, 1984).

Boddy, M., and C. Fudge, *Local Socialism* (Macmillan, Basingstoke, 1984).

Booth, T., *Developing Policy Research* (Avebury, Aldershot, 1988).

Bottomley, A.K., *Decisions in the Penal Process* (Martin Robertson, London, 1973).

Bottomore, T.B., *Elites and Society* (Penguin, Harmondsworth, 1966).

Braybrooke, D. and C.E. Lindblom, *A Strategy of Decision* (The Free Press, New York, 1963).

Brittan, S., *The Economic Consequences of Democracy* (Temple Smith, London, 1977).

Brown, M.K., 'The Allocation of Justice and Police–Citizen Encounters', in C.T. Goodsell (ed.), *The Public Encounter* (Indiana University Press, Bloomington, 1981).

Browne, A., and Wildavsky, A., 'Should Evaluation become Implementation', in J. Pressman and A. Wildavsky, *Implementation* (University of California Press, Berkeley, revised edition, 1984).

Bryant, C.G.A. and D. Jary (eds), *Giddens' Theory of Structuration* (Routledge, London, 1991).

Buchanan, J.M. and G. Tullock, *The Calculus of Consent* (University of Michigan Press, Ann Arbor Mich., 1962).

Bull, D., 'The Anti-Discretion Movement in Britain: Fact or Phantom?' *Journal of Social Welfare Law* (1980).

Bulmer, M. (ed.), *Social Science Research and Government* (Cambridge University Press, Cambridge, 1987).

Burnham, J., *The Managerial Revolution* (Putnam, London, 1942).

Burns, T. and G.M. Stalker, *The Management of Innovation* (Tavistock, London, 1961).

Burrell, G. and G. Morgan, *Sociological Paradigms and Organisational Analysis* (Heinemann, London, 1979).

Cain, M.E., *Society and the Policeman's Role* (Routledge & Kegan Paul, London, 1973).

Cartwright, D. and A. Zander (eds), *Group Dynamics* (Harper & Row, New York, 1968).

Cawson, A., 'Pluralism, Corporatism and the Role of the State', *Government and Opposition*, 13 (2) (1978).

Cawson, A. and P. Saunders, 'Corporatism, Competitive Politics and Class Struggle', paper prepared for a BSA/PSA Conference on Capital, Ideology and Politics (1981).

Chandler, A.D., *The Visible Hand: The Managerial Revolution in American Business* (Harvard University Press, Cambridge Mass., 1977).

Chandler, A.D., 'The Emergence of Managerial Capitalism', *Business History Review*, 58 (1984).

Chapman, R.A., *The Higher Civil Service in Britain* (Constable, London, 1970).

Child, J., 'Organization Structure, Environment and Performance: The Role of Strategic Choice', *Sociology*, 6 (1972).

Clegg, S., *Power, Rule and Domination* (Routledge & Kegan Paul, London, 1975).

Clegg, S., *The Theory of Power and Organization* (Routledge & Kegan Paul, London, 1979).

Clegg, S., *Frameworks of Power* (Sage, London, 1989).

Clegg, S., *Modern Organizations* (Sage, London, 1990).

Clegg, S. and D. Dunkerley, *Critical Issues in Organisations* (Routledge & Kegan Paul, London, 1977).

Clegg, S. and D. Dunkerley, *Organisation, Class and Control* (Routledge & Kegan Paul, London, 1980).

Cockburn, C., *The Local State* (Pluto Press, London, 1977).

Cousins, C., *Controlling Social Welfare* (Harvester Wheatsheaf, Hemel Hempstead, 1987).

Crenson, M.A., *The Unpolitics of Air Pollution* (The Johns Hopkins Press, Baltimore, 1971).

Crozier, M., *The Bureaucratic Phenomenon* (University of Chicago Press, Chicago, 1964).

Cunningham, G., 'Policy and Practice', *Public Administration*, 41 (1963).

Dahl, R.A., 'The Concept of Power', *Behavioural Science*, 2 (1957).

Dahl, R.A., 'A Critique of the Ruling-Elite Model', *American Political Science Review*, 52 (1958).

Dahl, R.A., *Who Governs?* (Yale University Press, New Haven, 1961).

Dalton, M., *Men Who Manage* (Wiley, New York, 1959).

Davis, K.C., *Discretionary Justice* (Louisiana State University Press, Baton Rouge, 1969).

Dearlove, J., *The Politics of Policy in Local Government* (Cambridge University Press, Cambridge, 1973).

Dearlove, J. and P. Saunders, *Introduction to British Politics* (Polity Press, Cambridge, 1991, 2nd ed.).

Degeling P. and H.K. Colebatch, 'Structure and Action as Constructs in the Practice of Public Administration', *Australian Journal of Public Administration*, 43 (4) (1984).

Dicey, A.V., *Lectures on the Relations between Law and Public Opinion* (Macmillan, London, 1905).

Djilas, M., *The New Class* (Thames & Hudson, London, 1957).

Donaldson, L., *In Defence of Organization Theory: A Response to the Critics* (Cambridge University Press, Cambridge, 1985).

Donaldson, L., 'Strategy, Structural Adjustment to Regain Fit and Performance: In Defence of Contingency Theory', *Journal of Management Studies*, 24 (2) 1987.

Donnison, D., 'Research for Policy', *Minerva*, 10 (4) (1972).

Donnison, D.V., 'Against Discretion', *New Society*, September (1977).

Downing P.B. and K. Hanf (eds), *International Comparisons in Implementing Pollution Laws* (Kluwer Nijhoff, Boston, 1983).

Downs, A., *Inside Bureaucracy* (Little Brown, Boston, 1967).

Dror, Y., 'Muddling Through – "Science" or Inertia?', *Public Administration Review*, 24 (1964).

Dror, Y., *Public Policymaking Re-examined* (Chandler, San Francisco, 1968).

Dror, Y., *Design for Policy Sciences* (Elsevier, New York, 1971).

Dror, Y., *Policymaking under Adversity* (Transaction Publications, New Brunswick, 1986).

Dunleavy, P., *The Politics of Mass Housing in Britain* (Oxford University Press, London, 1981a).

Dunleavy, P., 'Professions and Policy Change: Notes Towards a Model of Ideological Corporatism', *Public Administration Bulletin*, 36 (1981b).

Dunleavy, P., 'Bureaucrats, Budgets and the Growth of the State: Reconstructing an Instrumental Model', *British Journal of Political Science*, 15 (1985).

Dunleavy, P., 'Explaining the Privatization Boom: Public Choice versus Radical Approaches', *Public Administration*, 64 (1) (1986).

Dunleavy, P., *Democracy, Bureaucracy and Public Choice* (Harvester Wheatsheaf, Hemel Hempstead, 1991).

Dunleavy, P. and B. O'Leary, *Theories of the State* (Macmillan, Basingstoke, 1987).

Dunsire, A., *Implementation in a Bureaucracy* (Martin Robertson, Oxford, 1978a).

Dunsire, A., *Control in a Bureaucracy* (Martin Robertson, Oxford, 1978b).

Dworkin, R. *Taking Rights Seriously* (Duckworth, London, 1977).

Dye, T.R., *Policy Analysis* (University of Alabama Press, Alabama, 1976).

Easton, D., *The Political System* (Knopf, New York, 1953).

Easton, D., *A Systems Analysis of Political Life* (Wiley, New York, 1965a).

Easton, D., *A Framework for Political Analysis* (Prentice Hall, Englewood Cliffs N.J., 1965b).

Eckstein, H., *Pressure Group Politics* (Allen & Unwin, London, 1960).

Edelman, M., *Politics as Symbolic Action* (Markham, Chicago, 1971).

Elcock, H., *Change or Decay?: Public Administration in the 1990s* (Longman, London, 1991).

Elliott, M., *The Role of Law in Central–Local Relations* (SSRC, London, 1981).

Elmore, R., 'Organisational Models of Social Program Implementation', *Public Policy*, 26 (2) (1978).

Elmore, R., 'Backward Mapping: Implementation Research and Policy Decisions', *Political Science Quarterly*, 94 (1980).

Elmore, R., *Backward Mapping and Youth Employment*, unpublished paper prepared for the third meeting of the International Working Group on Policy Implementation (1981).

Elmore R., 'Forward and Backward Mapping', in K. Hanf and T. Toonen, *Policy Implementation in Federal and Unitary Systems* (Martinus Nijhoff, Dordrecht, 1985).

Engels, F., 'The Origins of Family, Private Property and the State', in K. Marx and F. Engels, *Selected Works*, Vol. 2 (Foreign Language Publishing House, Moscow, 1958).

Enthoven, A.C., *Reflections on the Management of the NHS* (Nuffield Provincial Hospitals Trust, London, 1985).

Etzioni, A., *A Comparative Analysis of Complex Organisations* (Free Press, New York, 1961).

Etzioni, A., 'Mixed-Scanning: A "Third" Approach to Decision-Making', *Public Administration Review*, 27 (1967).

Evans, P.B., D. Rueschemeyer and T. Skocpol (eds), *Bringing the State Back In* (Cambridge University Press, Cambridge, 1985).

Fayol, H., *Administration Industrielle et Générale* (Paris, 1916).

Feuer, L.S. (ed.), *Marx and Engels: Basic Writings on Politics and Philosophy* (Anchor Books, New York, 1959).

Finer, H., *The British Civil Service* (Allen & Unwin, London, 1937).

Flynn, R., 'Coping with Cutbacks and Managing Retrenchment in Health', *Journal of Social Policy*, 20 (2) (1991).

Follett, M.P., *Dynamic Administration* (Management Publications Trust, London, 1941).

Forrest, R. and A. Murie, *Selling the Welfare State* (Routledge, London, 1988).

Fox, A., *Beyond Contract: Work, Power and Trust Relations* (Faber & Faber, London, 1974).

Freeman, J. and M.T. Hannan, 'Growth and Decline Processes in Organizations', *American Sociological Review*, 40 (1975).

Friedrich, C.J., 'The Nature of Administrative Responsibility', *Public Policy*, 1 (1940).

Friedson, E., *Professional Dominance* (Atherton, New York, 1970).

Friend, J.K., J.M. Power and C.J.L. Yewlett, *Public Planning: The Inter-Corporate Dimension* (Tavistock, London, 1974).

Galdos, P., *Miau*, trans. J.M. Cohen (Methuen, London, 1963).

Galligan, D.J. *Discretionary Powers* (Clarendon Press, Oxford, 1986).

Gamble, A., *The Free Economy and the Strong State* (Macmillan, Basingstoke, 1988).

Gershuny, J.I., 'Policymaking Rationality: A Reformulation', *Policy Sciences*, 9 (1978).

Gerson, E., 'On the Quality of Life', *American Sociological Review*, 4 (1976).

Gerth, H.H. and C.W. Mills, *From Max Weber: Essays in Sociology* (Routledge & Kegan Paul, London, 1948).

Gerth, H.H. and C.W. Mills, 'A Marx for the Managers', in C.W. Mills, *Power, Politics and People* (Oxford University Press, New York, 1963).

Gibb, C.A., 'Leadership', in G. Lindley (ed.), *Handbook of Social Psychology* (Addison-Wesley, Reading Mass., 1954).

Giller, H. and A. Morris, 'What Type of Case is This? Social Workers' Decisions about Children who Offend', in M. Adler and S. Asquith (eds), *Discretion and Welfare* (Heinemann, London, 1981).

Glennerster, H., A. Power and T. Travers, 'A New Era for Social Policy: A New Enlightenment or a New Leviathan?', *Journal of Social Policy*, 20 (3), 1991.

Goldthorpe, J.H. et al., *The Affluent Worker: Industrial Attitudes and Behaviour* (Cambridge University Press, Cambridge, 1968).

Goodin, R.E., *Political Theory and Public Policy* (University of Chicago Press, Chicago, 1982).

Gordon, I., J. Lewis and K. Young, 'Perspectives on Policy Analysis', *Public Administration Bulletin*, 25 (1977).

Gough, I., *The Political Economy of the Welfare State* (Macmillan, London, 1979).

Gould, A., 'The Salaried Middle Class in the Corporatist Welfare State', *Policy and Politics*, 9 (4) (1981).

Gouldner, A.W., *Patterns of Industrial Bureaucracy* (Free Press, Glencoe Ill., 1954).

Gouldner, A.W., 'Metaphysical Pathos and the Theory of Bureaucracy', *American Political Science Review*, 49 (1955).

Gouldner, A.W., 'Cosmopolitans and Locals: Towards an Analysis of Latent Social Roles', *Administrative Science Quarterly*, 2 (1957–8).

Greenwood, E., 'Attributes of a Profession', *Social Work*, 2 (1957).

Greenwood, R., C.R. Hinings and S. Ranson, 'Contingency Theory and the Organisation of Local Authorities: Part One. Differentiation and Integration', *Public Administration*, 53 (1975).

Gregory, R., 'Political rationality or incrementalism? Charles E. Lindblom's enduring contribution to public policy making', *Policy and Politics*, 17 (2) (1989).

Griffith, J.A.G., *Central Departments and Local Authorities* (Allen & Unwin, London, 1966).

Griffith, J.A.G., *The Politics of the Judiciary* (Fontana, Glasgow, 1977).

Gunn, L., 'Why is Implementation so Difficult?', *Management Services in Government*, November (1978).

Gunn, L., 'Policy and the Policy Analyst, unpublished paper given to the Public Administration Committee Conference, University of York, 1980.

Gunn, L. and B. Hogwood, *Models of Policy-Making* (Centre for the Study of Public Policy, University of Strathclyde 1982).

Gunningham, N., *Pollution, Social Interest and the Law* (Martin Robertson, London, 1974).

Gustafsson, G., 'Swedish Local Government: Reconsidering Rationality and Consensus', in J.J. Hesse (ed.), *Local Government and Urban*

Affairs in International Perspective (Nomos Verlagsgesellschaft, Baden Baden, 1991).

Habermas, J., *Legitimation Crisis* (Heinemann, London, 1976).

Ham, C.J., *Policy Making in the National Health Service* (Macmillan, London, 1981).

Ham, C.J., *Health Policy in Britain* (Macmillan, London, 1982, 2nd ed., 1985, 3rd ed., 1992).

Ham, C.J., *Managing Health Services* (SAUS, Bristol, 1986)

Ham, C.J., 'Governing the Health Sector: Power and Policy making in the English and Swedish Health Services', *The Millbank Quarterly*, 66 (2), pp. 389–44 (1988).

Ham, C.J., 'Analysis of Health Policy – Principles and Practice', *Scandinavian Journal of Social Medicine*, Supplement 46, pp. 62–6, (1991).

Ham, C.J., R. Robinson and M. Benzeval, *Health Check* (Kings Fund Institute, London, 1990).

Hannan, M. and Freeman, J., 'The Population Ecology of Organizations', *American Journal of Sociology*, 82 (1977).

Hargrove, E.C., *The Missing Link* (The Urban Institute, Washington D.C., 1975).

Hargrove, E.C., 'The Search for Implementation Theory', in R. Zeckhauser and D. Leebaert (eds), *What Role for Government? Lessons from Policy Research* (Duke Press Policy Studies, Chapel Hill, North Carolina 1983).

Harrison, S., D.J. Hunter and C. Pollitt, *The Dynamics of British Health Policy* (Unwin Hyman, London, 1990).

Hasenfeld, Y. and D. Steinmetz, 'Client–Official Encounters in Social Service Agencies', in C.T. Goodsell (ed.), *The Public Encounter* (Indiana University Press, Bloomington, 1981).

Hawkins, K., *Environment and Enforcement: Regulation and the Social Definition of Pollution* (Oxford University Press, Oxford, 1984).

Heclo, H., 'Review Article: Policy Analysis', *British Journal of Political Science*, 2 (1972).

Heclo, H., *Modern Social Politics in Britain and Sweden* (Yale University Press, New Haven, 1974).

Heclo, H. and A. Wildavsky, *The Private Government of Public Money* (Macmillan, London, 1981 2nd ed.).

Heineman, R.A. et al, *The World of the Policy Analyst* (Chatham House, Chatham N.J., 1990).

Hennessy, P., *Whitehall* (Secker and Warburg, London, 1989).

Hewart, Lord, *The New Despotism* (London, 1929).

Hickson, D. et al., 'A Strategic Contingencies Theory of Intra-Organisational Power', *Administrative Science Quarterly*, 16 (2) (1971).

Hill, M., *Social Security Policy in Britain* (Edward Elgar, Cheltenham, 1990).

Hill, M., S. Aaronovitch and D. Baldock, 'Non-decision Making in Pollution Control in Britain: Nitrate Pollution, the EEC Drinking Water Directive and Agriculture', *Policy and Politics*, 17 (3) (1989).

Hill, M. and G. Bramley, *Analysing Social Policy* (Blackwell, Oxford, 1986).

Hill, M.J., 'The Exercise of Discretion in the National Assistance Board', *Public Administration*, 47 (1969).

Hill, M.J., *The Sociology of Public Administration* (Weidenfeld & Nicolson, 1972).

Hill, M.J., 'Some Implications of Legal Approaches to Welfare Rights', *British Journal of Social Work*, 4 (2) (1974).

Hirschman, A.O., *Exit, Voice and Loyalty* (Harvard University Press, Cambridge Mass., 1970)

Hjern, B. and C. Hull, 'Implementation Research as Empirical Constitutionalism', in B. Hjern and C. Hull (eds), *Implementation Beyond Hierarchy*, special issue of *European Journal of Political Research* (1982).

Hjern, B. and D.O. Porter, 'Implementation Structures: A New Unit of Administrative Analysis', *Organisational Studies*, 2 (1981).

Hogwood, B.W. and L.A. Gunn, *The Policy Orientation* (Centre for the Study of Public Policy, University of Strathclyde, 1981).

Hogwood, B.W. and L.A. Gunn, *Policy Analysis for the Real World* (Oxford University Press, Oxford, 1984).

Hogwood, B.W. and B.G. Peters, *Policy Dynamics* (Harvester Wheatsheaf, Hemel Hempstead, 1983).

Hood, C.C., *The Limits of Administration* (Wiley, London, 1976).

Hood, C.C., 'A Public Management for all Seasons', *Public Administration*, 69 (1) (1991).

Hudson, B., 'Michael Lipsky and Street-Level Bureaucracy: A Neglected Perspective' in L. Barton (ed.), *Disability and Dependency* (Falmer Press, Lewes, 1989).

Hughes, E.C., *Men and their Work* (Free Press, Glencoe Ill., 1958).

Hunter, F., *Community Power Structure* (University of North Carolina Press, Chapel Hill, 1953).

Hupe, P., 'Implementing a Meta-Policy: The Case of Decentralisation in the Netherlands', *Policy and Politics*, 18 (3) (1990).

Illich, I., *Limits to Medicine* (Penguin, Harmondsworth, 1977).

Jacques, E., *Equitable Payment* (Penguin, Harmondsworth, 1967).

Jenkins, W.I., *Policy Analysis* (Martin Robertson, London, 1978).

Jessop, B., *The Capitalist State* (Martin Robertson, Oxford, 1982).

Johnson, T.J., *Professions and Power* (Macmillan, London, 1972).

Jordan, A.G. 'Iron Triangles, Woolly Corporatism and Elastic Nets: Images of the Policy Process', *Journal of Public Policy*, 1 (1986).

Jordan, A.G. and J.J. Richardson, *British Politics and the Policy Process* (Unwin Hyman, London, 1987).

Jowell, J., 'The Legal Control of Administrative Discretion', *Public Law* (1973).

Jowell, J., 'Bargaining in Development Control', *Journal of Planning and Environmental Law* (1977).

Jowell, J., Contribution to SSRC sponsored workshops on discretion in social policy (unpublished, 1979). (See also Adler, M. and S. Asquith.)

Kennedy, I., *The Unmasking of Medicine* (Allen & Unwin, London, 1981).

Kingsley, J.D., *Representative Bureaucracy* (Antioch Press, Yellow Springs Ohio, 1944).

Klein, R., *The Politics of the NHS* (Longman, London, 1989, 2nd ed.).

Knoepfel, P. and H. Weidner, 'Formulation and Implementation of Air Quality Control Programmes: Patterns of Interest Consideration', *Policy and Politics*, 10 (1) (1982).

Krech, D. and R.S. Crutchfield, *Theory and Problems in Social Psychology* (McGraw Hill, New York, 1948).

Lambert, J.R., *Crime, Police and Race Relations* (Oxford University Press, London, 1967).

Lane, J-E., 'Implementation, Accountability and Trust', *European Journal of Political Research*, 15 (5) (1987).

Lasswell, H., 'The Policy Orientation', in D. Lerner and H. Lasswell (eds), *The Policy Sciences* (Stanford University Press, Stanford, 1951).

Latham, E., *The Group Basis of Politics* (Cornell University Press, Ithaca, 1952).

Lenin, V.I., *State and Revolution* (Foreign Languages Publishing House, Moscow, 1917).

Lidstrom, A. *Discretion: An Art of the Possible* (University of Umea Ph.D Thesis, Research Report, Department of Political Science, 1991).

Lijphart, A., *Verzuiling, pacificatie en kentering in nederlandse politiek* (De Bussy, Amsterdam, 1982).

Lindblom, C.E., 'The Science of "Muddling Through" ', *Public Administration Review*, 19 (1959).

Lindblom, C.E., 'Contexts for Change and Strategy: A Reply', *Public Administration Review*, 24 (1964).

Lindblom, C.E., *The Intelligence of Democracy* (The Free Press, New York, 1965).

Lindblom, C.E., *Politics and Markets* (Basic Books, New York, 1977).

Lindblom, C.E., 'Still Muddling, Not Yet Through', *Public Administration Review*, 39 (1979).

Lipset, S.M., *Agrarian Socialism* (University of California Press, Berkeley, 1950).

Lipsky, M., *Street-Level Bureaucracy* (Russell Sage, New York, 1980).

Litter, C.R., 'Understanding Taylorism', *British Journal of Sociology*, 29 (2) (1978).

Lowi, T.A., 'Four Systems of Policy, Politics and Choice', *Public Administration Review*, 32 (1972).

Lukes, S., *Power: A Radical View* (Macmillan, London, 1974).

MacRae, C.D., 'A political model of the business cycle', *Journal of Political Economy*, 85 (1977).

Majone, G. and A. Wildavsky, 'Implementation as Evolution', *Policy Studies Review Annual* (1978).

Marris, P. and M. Rein, *Dilemmas of Social Reform* (Routledge & Kegan Paul, London, 1967).

Marx, F.M., *The Administrative State* (University of Chicago Press, Chicago, 1957).

Maslow, A.H., *Motivation and Personality* (Harper, New York, 1954).

Mayo, E., *The Human Problems of an Industrial Civilization* (Harvard University Press, Cambridge Mass., 1933).

McGregor, D., *The Human Side of Enterprise* (McGraw Hill, New York, 1960).

McLellan, D., *The Thought of Karl Marx* (Macmillan, London, 1971).

McLennan, G., *Marxism, Pluralism and Beyond* (Polity Press, Cambridge, 1989).

Meltsner, A.J., *Policy Analysts in the Bureaucracy* (University of California Press, Berkeley, 1976).

Merelman, R.M., 'On the Neo-Elitist Critique of Community Power', *American Political Science Review*, 62 (1968).

Merton, R.K., *Social Theory and Social Structure* (Free Press, Glencoe Ill., 1957).

Michels, R., *Political Parties*, trans. E. and C. Paul (Constable, London, 1915).

Middlemas, K., *Politics in Industrial Society* (André Deutsch, London, 1979).

Middlemas, K., *Power, Competition and the State*, Vol. 1 (Macmillan, London, 1986).

Miliband, R., *The State in Capitalist Society* (Weidenfeld & Nicolson, London, 1969).

Miliband, R., *Marxism and Politics* (Oxford University Press, Oxford, 1977).

Mills, C.W., *The Power Elite* (Oxford University Press, New York, 1956).

Mills, C.W., 'Culture and Politics', in C.W. Mills, *Power, Politics and People* (Oxford University Press, New York, 1963).

Milward, H.B. and R.A. Francisco, 'Subsystem Politics and Corporatism in the United States', *Policy and Politics*, Vol. 11 (3) (1983).

Minogue, M., 'Theory and Practice in Public Policy and Administration', *Policy and Politics*, 11 (1983).

Minogue, M., *Problems in Teaching Public Policy* (Department of Administrative Studies, University of Manchester, not dated).

Minzberg, H., *Power in and Around Organizations* (Prentice Hall, Englewood Cliffs N.J., 1983).

Mishra, R., *The Welfare State in Crisis* (Harvester Wheatsheaf, Hemel Hempstead, 1984).

Mosca, C., *The Ruling Class*, trans. H.D. Kahn (McGraw Hill, London, 1939).

Mosley, P., *The Making of Economic Policy* (Harvester Wheatsheaf, Hemel Hempstead, 1984).

Mountjoy, R.S. and L.J. O'Toole, 'Towards a Theory of Policy Implementation: An Organisational Review', *Public Administration Review* (1979).

Moynihan, D. P., *Maximum Feasible Misunderstanding* (Free Press, New York, 1969).

Newton, K., *Second City Politics* (Oxford University Press, Oxford, 1976).

Niskanen, W.A., *Bureaucracy and Representative Government* (Aldine-Atherton, New York, 1971).

Nixon, J., 'The Importance of Communication in the Implementation of Government Policy at the Local Level', *Policy and Politics*, 8 (2) (1980).

Nordhaus, W., 'The Political Business Cycle', *Review of Economic Studies*, 42 (1975).

Nordlinger, E.A., *On the Autonomy of the Democratic State* (Harvard University Press, Cambridge Mass., 1981).

O'Connor, J., *The Fiscal Crisis of the State* (St. Martin's Press, New York, 1973).

Offe, C., 'Structural Problems of the Capitalist State', in K. von Beyme (ed.), *German Political Studies*, Vol. 1 (Sage, London, 1974).

Offe, C., 'The Theory of the Capitalist State and the Problem of Policy Formation', in L. Lindberg, R. Alford, C. Crouch and C. Offe (eds), *Stress and Contradictions in Modern Capitalism* (Lexington Books, Lexington Mass., 1975).

Offe, C., 'Political Authority and Class Structures', in P. Connerton (ed.), *Critical Sociology* (Penguin, Harmondsworth, 1976).

Offe, C., *Contradictions of the Welfare State* (Hutchinson, London, 1984).

Olsen, M., *The Logic of Collective Action* (Harvard University Press, Cambridge Mass., 1965).

Olson, M., *The Rise and Decline of Nations* (Yale University Press, New Haven, 1982).

Page, E.C. and M.J. Goldsmith, *Central and Local Government Relations* (Sage, London, 1987).

Pahl, R., *Whose City?* (Penguin, Harmondsworth 1975, 2nd ed., 1975).

Pahl, R., 'Managers, Technical Experts and the State', in M. Harloe (ed.), *Captive Cities* (John Wiley, London, 1977).

Panitch, L., 'Recent Theorisations of Corporatism: Reflections on a Growth Industry', *British Journal of Sociology*, 31 (2) (1980).

Parry, G., *Political Elites* (Allen & Unwin, London, 1969).

Parry, G. and P. Morriss, 'When is a Decision not a Decision?', in I. Crewe (ed.), *British Political Sociology Yearbook*, Vol. 1 (Croom Helm, London, 1974).

Parry, N. and J. Parry, *The Rise of the Medical Profession* (Croom Helm, London, 1976).

Paulus, I., *The Search for Pure Food* (Martin Robertson, London, 1974).

Perrow, C., *Complex Organizations: A Critical Essay* (Scott Foresman, Glenview Ill., 1972).

Pfeffer, J. and C. Salancik, *The External Control of Organizations* (Harper & Row, New York, 1978).

Pollitt, C., *Managerialism and the Public Services* (Blackwell, Oxford, 1990).

Polsby, N.W., *Community Power and Political Theory* (Yale University Press, New Haven, 1963).

Polsby, N.W., *Community Power and Political Theory: A Further Look at Problems of Evidence and Inference* (Yale University Press, New Haven, 1980, 2nd, enlarged ed.).

Popper, K.R., *The Open Society and its Enemies* (Routledge & Kegan Paul, London, 1966, 5th ed.).

Poulantzas, N., 'The Problem of the Capitalist State', in J. Urry and J. Wakeford (eds), *Power in Britain* (Heinemann, London, 1973a). Poulantzas' article was originally published in *New Left Review*, 58 (1969).

Poulantzas, N., *Political Power and Social Classes* (New Left Books, London, 1973b).

Premfors, R., 'Review Article: Charles Lindblom and Aaron Wildavsky', *British Journal of Political Science*, 11 (2) (1981).

Pressman, J. and A. Wildavsky, *Implementation* (Berkeley, University of California Press, 1973).

Prosser, T. 'The Politics of Discretion: Aspects of Discretionary Power in the Supplementary Benefits Scheme', in M. Adler and S. Asquith, *Discretion and Welfare* (Heinemann, London, 1981).

Prottas, J.M., 'The Power of the Street-Level Bureaucrat in Public Service Bureaucracies', *Urban Affairs Quarterly*, 13 (3) (1978).

Prottas, J.M., *People Processing: The Street-Level Bureaucrat in Public Service Bureaucracies* (D.C. Heath, Lexington Mass., 1979).

Rein, M., *Social Science and Public Policy* (Penguin, Harmondsworth, 1976).

Rein, M., *From Policy to Practice* (Macmillan, London, 1983).

Reissman, L., 'The Study of Role Conceptions in Bureaucracy', *Social Forces*, 27 (1949).

Rex, J. and S. Tomlinson, *Colonial Immigrants in a British City* (Routledge & Kegan Paul, London, 1979).

Rhodes, R.A.W., 'Research into Central–Local Relations in Britain: A Framework for Analysis', *Report of the Social Science Research Council's Panel on Research on Central–Local Relations* (SSRC, London, 1979).

Rhodes, R.A.W., *Public Administration and Policy Analysis* (Saxon House, Farnborough, 1979).

Richardson, J.J. and A.C. Jordan, *Governing under Pressure* (Martin Robertson, Oxford, 1979).

Roethlisberger, F.J. and W.J. Dickson, *Management and the Worker* (Harvard University Press, Cambridge Mass., 1939).

Room, G., *The Sociology of Welfare* (Blackwell, Oxford, 1979).

Sabatier, P., 'Top-Down and Bottom-Up Approaches to Implementation Research: A Critical Analysis and Suggested Synthesis', *Journal of Public Policy*, 6 (1) (1986).

Sabatier, P. and D. Mazmanian, 'The Conditions of Effective Implementation: A Guide to Accomplishing Policy Objectives, *Policy Analysis* (1979).

Salaman, G., *Work Organisations* (Longman, London, 1979).

Salaman, G., *Class and the Corporation* (Fontana, London, 1981).

Salisbury, R.H., 'Why No Corporatism in America?', in P. Schmitter and G. Lehmbruch (eds), *Trends Towards Corporatist Intermediation* (Sage, Beverly Hills, 1979).

Satyamurti, C., *Occupational Survival* (Blackwell, Oxford, 1981).

Saunders, P., *Urban Politics* (Penguin, Harmondsworth, 1980) (first published by Hutchinson in 1979).

Saunders, P., *Social Theory and the Urban Question* (Hutchinson, London, 1981a).

Saunders, P., 'Notes on the Specificity of the Local State', in M. Boddy and C. Fudge (eds), *The Local State: Theory and Practice* (School for Advanced Urban Studies, University of Bristol, 1981b).

Schattschneider, E.E., *The Semi-Sovereign People* (Holt, Rinehart and Winston, New York, 1960).

Scheingold, S.A., *The Politics of Rights* (Yale University Press, New Haven, 1974).

Schmitter, P., 'Still the Century of Corporatism?', *Review of Politics*, 36 (1974).

Schumpeter, J., *Capitalism, Socialism and Democracy* (Allen & Unwin, London, 1947) (2nd revised edition).

Self, P., *Political Theories of Modern Government* (Allen & Unwin, London, 1985).

Selznick, P., *TVA and the Grass Roots* (University of California Press, Berkeley, 1949).

Selznick, P., *Leadership in Administration* (Harper & Row, New York, 1957).

Sharpe, L.J., 'The Social Scientist and Policy-Making: Some Cautionary Thoughts and Transatlantic Reflections', *Policy and Politics*, 4 (2) (1975).

Silverman, D., 'Accounts of Organisations', in J.B. McKinley (ed.), *Processing People* (Holt, Rinehart & Winston, London, 1975).

Simmie, J., *Power, Property and Corporatism* (Macmillan, London, 1981).

Simon, H.A., *Administrative Behaviour* (Free Press, Glencoe Ill., 1945, 1st ed., Macmillan, New York, 1957, 2nd ed.).

Smith, B.C., *Bureaucracy and Political Power* (Harvester Wheatsheaf, Hemel Hempstead, 1988).

Smith, G., 'Discretionary Decision-Making in Social Work', in M. Adler and S. Asquith (eds), *Discretion and Welfare* (Heinemann, London, 1981).

Smith, G. and D. May, 'The Artificial Debate Between Rationalist and Incrementalist Models of Decision-Making', *Policy and Politics*, 8 (2) (1980).

Strauss, A., *Negotiations* (Jossey-Bass, San Francisco, 1978).

Taylor, F.W., *The Principles of Scientific Management* (Harper, New York, 1911).

Thomas, P., *The Aims and Outcomes of Social Policy Research* (Croom Helm, Beckenham, 1985).

Titmuss, R.M., 'Welfare Rights, Law and Discretion', *Political Quarterly*, 42 (1971).

Tullock, G., *The Politics of Bureaucracy* (Public Affairs Press, New York, 1967).

Tullock, G., *The Vote Motive* (Institute of Economic Affairs, London, 1976).

Urwick, L.F., *The Elements of Administration* (Pitman, London, 1943).

Van Meter, D. and C.E. Van Horn, 'The Policy Implementation Process, a Conceptual Framework', *Administration and Society*, 6 (4) (1975).

Vickers, G., *The Art of Judgement* (Chapman & Hall, London, 1965).

Wade, H., *Administrative Law* (Clarendon Press, Oxford, 1967).

Wallas, C., *Human Nature in Politics* (Constable, London, 1948).

Walsh, K., B. Hinings, R. Greenwood and S. Ranson, 'Power and Advantage in Organisations', *Organisation Studies*, 2 (2) (1981).

Weatherley, R., *Reforming Special Education: Policy Implementation from State Level to Street Level* (MIT Press, Cambridge Mass., 1979).

Weatherley, R., 'Implementing Social Programs: The View from the Front Line', paper delivered at the Annual Meeting of the American Political Science Association, Washington D.C. (1980).

Weatherley, R. and M. Lipsky, 'Street-Level Bureaucrats and Institutional Innovation: Implementing Special Education Reform', *Harvard Educational Review*, 47 (2) (1977).

Webb, A. and G. Wistow, *Whither State Welfare* (RIPA, London, 1982).

Weber, M., *The Theory of Social and Economic Organization*, trans. A.M. Henderson and T. Parsons (Free Press, Glencoe Ill., 1947).

Weiss C., 'Research for Policy's Sake: The Enlightenment Function of Social Research', *Policy Analysis*, 3 (4) (1977).

Westergaard, J., 'Class, Inequality and "Corporatism" ', in A. Hunt (ed.), *Class and Class Structure* (Lawrence & Wishart, London, 1977).

Whitmore, R.,'Modelling the policy/implementation distinction', *Policy and Politics*, 12 (3) (1984).

Whyte, W.H., *The Organization Man* (Simon & Schuster, New York, 1956).

Wildavsky, A., *Speaking Truth to Power: The Art and Craft of Policy Analysis* (Little Brown, Boston, 1979).

Wilding, P., *Professional Power and Social Welfare* (Routledge & Kegan Paul, London, 1982).

Wilensky, H.L., 'The Professionalisation of Everyone', *American Journal of Sociology*, 70 (1964).

Williams, F., *Social Policy: A Critical Introduction* (Polity Press, Cambridge, 1989).

Williamson, O.E., *Markets and Hierarchies* (Free Press, New York, 1975).

Williamson, O.E., 'The Economics of Organization', *American Journal of Sociology*, 87 (1981).

Wilson, J.Q., *Varieties of Police Behavior* (Atheneum, New York, 1970).

Winkler, J., 'Corporatism', *Archives Européennes de Sociologie*, XVII (1) (1976).

Wiseman, C., 'Selection of Major Planning Issues', *Policy Sciences*, 9 (1978).

Wiseman, C., 'Policy Making for the Scottish Health Services at National Level', in H. Drucker and N. Drucker (eds), *The Scottish Government Yearbook 1980* (Paul Hams, Edinburgh, 1979).

Wittfogel, K.A., *Oriental Despotism* (Yale University Press, New Haven, 1963).

Wolfe, A., *The Limits of Legitimacy* (The Free Press, New York, 1977).

Wolfinger, R.E., 'Nondecisions and the Study of Local Politics', *American Political Science Review*, 65 (1971).

Young, H., *One of Us: A Biography of Mrs Thatcher* (Macmillan, London, 1989).

Zimmerman, D.H., 'The Practicalities of Rule Use', in J.D. Douglas (ed.), *Understanding Everyday Life* (Routledge & Kegan Paul, London, 1971).

INDEX OF NAMES

INDEX OF SUBJECTS